How the Universe Was Created and Our Purpose In It

The Eastern Answers to the Mysteries of Life

VOLUME FOUR

Find out more about
The World Relief Network
Stephen Knapp and his books at:
http://www.Stephen-Knapp.com

By

Stephen Knapp

Dedicated to all
who feel that the search to discover who you are
includes the quest to find out from where you have come.
May this book show the reality and potential that exists within all of us.

All photographs taken by the author during his travels in India.

Cover design by Stephen Knapp. Cover painting by Rangadevi dasi. In the center of the painting is the sacred syllable *om*. It is the seed and root of all creation and dissolution from which everything is a development, and in which is found all past, present, and future. It is spiritual, eternal, beyond restrictions, and the name of God upon which many sages have meditated since the beginning of time. It is also the vibrational frequency of the universe and, thus, pervades it.

ISBN: 0-9617410-8-2
Library of Congress Catalog Card Number: 90-71652

PUBLISHED BY

PROVIDING KNOWLEDGE
OF
REALITY DISTINGUISHED FROM ILLUSION
FOR THE WELFARE OF ALL

The World Relief Network
P. O. Box 15082
Detroit, Michigan
48215-0082

Other books by the author:
The Secret Teachings of the Vedas: The Eastern Answers to the Mysteries of Life
The Universal Path to Enlightenment
The Vedic Prophecies: A New Look into the Future
Toward World Peace: Seeing the Unity Between Us All
Facing Death: Welcoming the Afterlife
Proof of Vedic Culture's Global Existence

Contents

Contents

Introduction

This book takes information that is widely scattered throughout many volumes of Vedic literature and condenses it into the present work for a concise explanation of the Vedic process of creation. Regardless of one's background, or the reason why you may want to read this book, there will be many examples found within that will provide much insight into the cause, purpose, or the plan behind this universe, and the way to utilize our existence in this creation. Even if one has little regard for the Vedic system, or is a theologian from another religious persuasion, you will still find many interesting points that you can use for your own reasoning, especially regarding how the universe is not a mechanistic phenomena, or a miracle of chance, but is a manifestation that is overseen by a Supreme Creator.

The Vedic texts, being ancient but important spiritual literature, gives explicit information about a wide variety of topics, including our spiritual identity, the Supreme Being, His incarnations, the material creation, and about the important spiritual processes that people can use for getting free from material existence. In relating this information, I have tried to use specific references from the Vedic texts whenever possible to let them speak for themselves. That way we can understand as clearly as possible what they say.

For some readers, the information in this book may seem so different that it may border the fantastic and be quite controversial. For others, it may make a lot of sense and provide an understanding of life for which they have long been searching. For others, it may kindle a reawakening of what, deep in their hearts, they already know but could not quite remember. Nonetheless, it will provide you with a deeper look into a new level of being and of comprehending who you are and the significance of your life.

If any readers have specific questions, or would like to know good sources for acquiring more books on this subject, I will be glad to correspond with you anytime, as long as I am not traveling in India. During my travels I have little contact with anyone beyond my personal location, which can often change every few days. So please use the following address and I will be glad to give further assistance:

The World Relief Network
P. O. Box 15082
Detroit, Michigan U.S.A.
48215-0082

Further information on the knowledge of the East is supplied in Volume One of this series, *The Secret Teachings of the Vedas*, and in Volume Two, *The*

Universal Path to Enlightenment. Volume Three, *The Vedic Prophecies: A New Look into the Future,* is also of much interest and continues the presentation of this information by explaining many of the most ancient prophecies in the world. It also explains how the material creation is finally annihilated and merged back into the spiritual atmosphere. If you would also like to have the addresses of temples and organizations in the West that are based on the philosophy of the East, please write for a free listing.

To help make these books more authentic and complete, I have included a section on seeing the spiritual side of India, mixing travel and adventure with philosophy, and adding diversity to the book. In this volume are more than seventy photographs of temples, holy sites, people, and life in India. Thus, you will be able to read and see what it is like to travel to the holy places and how this spiritual knowledge is applied today, and how people utilize their interest in adventure to make spiritual advancement while on the road to enlightenment. The hardest part about doing this section is choosing the photographs from the thousands of slides I have, and deciding which stories to relate. There are too many photos and more stories I would like to include, but not enough time or space. In this volume we will journey through Northern India from New Delhi in North Central India to all of the major holy places in the north. We will learn about the legends and special traits that make these places sacred. In the other volumes we continue our travels through other sections of India to see some of the holiest cities in the world.

Since this is the last volume in *The Eastern Answers to the Mysteries of Life* series, this is also the last of the travel sections for *Seeing Spiritual India.* I sincerely hope you have enjoyed these books and have benefitted from them. However, this is not the end. More books will follow.

A NOTE TO SCHOLARS

As most scholars on Vedic philosophy know, when you say *Vedas* you refer to the original four *Vedas*: the *Rig, Yajur, Sama,* and *Atharva Vedas.* From the four main *Vedas* are branches or appendices called *Brahmanas,* which relate to rituals and ceremonies. From these are derived the *Aranyakas.* The *Upanishads* are the appendices (the secret and esoteric knowledge) of the *Aranyakas.* When you say *Veda* (without the *s*) you not only refer to the four *Vedas*, but also to the *Brahmanas, Aranyakas,* and *Upanishads*: All the texts that are considered *Shruti.* *Shruti* is considered the original revealed knowledge. The remaining parts of Vedic literature consist of the *Mahabharata* and *Bhagavad-gita,* the *Ramayana,* and the *Puranas.* These are the *Itihasas* or histories and supplemental portions of the Vedic literature, which they call *Smriti,* or that which is remembered. "Vedic literature" refers to both *Shruti* and *Smriti* in a general way. However, some scholars think that the *Shruti* is more important than the *Smriti.* So some may object to the way I alternately use the words "*Vedas*" and "Vedic literature" to refer to the same thing, which is all of the Vedic texts, both *Shruti* and *Smriti*.

The reason I do this is that I present Vedic evidence from any portion of the Vedic literature, and I often use quotes from the *Puranas*. To leave out the supplemental portions of the Vedic literature would deprive the reader of an enormous amount of Vedic knowledge and elaborated explanations. And for this book in particular, it would leave out many of the best portions of Vedic descriptions of the process of universal creation and its purpose. Furthermore, some of the greatest of spiritual authorities, like Shankaracarya, Ramanujacarya, Madhvacarya, and others, have presented *Smriti* as valid evidence of spiritual truths and wrote commentaries on *Bhagavad-gita*. In fact, Madhvacarya, in his commentary on the *Vedanta-sutras* (2.1.6), quotes the *Bhavishya Purana*, which states: "The *Rig-veda, Yajur-veda, Sama-veda, Atharva-veda, Mahabharata, Pancaratra*, and the original *Ramayana* are all considered Vedic literature. The Vaishnava supplements, the *Puranas*, are also Vedic literature." Even the *Chandogya Upanishad* (7.1.4) mentions the *Puranas* as the fifth *Veda*. The *Srimad-Bhagavatam* (1.4.20) also clearly agrees with this: "The four divisions of the original sources of knowledge (the *Vedas*) were made separately. But the historical facts and authentic stories mentioned in the *Puranas* are called the fifth *Veda*."

The *Brihadaranyaka Upanishad* (4.5.11) also relates: "The *Rig, Yajur, Sama*, and *Atharva Vedas*, the *Itihasas, Puranas, Upanishads*, verses and *mantras, sutras*, and the spiritual knowledge and explanations within, all emanate from the Supreme Being." Thus, they all have importance in presenting Vedic information. The *Mahabharata* (*Adi Parva* 1.267) explains the necessity of understanding Vedic knowledge with the help of the *Puranas*: "One should expand and accept the meaning of the *Vedas* with the help of the *Itihasas* and *Puranas*. The *Vedas* are afraid of being mistreated by one who is ignorant of the *Itihasas* and *Puranas*." This is quite similar to what is related in the *Prabhasa-khanda* section of the *Skanda Purana*, where it is said, "I consider the *Puranas* equal to the *Vedas*. . . The *Vedas* feared that their purport would be distorted by inattentive listening, but their purport was established long ago by the *Itihasas* and *Puranas*. What is not found in the *Vedas* is found in the *smritis*. And what is not found in either is described in the *Puranas*. A person who knows the four *Vedas* along with the *Upanishads* but who does not know the *Puranas* is not very learned." The *Naradiya Purana* goes so far as to explain, "I consider the message of the *Puranas* to be more important than that of the *Vedas*. All that is in the *Vedas* is in the *Puranas* without a doubt." So I point this out simply for those scholars who feel that there should be some distinction between *Shruti* and *Smriti* and may object to the way I use the terms "*Vedas*" and "Vedic literature" to mean the same thing, although many parts of the Vedic literature point to the need for using the *Puranas* and other portions of the *Smritis* to understand the depths of Vedic knowledge.

PART ONE

THE SOURCE OF THE MATERIAL CREATION

CHAPTER ONE

Why Understand the Creation of the Universe

Why should we understand how the universe was created? Because it gives us a clearer understanding of where we have come from, where we are going, who and what we are, and what our purpose is here. There have been many scientific theories over the years about the origin of life and how the universe may have been created. However, science makes little comment on the purpose of the universe or the reason for life. But why would something come to be without a purpose? Once you consider that there is a purpose to life, the search for life's origins may very well lead you into a different direction than simply trying to find an explanation for a mechanical or chemical process of creation. In this book we are going to deal with these points, and more.

We are going to take a look at a different approach to the origin of the universe, the Vedic approach. The difference between most scientists and the Vedic approach is that the Vedic system accepts a descending channel of knowledge coming from previous authorities. Scientists accept no prior authority, except for other scientists, and try to discover the mysteries of the universe through their own perceptions by various instruments, experiments, and the use of mathematical formulas to try to verify their theories. This is called the ascending process. However, if one should diligently take this process to its ultimate conclusion, one will reach the same line of thought as the descending method.

For example, in the 1930s, Sir James Jeans concluded in his book, *The Mysterious Universe* (1930), that the universe consists of pure thought, which means the creation must have been an act of thought. However, he felt that the "thinker" had to have been a mathematical thinker working outside the boundaries of time and space, which is part of His creation. Thus, the "thinker" had to have been "beyond what He created." Sir Arthur Eddington also concluded in his book, *The Nature of the Physical World* (1935), that, "The stuff of the world is mind stuff." In part, both of these theories are corroborated in the Vedic texts because it is described that the Supreme Creator produces the material world by His dreaming in *yoga-nidra*, His mystic slumber. Thus, the material creation is the Supreme Being's dream, or a display of His thought energy. Furthermore, the Vedic literature describes how the Supreme Being exists outside the boundaries of the material manifestation from where He begins the process of creation. So, He is indeed "beyond what He created."

It was also in the 1930s when scientists played with the idea that all life and consciousness began from a "primordial soup." This would be a soup of all the necessary chemicals needed to produce a living cell that would somehow combine in just the right way to spark a living organism.

Another idea was the theory of the BIG BANG, that all creation started from a single point or particle. This particle had unlimited depth and weight that somehow exploded to produce the universe. This, however, is mathematically indescribable. It is called a singularity, which means it is impossible. Nonetheless, this theory, as with the theory of evolution, is often taken to be a fact, upon which many other theories become based. However, they do not explain from where or how the original particle appeared.

The theories of the primordial soup and BIG BANG depend on the idea that inert matter can randomly organize itself into complex structures and various species of life. That is the fundamental trouble with both of these theories: How can inert matter by itself develop the incredible molecular arrangements to produce even the simplest cell? Matter does not organize itself that way. In fact, it can be seen that matter, once put into some form of construction and then left alone, always deteriorates. As scientists develop newer instruments to take a closer look at cells, they understand how truly miraculous such a random occurrence could be. Thus, it becomes obvious that nature needs to be directed by some higher force or intelligence for such combinations of material ingredients to come together to produce life. This immediately nullifies Darwin's theory of evolution. Even Darwin admitted that there were problems with his theory.

However, the modern theory and the Vedic description of evolution are similar, but there is one big difference. The modern theory teaches that one simple species produces another species through variations of genetic reproduction until we have a variety of progressively more complex life forms. The Vedic system, on the other hand, teaches that evolution starts in the opposite way. From a complex species, such as God, and then the *devas* or demigods who are the co-creators, and through the process of reproduction and genetic variations, there is a production of continually less complex species. This could be called the process of inverse evolution. However, the modern theory cannot explain why there are galaxies, or how the simplest of cells were formed. So there are many gaps in the modern theories of creation and evolution that are still waiting for further evidence to be solved. So why should science not look at the Vedic view as well?

My suggestion is that the assumption of a BIG BANG is the scientists interpretation of evidence that indicates an exceedingly sudden arise of material elements as they were manifested from the Supreme Being. The Supreme Creator is, of course, spiritual and would be undetectable and beyond observation in the material sense by our limited senses and ordinary instruments. Thus, there would be nothing that we could see to indicate His presence in the universe before the creation. So it may certainly look as if this universe did come from nothing. Nonetheless, the process of the sudden development of the stars, planets, and galaxies could have been similar to the ideas that the scientists have put forth.

The problem is that even if something like the BIG BANG did occur without the supervision of a higher authority, what you would really end up having is a universe filled with dust. Why would such solid planets, suns, stars, and galaxies form out of this floating dust? And there certainly has been no scientific explanation why there is consciousness that inhabits the millions of species of beings. How could a BIG BANG bring about consciousness? From where did it come? These things are not explained by science. So it is not unreasonable to consider other theories about how this universe came into being, and how there was a development of so many species of life that have consciousness.

Another problem is that trying to apply simple physical laws on complex phenomenon like the creation requires the use of assumptions and guesswork which make such scientific theories no better than superstitions, even if such ideas are supported by other scientists or mathematicians. Their conclusions are misleading. This is why scientists are always changing or updating their conclusions as they make new discoveries. If they did not have it right the first time, why should we think they may have it right later on? And they will never get it right if they have only one theory and simply try to make all of their evidence fit that theory. They need to look at other possibilities.

Furthermore, the whole idea of a random reorganization of matter directly opposes the second law of thermodynamics. This law states that as time goes on, there is an increase in entropy, which is an increase in the state of random disorder or deterioration. This means that without a higher intelligence to intercede in the steady disorganization of elements, the universe is in a constant state of gradual decline. This is directly opposite to the idea that matter could organize itself into increasingly complex systems of stars, planets, and galaxies, or even cells, bodies, and various species. So such an organization of matter after a BIG BANG could never have taken place, nor could a BIG BANG have occurred. How could there have been a single particle of unlimited depth and weight floating around in the void universe waiting to explode? Someone had to have put it there. And how could it have exploded into unlimited atoms that formed the universe? Such theories are simply more scientific myths. So how else could the universe have been formed and from where does consciousness come?

First of all, consciousness does not come from a combination of chemicals. Consciousness is a non-material energy. Thus, consciousness exists before, during, and after the material creation. This means that the origin of the material cosmos and all life within it must also be consciousness, a Supreme Consciousness from whom come all other forms of consciousness that take up residence in the varieties of material bodies or species found in this material creation. This origin must also have intelligence and the ability to design in order to make the various combinations of elements come together to form even the simplest of cells. A single cell is formed by a combination of 300 amino acids that come together in a certain chain or pattern. Even scientists cannot figure out how that happened. And nature cannot do it by itself, as explained above. So there had to have been a guiding Creator to put this all together.

So if there is such a Supreme Creator with consciousness and intelligence, it is also quite possible that He would allow a way for us to communicate with Him. It is also quite possible that He provides us with the knowledge we need for us to know how to do this and to understand what we are and the purpose of life. For example, according to Vedic science, as the Supreme Creator creates the cosmos, the creative potency descends among other beings who are created, called demigods in the Vedic system, to assist the Supreme in manifesting the material worlds. So, the Supreme expands Himself and also creates positions within the material cosmos which are taken by co-creators or demigods who assist in creating and maintaining the material manifestation. They also help distribute the spiritual knowledge among all others. This is the descending process of acquiring knowledge by which we understand the mysteries of life. It is the information provided by the Supreme Creator that descends through the ancient sages and scriptures, and His pure representatives. In this way, we can learn about the universe and its purpose rather than trying to understand it only by analyzing minute cells and parts of the cosmos, the way of modern science.

We need to be aware that scientists may continue to try to find the cause and origin of the universe for thousands of years, but they will not find it. They will never find the source by examining the elements within the universe. They may get clues through such a process and realize that all molecules and elements are like signs that point to a Creator, but you have to reach the Creator to understand how everything happened. Therefore, the reason why they will never find the cause of the universe by only using this method is that the original cause of the creation exists OUTSIDE the universe. It is like analyzing the elements within a house to find its cause when the designer lives somewhere else outside the house. Thus, until the scientists can reach the Creator through spiritual understanding, examining the universe to find its cause or source is like a maze that has no end.

Our premise, on the other hand, is that all life comes from God. Almost every religion accepts this. Unfortunately, the problem is that most religions and traditions provide only a short and unscientific story or allegory of the universal creation. However, the Vedic literature, such as the *Srimad-Bhagavatam*, explains that the universal creation is but an expansion or a development from the original spiritual elements. These exist prior to, during, and after the material creation. By understanding the Supreme Creator and the spiritual nature, the cause of the material manifestation can be understood. Not the other way around.

The universe started in a state of perfect simplicity. The design of this universe comes from that dimension of ultimate cause and simplicity, which is that of the spiritual. This is beyond the material strata and where the cause of the universe and the seed of its manifestation exists. The Vedic literature points the way to this region and presents the blueprints of the universe and all life within.

The energies of matter and spirit are energies that vibrate at different frequencies and manifest on diverse levels. However, they both originate from the same source, which is consciousness, the pure consciousness of the Supreme Being. Yet, the spiritual strata is eternal while the material is temporary. Thus, the material plane is subservient to, and pervaded by, the unlimited spiritual energy. It is this spiritual energy which is the foundation of the material realm and interacts with it in all phases, although unbeknownst to those who are spiritually unaware. To know the universe is to know that each atom is but a reflection of the Supreme Creator's potency.

The Vedic literature explains how the material elements are created, and how they make systems and arrangements of forms from planets to various species of life. It describes how the material energy is directed and maintained to prevent it from sliding into deterioration, and how it is finally destroyed or wrapped up to merge back into the spiritual atmosphere. So in this book we will show by Vedic descriptions how the temporary material cosmic creation comes from the Supreme Being and the eternal spiritual nature, and what we are supposed to do while living here.

CHAPTER TWO

Comparisons Between Some of the Creation Legends

There are many stories about the creation of the universe from around the world, and it would be to our benefit for us to take a brief look at some of these before we proceed into the Vedic version. One of the best known traditions of the universal creation, and maybe least understood, is that found in the book of *Genesis*. The story is found in the first three chapters of the book. Therein, it is described that in the beginning God created the heaven and earth. The earth was without form, and void; and darkness was upon the face of the deep, and the spirit of God moved upon the face of the waters.

This means that there was already water somewhere, which was deep, and darkness filled the area. As we will read in the chapters in this volume, this description in the Bible sounds quite similar to the Vedic process of creation. The deep water was likely the Garbhodaka Ocean, situated at the bottom of the universe. The spirit of God was likely a reference to the form of Vishnu who floats on the Garbhodaka Ocean. And the planets, such as earth, had not yet been formed.

Then, after God created the heavens and the earth, he said, "Let there be light," and there was light. Then, after calling the light Day and the darkness Night, the first day's work was done.

Thereafter, God made the firmament, which was both under and above the waters. So these were not ordinary waters, but were encompassing the firmament, or the universal manifestation. This water was likely the Karana Ocean, which had previously been manifested and envelopes the universes that float in its water. This completed the second day.

Then God made the dry land, or the earth, and gathered the water together to create the seas. Thereafter, God had the earth bring forth grass, the herb yielding seeds, and the fruit bearing trees. This completed the third day.

Then the Lord made the sun for the day, the moon for the night, and the stars in the heavens. This completed the fourth day.

Then God made the waters to bring forth abundantly the living and moving creatures, and every winged fowl. And God created great whales and every living creature, which the waters brought forth. God blessed them to be fruitful and multiply, and fill the waters in the seas, and let the fowl multiply the earth. That was the fifth day.

On the sixth day, God let the earth bring forth the living creatures, and the cattle, the creeping things, and the beasts. Then God said, "Let us make man in *our* image, after *our* likeness: and let them have dominion over the fish of the sea, and over the fowl, the cattle, and over all the earth, and over every creeping thing." So God created man in His own image, male and female. God blessed them and said to be fruitful, and multiply over the earth. God said that for food, every creature was provided the herb bearing seed and fruits, which shall be for their food. And that concluded the sixth day.

This means that man was the last to be created. Again, we find that this description is similar to that presented in the ancient Vedic literature, except less detailed. Furthermore, if the creatures were made in a way to be satisfied to eat seeds or grains and fruits, it must have been a very paradisaical time, which is the way the Bible describes it. There was no need for hunting, killing, or slaughter. Similarly, in the Vedic version, this would have been the peaceful and harmonious time called the age of Satya-yuga, when all mankind and creatures lived in peace, and the earth supplied all necessities without endeavor.

Thereafter, in the second chapter of *Genesis*, it is explained that God rested, having seen that His creation was complete.

Interestingly, another version of the creation, quite different from the first, immediately starts in the fourth verse of the second chapter of *Genesis*. In this account, the Lord does not take six days to manifest the creation, but creates the earth and the heavens in a single day. It explains that the Lord had not made it to rain upon the earth, nor was there a man to till the ground, so there were no plants or herbs of the field. But there went up a mist from the earth which watered the whole face of the land. Only then did God form a man from the dust of the ground, and breathed life into him through his nostrils.

The Lord then planted a garden east of Eden and put the man into it. In the garden, the Lord also put every tree that is pleasant for sight and for food, as well as the tree of life and the tree of knowledge of good and evil. A river went out of Eden to water the garden and then divided into four branches. The first branch was named Pison, which encompassed the whole land of Havilah. The second branch was Gihon, which went around the land of Ethiopia. The third branch was Hiddekel, which went into the land of Assyria, and the fourth was the Euphrates.

The Persian account of paradise also relates that four great rivers came from Mount Alborj; two going to the north and two to the south. The Chinese description of their paradise mentions that the waters issued from a fountain of immortality and then became divided into four rivers. The Vedic literature also relates that four sacred rivers started from the holy land of Mount Meru. So the biblical description of four rivers coming from paradise is a view shared by many cultures.

After this, the biblical legend relates how the Lord established that man could eat from any tree in the garden except the tree of the knowledge of good and evil. If he should eat from that tree, he would surely die that day.

Then the Lord considered that it was not good that man should live alone. Then from out of the ground the Lord formed every beast of the field, and every fowl of the air, and brought them unto Adam so he could name them. After Adam had given names to the animals, there was still not found a helper for him. So the Lord caused a deep sleep to fall upon Adam, and the Lord took one of his ribs and then closed up the flesh. With the rib from Adam, the Lord made a woman and brought her to Adam. Then Adam named her Woman since she had been taken out of man.

Muslims also believe that Allah created the first man, Adam, and first woman, Hawa, in paradise, which was in a perfect and far larger universe. There they lived a most happy life. However, after being tricked by Satan, who was jealous of God, they engaged in the direct disobedience to God's orders and were sent out of paradise to earth.

The Tahitians have a similar story. After the God Taarao manifested the world, he created man out of the red earth, which was also the food of man until bread was made. Taarao one day called the man by name. When he came, he caused him to fall asleep and then took out one of his bones. With it, he made a woman whom he gave to the man as his wife. They became the progenitors of mankind. The woman was named Ivi, which signifies a bone. (Notice the linguistic similarity between Eve and Ivi.)

Continuing with the biblical account, after this everything was supposed to have gone most harmoniously until the nasty serpent shows up to temp the woman, who thereafter was called Eve. As a result, the serpent convinced Eve to eat of the tree of knowledge because even if she ate of it she would not die, as the Lord had proclaimed, but would be as *gods*. So she did eat and gave it also to Adam, and the result was not death. However, their eyes were opened and they could now recognize that they were both naked and they sewed fig leaves together for aprons. When they heard the voice of God walking in the garden they hid themselves. When the Lord understood what had happened, that they had eaten from the tree of knowledge, he cursed Adam in various ways, above all cattle, and above every beast of the field, and that he would eat bread only by the sweat of his face, till he returned to the ground as the dust from which he was made. And the woman was cursed to greatly multiply in sorrow and during conception; in sorrow she would bring forth children; and her desire would be her husband, and he would rule over her.

Then the Lord made coats of skins and clothed the two. And the Lord said, "Behold, the man is become as one of *us*, to know good and evil; and now, lest he put forth his hand and eat from the tree of life and live forever," so the Lord sent them from the garden of Eden to till the ground from whence he was taken. The Lord placed Cherubims on the east side of the garden and a flaming sword which turned every way to guard the way to the tree of life.

* * *

So herein we have two different versions of the creation found in the very beginning of the Bible. They differ in the order of events and in the purpose of mankind after his fall from grace. By studying these accounts we can see that in the first account the earth was created or emerged from the waters and was saturated with moisture, which had to be gathered in one place so the dry land could appear. In the second version, the whole face of the ground required to be moistened.

In the first version, the birds and beasts are created before man, and in the second, man is created first. In the first account, all fowls that fly are made out of the waters, while in the second they are made out of the ground. In the first story, man is created in the image of God, while in the second man is made out of the dust and animated by the breath of life. Only after eating the forbidden fruit does the Lord say that because of this man has become as one of *us* and knows the good and evil.

In the first account, man is made lord of the whole earth, while in the second he is merely placed in the garden to dress and keep it. And again, in the first account the man and woman are created together as the completion work of the whole process of creation, while in the second version, the beasts and birds are created after the appearance of the man and before the creation of the woman.

The conclusion is that the second version was composed by a different writer than the first. Further evidence of this can be seen in that the first version refers to God by the name Elohim (plural), whereas throughout the second account He is called Jehovah Elohim. Thus, the accounts of two writers have been joined together with no reference to their inconsistencies. This makes it obvious that these versions of the creation came from another source and were merely adopted or added to this scripture. The next step is to find from where these legends of creation originated.

One point to consider is that in regard to the stories of the creation, the biblical version is one of the more modern. There are many versions from other cultures which are much more ancient. For example, in the biblical account, God's work of creation took place over six days. The older Persian tradition agrees with this. However, we can ask, is it six days of the humans on earth, or is it six days of the demigods, which consist of many thousands of human days? For example, the ancient Etruscan legend, which is almost the same as the Persian, relates how God created the universe not in six days, but in six thousand years. In the first thousand, He created the heaven and earth; in the second, the firmament; in the third, the waters of the earth; in the fourth, the sun, moon, and stars; in the fifth, the animals belonging to air, water, and land; and in the sixth, man alone. Again, this order of events is quite similar to the Vedic version from India. Not only this, but the cosmogony of the Babylonians, the Phoenicians, and the Chaldeans contain some of the same similarities.

The *Zend Avesta*, the sacred text of the Parsees, also relates that the Supreme Being, Ahuramazda, created the universe and man in six periods of time. First it was the heavens, then the waters followed by the earth, then trees and plants, then animals, and finally man. After the Creator finished His work, he rested. The teachings of Zoroaster, the one known as Zarathustra, were put together sometime around 628 B.C. However, these were, basically, the collected teachings of the previous two Zoroasters, one of which had lived nearly 7000 years ago, and the other around 2000 to 3000 years later. This means that this philosophy and culture, and their rendition of the creation story, are much older than the books of the Bible.

Furthermore, according to this version, after the first man and woman had been created, they lived in purity and innocence. Perpetual happiness was promised them by the Creator if they persevered in their virtue. However, an evil demon, sent by Ahriman, the prince of devils, came to them in the form of a serpent and gave them fruit from a powerful tree, which imparted immortality. Evil inclinations then entered their hearts, and all their moral excellence was destroyed. For this reason they fell and lost the eternal happiness for which they had been destined. They killed beasts and clothed themselves in the skins. The evil demon obtained still more power over their minds and called forth envy, hatred, discord, and rebellion, which raged in the hearts of the families that followed.

From this evidence we can consider, as stated by Bishop Colenso [1] (quoted from *The Pentateuch and Book of Joshua Critically Examined*), that for such accounts and legends to exist outside of Israel, we must, therefore, conclude that the author of *Genesis* had no vision before him but merely used a tradition which had been passed down from other cultures from which he based his writing.

Another interesting fact is that around the time of 1873, Mr. George Smith of the British Museum learned of cuneiform inscriptions that show conclusively that the Babylonians had this legend of the creation some 1500 years or more before the Hebrews had ever heard of it. However, the inscriptions, which had been discovered by English archeologists, were not complete. The portions regarding the tree and serpent have not been found, but Babylonian engravings found on gems show these incidents were evidently a part of the original legend. The tree of life in the book of *Genesis* appears to correspond with the sacred grove of Anu, which was guarded by a sword turning to all four points of the compass.

In this regard, Mr. Smith, in his book, *The Chaldean Account of Genesis* (pp. 13-14), relates that, "Whatever the primitive account may have been from which the earlier part of the book of *Genesis* was copied, it is evident that the brief narration given in the Pentateuch omits a number of incidents and explanations--

for instance, the origin of evil, the fall of the angels, the wickedness of the serpent, etc. Such points as these are included in the cuneiform narrative."

* * *

Another point that seems to have been a prominent part of the creation tradition that is found in many parts of the world is the idea of happiness in a special garden, like Eden, or a time of harmony between God and the first of the humans. The troubles that followed were brought about by inquisitiveness, or the loss of control of desires, which is a trait shared in the legends of many cultures. For example, in the Greek tradition, Epimethens received from the god Zeus a gift in the form of a beautiful woman, Pandora. She brought with her a vase, the lid of which was meant to remain closed. The curiosity of her husband tempted him to open it, and suddenly there escaped from it such things as troubles, weariness, and illness from which mankind was never free. Thereafter, hope was all that remained.

The Tibetans also had a paradisaical time, which was more complete. However, the desire to eat of a certain sweet herb deprived men of their spiritual life. Then there arose in men a sense of shame, and the need to clothe themselves. Necessity forced them into agriculture, and then the virtues disappeared, and murder, adultery, and other vices became apparent.

The black people of East Africa also have legends of how the fall of man is connected with the need to engage in agriculture. Especially the Calabar legend of the creation presents many interesting points similar to the biblical story. There we find that the first human pair are called by a bell at meal-times to Abasi, the Calabar God, in heaven. In place of the forbidden tree of *Genesis*, we find that Abasi had prohibited the use of agriculture and propagation. Man fell into trouble when he transgressed these commands and used implements of tillage to which the woman was tempted by a female friend. From that moment man became mortal, and, like the biblical account, he could eat bread only by the sweat of his brow.

The Persians also record a region of bliss and happiness called Heden, more beautiful than the rest of the world. This was the abode of the first men, where a great river flowed through it. This was before they had been tempted by an evil spirit in the form of a serpent to partake of the forbidden fruit tree known as Hom.

Another parallel to the Eden myth is found with the ancient Greeks in their tradition that the islands of the blessed, the Elysium, located on the borders of earth, abounded in every charm of life. In the garden of the Hesperides, the paradise, there was a tree bearing golden apples of immortality. It was guarded by three nymphs, and a serpent, or dragon, called Ladon. It was one of the requirements of Hercules to gather some of these apples of life. When he arrived, he found the garden protected by the dragon. Ancient medallions or coins show a tree with a serpent wrapped around it. In the depictions, Hercules has gathered an apple, and near him stand the three nymphs, the Hesperides.

The ancient Egyptians also had the legend of the tree of life. It is mentioned in their sacred books that Osiris ordered the names of some souls to be written on this tree of life, of which the fruit made those who ate it to become as gods.

The Chinese also have their time of virtue when nature provided plenty of food without labor. The seasons were untroubled by wind or storms, and man lived peacefully, surrounded by all the beasts, with no calamity, sickness, or death. In their sacred books we find a story of a mysterious garden where a special tree grew apples of immortality. This was guarded by a winged serpent, called a dragon. Waters flowed from a fountain of immortality, from where four rivers had their source.

The ancient *Edda* of the Scandinavians also relates a time called the golden age when all was pure and harmonious. This age lasted until the arrival of a woman who came from Jotunheim, the region of the giants, who corrupted the age.

Even the inhabitants of Madagascar had a similar legend to the Eden story. Their account relates how the first man was also made of the dust of the earth and placed in a garden where he encountered no ills or death. Though surrounded by delicious fruits, he had no bodily appetites. Though beautiful streams were everywhere, he had no thirst. The Creator strictly forbade him to eat or drink [which would refer to indulging in material or bodily desires]. Then a great enemy came to him and described in great colors the delightful taste of the apple, the lusciousness of the date, and sweetness of the orange. Thus, after having resisted these temptations for so long, the man at last ate the fruit and fell into mortality.

From the above evidence, we can see that the idea of an early paradise or spiritual garden, and a time of peace and harmony, as well as the fall of mankind, were not exclusive to the early history of the Hebrews. Indeed, most of the ancient nations and cultures also have their stories relating to an early and most happy time, or a special abode wherein concern was not known, and the need to work was absent. In this way, we can recognize how the first two chapters of *Genesis*, and many other short versions of the story of creation, are written in an Eastern style. They are merely summarized versions of a more ancient legend of the world's creation and the fall of man. Thus, such summarizations cannot be expected to be the full word of God, as some people proclaim. There are most likely other references and texts which contain more of the word of God. This is also the reason why some of these stories, two of which we find in the Bible, will naturally contain a variety of differences in the versions they present. For this reason, we can also anticipate that it will not hold the complete truth regarding the nature of mankind and the purpose of the creation. Older traditions may indeed contain a more complete version and a deeper understanding of the process of the material creation and of who and what we are, as we will see.

* * *

The Mayan *Popol Vuh* offers another view of the creation legend. It describes that in the beginning there was not one person, nor any animal, bird, fish, tree, nor any canyon, meadow, or forest. Only the sky was there, and the face of the earth was not yet developed. Under all the sky was the pooled sea. There was nothing else. Everything was at rest. Whatever there might be was not there, only the sea and the darkness. Only the Maker, the Modeler alone, and the Plumed Serpent, the begetters, were in the water.

[Now this certainly sounds much like the Vedic description of the beginning of the material manifestation, as described in the chapters that follow in this book. For therein we also find that in the beginning there was nothing but the Gharbhodaka Ocean at the bottom of the universe under the sky, and nothing else had yet been developed. All was in darkness, and nothing stirred. There was only Lord Vishnu resting on the water, on the coils of the great serpent, Seshanaga, whose many hoods appear swaying in the air. Is the "Plumed Serpent" originally a reference to Seshanaga? These are the "begetters" of the material universe.]

Continuing with the *Popol Vuh*, then came His word in the early dawn of creation, in the blackness of the universe. Then they joined their words and thoughts, and things became clear for the process of creation. Then the seed of humanity developed, along with the generation of trees, bushes, and the growth of life, of humankind, in the blackness. This was because of the Heart of Sky, named Hurricane. Thunderbolt Hurricane came first, then Newborn Thunderbolt, and then Raw Thunderbolt. Thus, three of them came to the Plumed Serpent when the dawn of life was conceived.

[The "word" of the Lord could be compared to the word of Lord Vishnu to Brahma, which was *tapa*, meaning austerity. Lord Brahma was the first living being from Lord Vishnu and the secondary engineer of the universe. It was through the performance of austerity that Brahma attained a clear understanding of how to proceed with the creation process. Furthermore, the three thunderbolts mentioned above can practically be compared to the three modes of material nature, namely goodness, passion, and ignorance, which agitated the ingredients of material nature to bring about the cause of creation.]

Then, after some discussion, earth arose because of their word, and like a mist it formed and unfolded. Then the great mountains came forth, and appeared on the mountain with instant groves of cypress and pine. Then channels of water branched around the mountains. Then in the midst of the waters, the sky and the earth were set apart, or divided.

Next they planned the animals of the mountains, such as the deer, birds, jaguars, rattlesnakes, and guardians of the bushes. When the animals were asked to speak, they just made noises or squawked, chattered or howled. They did not offer prayers. So the begetters were not pleased with their creations and set about to create another form of beings. Then they invoked the daykeepers, diviners, and midmost seers. However, there was still a concern to model a person who would be a provider, and one who would recognize and call upon the creators.

[This much also is similar in ways to the Vedic version in the order of what was created. And even as Lord Brahma was creating the various creatures, he also had a little difficulty in the results of the creatures he was creating, like those of the *Popol Vuh*. Since the Vedic version is much older than that of the Maya, it becomes easy to assume that various portions of the *Popol Vuh* are but carry-overs from that found in the Vedic literature, limited in respect to what was remembered, and changed according to the language and preferences of the people of the time.]

Thereafter, as the *Popol Vuh* goes on, came the midwife, the grandmother, Xmucane, and grandfather, Xpiyacoc. From these came the peopling of the face of the earth, human in looks and in speech. Then they multiplied with sons and daughters. However, according to the legend, they were as manikins, carved of wood, with no heart, no blood, and nothing in their minds. Thus, a great flood was devised and all were killed.

From this point, the story of the *Popol Vuh* takes many turns that are unique to the culture of the Maya. Nonetheless, we can see that here is another reference to a great deluge that affected the whole earth, which is common in almost every culture of the world, including the Vedic literature, which contains one of the oldest versions available. Thus, we have to again come to the conclusion that there had once been a common source for most of the world's traditions, which is a thread that can still be recognized running through the various traditions today. In any case, the similarities are fascinating and certainly point to India as a source of the world's spiritual heritage.

Another culture that corroborates this point, and has additional resemblances to the Vedic story of creation, is that of the Chinese. It also refers to how there was nothing that existed at the beginning of time, and anything that manifested did so only by the power of God. The Chinese have a story of the original man, Pangu [similar to Brahma of the Vedic tradition], who brought about the creation. The story relates how at first nothing was manifest, but only chaos existed in a mixture of yin yang--a combination of the male and female energies. [This would be similar to the Shiva/Durga principles of the Vedic story.]

Everything was within the egg of creation, including Pangu, who broke from it and separated chaos into its individual parts, including earth and sky. Then for 18,000 years Pangu grew each day, creating a distance between the earth and sky that reached 30,000 miles. Then he carved out the hills and valleys, rivers, and seas from the earth, and also made the sun, moon, and stars. When he died, his body became the additional parts of the creation, such as the wind from his breath, the rivers from his blood, the soil from his skin, and the fleas in his hair became people. Evil and pain entered only within the space left by Pangu's death.

The Egyptians also have their legends of the creation that offer similarities to the Vedic version. One of the principle stories is elaborated in what is called *The Book of Overthrowing Apophia*. In it the Supreme Being, Khepri, explains that no beings exist before he appears. From his mouth come innumerable beings before there was the physical manifestation of any heaven, earth, or other creatures. In weariness, he had been bound to the deep watery abyss [the Garbhodaka Ocean], and in his heart he had planned or meditated into being all forms of life, which became as his children. [This most likely refers to the way Lord Brahma, though called by a different name in this story, had the seeds of all life within him and simply needed to use the power of his mind through meditation to make them manifest.] Then from him came Shu, and he spat out Tefnut, all of whom became the three principal gods. From Shu and Tefnut came many of the other main personalities of the Egyptian tradition, namely Geb and Nut, who produced Osiris, Horus, Seth, Isis, and Nephthys.

Here again we have a story of the creation that seems so short and allegorical that it can hardly be understood. However, by comparing it with other references, it can begin to make sense regarding what it means. Furthermore, it also seems to contain references to a more complete and older rendition of the story of how God manifested the universe.

The oldest written account of the creation of the world is found in the Vedic literature, the compilation of which dates back 5,000 years, and a tradition which dates back thousands of years further. Actually, there is no date to which the beginning of the Vedic culture can be set. It has existed from beyond recorded history. It is also the Vedic version of the creation which describes that when mankind was first manifested in this world, it was in the age of Satya-yuga, which is called the Golden Age, a time of peace and harmony to which many legends refer. It was only with time that mankind gave way to the dictates of his lust and avarice, because of which life became more difficult.

The Vedic version also describes the darkness and void of the universe before anything was manifested, and how the Supreme Being expanded Himself from the spiritual world and manifested Himself within the universe as Lord Vishnu and gave birth to Brahma. Brahma then began the secondary stage of the universal creation, which included the formation of the planets and all species of life, including the first of the human species in the golden age of Satya-yuga. This is to what most traditions refer, however much the names and activities of the characters may have changed.

We can also recognize that most legends depict man being created as a perfect spiritual being, only to become a fallen and broken reflection of what he once was. This is even more closely related to the Vedic version once we understand the Vedic descriptions of how the soul is manifested and then appears in the material world, or falls from his spiritual identity. Indeed, the garden of paradise, to which so many cultures refer, may indeed be a reference to the spiritual world, or the spiritual nature of the living being, from which the living being falls and enters material existence. It is this from which the living entity must be redeemed by regaining his spiritual identity.

So as we read the chapters that follow in this book on the Vedic story of the creation of the universe, we will acquire many more details about how the world was manifested, from where it came, and how the living being takes birth in such an existence. Through this means, we will also more deeply understand the versions of other cultures, and receive a view and comprehension of our origins and identity the likes of which no other culture has to offer.

SUMMARY OF THE VEDIC PROCESS OF CREATION
FROM THE MANU-SAMHITA

To help show how other legends from various cultures tie into the Vedic version, or how they contain references that lead back to the more complete Vedic description, I will now present a summary of the creative process as found in the *Manu-samhita*. The information in the *Manu-samhita* is itself a shorter version of the more complete details found in the *Puranas*, but I will present and elaborate on the finer points in the chapters that follow.

Our story begins with the time when the great sages of the world approached Manu. He was seated with a collected and equipoised mind. After duly showing him their respects, they spoke to him. They asked if he might share his knowledge of the sacred laws of the four *varnas*, or social divisions, for he alone knew the full knowledge of the soul, which is unfathomable, as taught by He who is self-existent.

Manu, whose power and knowledge are immeasurable, having been asked by those sages who were possessed of great minds, answered, "Listen." He then proceeded to explain to them the answer to all of their questions by starting at the beginning of time.

The universe originally existed in a state of darkness, unperceivable, without distinctions or separated parts. It was unknowable by reasoning or logic, wholly immersed in a state of dormancy. Then the divine self-existent one, Lord Vishnu, capable of making all of the universal elements discernable, appeared with full creative power, and dispelled the darkness. He who is subtle, indiscernible, and eternal, who contains all created beings, who is perceived only by the internal organ developed by devotion, shone forth by His own will.

Desiring to produce many kinds of beings from His own body, He first created the waters [the Karana or Causal Ocean] by a thought, and placed His seed, or energy, in them in the form of the innumerable universes. Those seeds took the shape of golden eggs, the universes, each one brilliant like the sun. Then in each egg He expanded himself [into Garbhodakashayi Vishnu], and then took the form of Brahma, the [first living entity and] progenitor of the world. The waters, called *narah*, are the offspring of Nara; and as they were his first residence, he is called Narayana. He is also called so because He is the ultimate shelter of all living beings.

Brahma resided in that egg for a whole year [of the demigods], and then by himself, through thought alone, divided it into the heaven and the earth. Between them was the middle sphere, and the eight directions, and the waters. From himself, he drew forth the mind, and sense of ego [the material false ego]. From the three qualities, the material modes of passion, ignorance, and goodness, came the organs of sense perception. By joining those particles with his own energy, he created all beings.

In the beginning, he assigned the names, actions, and functions to all created beings, according to the instructions of the *Veda*. [Thus, the *Veda* is the blueprint for the creation of the material worlds.] Thereafter, he created the class of demigods who are endowed with life [for the maintenance of the universe], and the eternal rituals or sacrifices for the well-being of all. Then he drew forth the threefold *Vedas*, namely the *Rig*, *Yajur*, and the *Sama*, for the due performance of such sacrifices.

In the process of creation, such things were manifested as time and the divisions of time, the lunar mansions and planets, the rivers, oceans, mountains and plains, along with austerity, speech, pleasure, desire, and anger. All that is in the whole creation he likewise produced, as he desired to bring all such things and beings into existence.

Then he separated merit from demerit, and caused the creatures to be affected by the dualities of pain and pleasure. [This is also the beginning of effective *karma* on the living entities.] To whatever tendency was assigned each kind of being, whether gentle or harmful, sinful or virtuous, truthful or with falseness, that quality is spontaneously accepted by each creature in all succeeding creations. Thus, of their own accord, the living beings assume their own tendency or accepted course of action in new births.

The creator also caused the manifestation of the social divisions, four *varnas*, of humans, namely the *brahmana*, *kshatriya*, *vaishya*, and *shudra*, which represents the power of his mouth, arms, legs, and feet respectively.

The ten great mind-born sages were created, namely Marichi, Atri, Angiras, Pulastya, Pulaha, Kratu, Prachetas, Vishishtha, Bhrigu, and Narada. They created other Manus possessing great clarity and brilliance, as well as other classes of gods and sages. Then other beings were manifested, such as the Yakshas, servants of Kubera, and the demons called the Rakshashas and Pishakas, the Gandharvas, or angel-like musicians of the gods, and the heavenly dancers called the Apsaras. Also, the snake-like beings known as the Nagas and Sarpas, and the bird-like beings called Suparnas, along with several classes of ancestors were created.

Within the material creation also came the lightning bolts, clouds, rainbows, falling meteors, comets, and heavenly lights. Other creatures that were created included the Kinnaras, monkeys, fishes, many kinds of birds, cattle, deer, carnivorous beasts, and other classes of men. There also came small and large worms, beetles, moths, lice, flies, and all stinging and biting insects, and other kinds of immovable entities, or plants. Thus, this whole creation and all creatures within it, both movable and immovable, were produced by the high-minded ones by means of their strength of austerities, and at the Lord's command.

When that divine one, Brahma, the first living being from Lord Vishnu, wakes, then this world stirs. Nothing exists before his power awakens that which is to be manifested. However, when he slumbers, then the universe sinks into sleep, inertia, and destruction. Thus, as the eternal and imperishable one enters alternate states of wakefulness and sleep, he incessantly revives and destroys this whole creation. The times the worlds are created are numberless, and Brahma repeats it again and again.

After the world is created in completeness, the beginning of humankind is in the age of Satya or Krita-yuga when religion and piety are wholly manifested, people live for hundreds of years, and truth and harmony prevail in the lives of all. The activities of men hold no unrighteousness. Thus, it is a most peaceful and pleasant time to live in which the world provides all necessities like a garden or a heaven. Only through the desire for easy gain and pleasure by unrighteous means does the world lose its religiosity and peace, and does theft, falsehood, and fraud become prevalent. Thus, life becomes increasingly difficult for all, [and mankind gradually needs to acquire necessities through labor].

In this way, even though this is merely a summary of the Vedic process of how the world is manifested, as found in the *Manu-samhita*, we can see how many of the world's legends of creation can tie into the Vedic version. We can recognize many aspects mentioned earlier in this chapter from the stories in the Bible, the *Popol Vuh*, and in those found from the Egyptians, Chinese, Africans, etc., that can be traced to this most ancient description from the Vedic culture. Many details that have not been included in the *Manu-samhita* are presented in other portions of the Vedic literature, which we will glean and explain in the following chapters. Then even more information regarding the hidden meanings in the narratives of other cultures, and their similarities and references to Vedic traits, will come to light. In conclusion, we will be able to more clearly understand the universal story of the creation through this study. Furthermore, another aspect of our ancient and spiritual past we begin to open up to us.

DESCRIPTIONS OF THE BEGINNING OF CREATION
FROM OTHER EARLY VEDIC TEXTS

There are many other early Vedic texts which offer descriptions of the creation of the cosmos. These include the main Vedic *Samhitas*, such as the *Rig-veda* and *Atharva-veda*, as well as the *Upanishads*, such as the *Chandogya* and *Aitareya*, and others. All of them relate various aspects of how the material manifestation comes from the Supreme Creator. For example, one of the oldest of the Vedic *samhitas*, the *Rig-veda* (10.129.1-6), explains that everything originally came from the Supreme Being. It describes that in the beginning of the creation there was neither non-existence nor existence. There was no realm of air or sky beyond it. There was no water, nor death or immortality. There was neither day nor night. Only that One Thing, the Supreme, breathed by its own nature. Apart from it was nothing whatsoever but darkness. At first all was indiscriminate chaos concealed in that darkness. All that existed then was void and formless. Thereafter, arose desire in the beginning. Desire, which is the primal seed and germ of Spirit.

The *Rig-veda* (10.121.1) goes on to describe that in the beginning rose Hiranyagarbha, the Supreme Creator, born the only Lord of all created beings. He fixes and holds up this earth and heaven. What other God shall we adore with our oblation?

The *Atharva-veda* (8.9.2, 5, 8, 9) also points out the process by which everything comes from the Supreme Being: God agitates matter. Preparing a threefold home through His greatness, He pervades all objects. God, the Fulfiller of all wishes, the One who envelopes matter, creates in the atmosphere vast different worlds. . . This material world evolves out of the subtle primary matter. God changes the subtle matter into material objects. Intellect is born of God the embodiment of intellect. God lords over the soul. . . With the dissolution of matter into its nascent atomic state, the worlds disappear. With its reappearance the worlds reappear. Under whose law and behest this universe comes into existence, that God is Supreme, and protector of the world. Breathless matter moves by breath of living creatures. Lifeless matter goes closely after the self-luminous Supreme Being. Some wise persons behold and some ignorant persons do not behold the matter when it assumes different forms by the touch of the all-pervading God.

In this way, the *Atharva-veda* points out how those people with spiritual knowledge can understand how all matter and its varied forms are products of the energy of the Supreme. However, those without such knowledge consider that lifeless matter creates forms by itself and of its own accord.

The *Brihadaranyaka Upanishad* (1.4.7) relates this same fact in a similar way: Verily, before Brahma became the secondary or instrumental cause of the creation of the *jivas*, the world was remaining in its unmanifested form within the hold of its efficient cause: *atmaivedamagra asit*. It became manifest just by the providence of God with its name and form, viz. with its varieties of twenty-four distinctiveness, or elements. Even today this world is characterized by its variegated elements in the same way a person is identified by his name and personality. So, it is by the providence of God who entered within the creation, and His ruling so encompassing even to the tips of the fingernails that He sustains the world. People cannot see that sustainer of the world, who is the final resort of all, because of their own incompleteness. Nonetheless, when one breaths it is only by His providence. Accordingly, when speaking, seeing, hearing, thinking-- everywhere His power is ruling.

The *Aitareya Upanishad* (1.1.1-3) explains things a little further, like so: Before the creation of the universe, verily the Brahman (the Supreme Personality of Godhead in the form of Lord Vishnu) along with His own potency was existent and nothing else remained separately. Thereby it is to be known that His *tatasthashakti* (the potency that encompasses the individual *jiva* souls), and *maya*, His external potency, were not separately existing but they were within Him. So He, the Self-same Almighty, thought, "Let me create the worlds." He created these worlds: Ambahas, Marichi, Maram, and Apah. That Ambahas is above the Dvaus or Svarga or heaven, but the ever-existing Transcendental abode of the Supreme Divinity is the Substratum [beyond the material strata]. Marichi is the middle region. This earth is Mara, or death, because all beings on earth die within a very short span of life. The region of waters below the earth is the Apah. He, the Lord, thought: "These indeed are the worlds (I have created). Let Me now create the custodians of these worlds." Right from the waters He drew forth and shaped a person (*purusha*). And this was the person who became Lord Brahma.

This shows how there are many references in the essential Vedic literature regarding how the Supreme Being began the process of creating the material world. In some places, however, they do go into more detail in their descriptions. Most of the above quotes, however, are rather short and lack the details we need to get a better understanding of the full process that takes place. Only in the *Puranas* do we find the necessary details that allow us to get a complete explanation of the process of the cosmic creation.

The meaning of the word "*Purana*," comes from the Sanskrit *Pura Anati*, which means that it is ancient but still living.[2] The *Puranas* are meant for all classes of people. Since all men are not on the same level of consciousness and are spread over many different types of thinking, feeling, and desiring, the *Puranas* are divided so that any class of people can take advantage of them and utilize them for their own individual spiritual advancement, even to the point of getting out of the material entanglement either gradually or rapidly. So, depending on their position in life, people may use the particular *Puranas* that are most suited for them.

The *Puranas* are divided into two groups consisting of the primary *Mahapuranas* and the secondary *Upa-puranas*. The *Upa-puranas* consist of eighteen, entitled: *Sanatkumara, Narasimha, Naradiya, Shiva, Durvasasa, Kapila, Manava, Ausanasa, Varuna, Kalika, Samba, Nandi, Saura, Parasara, Aditya, Mahesvara, Bhagavata* or *Bhargava*, and *Vasistha*.

The eighteen *Mahapuranas* are divided into three groups. One group considered to be related to *Tamasa*, the mode of ignorance or darkness, which consists of the *Linga, Skanda, Agni, Matsya, Kurma,* and *Shiva* (or sometimes the *Vayu*) *Puranas*. These are usually related to Lord Shiva. The next group is usually related to Lord Brahma and is considered connected to *Rajas*, the mode of passion. These consist of the *Brahma, Brahmanda, Brahma-vaivarta, Markandeya, Bhavisya,* and *Vamana Puranas*. The third group relating to Lord Vishnu with *Sattva*, the mode of purity or goodness prevailing, are the *Vishnu, Bhagavata, Narada* or *Naradiya, Garuda, Padma,* and *Varaha Puranas*.

Out of all the *Puranas,* many scholars seem to agree that the *Vishnu Purana* seems to conform most closely to what a *Purana* is expected to be. It contains the five essential subjects that a *Purana* is supposed to relate and also contains many other topics that are dealt with in detail. The central theme is praise of Vishnu, and it describes many aspects and incarnations of Lord Vishnu along with many stories of Lord Krishna in Vrindavana and Mathura. This *Purana* is quite similar to the contents of the *Bhagavata Purana,* otherwise called *Srimad-Bhagavatam,* which is also centered around the theme of praise of Lord Krishna, the source of all other incarnations of God. This *Purana* also describes many of the pastimes of Lord Krishna in this material creation. This *Purana* is also described as the most ripened fruit of all Vedic knowledge because it was Srila Vyasadeva's own commentary on all the other Vedic literature, most of which he had composed. This is why the *Puranas* give us the most information about how the material realm is manifested.

However, even in the *Puranas* we find variances in the descriptions about the creative process. One reason for this is that the creation is not always the same each time it takes place. This is because the creation is not merely a mechanistic process, but is overseen by a Supreme Being who interacts with those energies and beings that He creates. So the order of this interaction may change from time to time, which is natural when it is based on the interactions between personalities.

Another reason for the differences in descriptions is that there are different classifications of the *Puranas,* as pointed out above, and each one may focus on different aspects of the creation, which then provides slight differences in the explanation or order of events. Reasons for this will become more apparent later in the book. After reviewing the many *Puranas,* I have included the descriptions that are agreed to by most of them. I have used primarily the *Puranas* that are based on the *Sattvic* principle, and the *Srimad-Bhagavatam,* because in most cases they are the more developed in this topic and contain the most information. So now let us begin uncovering the details of how the universe is created and from where it has come and why.

CHAPTER THREE

Everything Comes From the Absolute Truth

Scientists agree that all time, all history, and all creation start from a single point. And that point would have to be the ultimate or Absolute Truth. So what exactly is the Absolute Truth? How do we go back through time and space to find the original source of everything? Even if we research the Bible, the Koran, the Jewish writings, or even the Sikh, Zoroastrian, or Buddhist texts, we will find limited information on what is the Absolute Truth. And forget about depending on modern science, they are still searching and have many varying theories to offer.

Fortunately, the Vedic texts of India have always been a guiding light to provide knowledge of what is the Absolute Truth. For example, the second verse of the *Vedanta Sutras* (1.1.2) clearly explains, "The Absolute Truth is that omniscient, omnipotent, all-merciful Being from whom proceeds all things (origins, sustenance, and dissolution)."

This is similar to the *Aitareya Upanishad* (1.1.2) which states, "He (the Supreme Person) created this entire material world."

Herein we start to understand that the Absolute Truth is a person, the Supreme Person, who is all-powerful, fully merciful, and the origin and source of everything. Thus, the single point from which all time, history, and creation originate is this Supreme Person, God. Actually, this is only logical because material nature is inert. It cannot be the cause of its own creation. Thus, a living brain is behind the great plan for this manifestation. Seeing how everything is wonderfully arranged in this material world for its continued existence, we should understand that a living brain, a person, is the cause of this development, just as a building cannot develop and build itself.

The *Aitareya Upanishad* (3.11) goes on to explain, "He saw, and His power sent forth the creation." The *Brihadaranyaka Upanishad* (4.4.22) continues, "He is the Lord and controller of everyone."

The *Vishnu Purana* (1.3.2) also explains that all creative energies that act in

23

the process of creation, maintenance, and annihilation are the natural characteristics of the Supreme Truth, just as heat and light are the natural energies of fire. Therefore, we can understand that everything in the cosmic creation emanates from this Absolute Truth, and even after its annihilation the material energies again enter the same Absolute Truth.[1]

The definition of this Absolute Truth is presented in the *Vishnu Purana*,[2] that He is the all-pervasive, all-increasing, changeless soul of all. Furthermore, He is one without a second, without whom nothing can exist.[3]

The *Svetasvatara Upanishad* (6.1-5) goes on to explain that God is the ultimate cause of all causes. It is He, the Supreme Person, who pervades the whole world with His consciousness and power. He is the controller of time, through which the creation itself unfolds. It is He who sets the creation in motion and then rests peacefully, after uniting the individual *jiva* souls with the principles of matter. He is the primal cause of the universal creation and propels the living beings toward their material desires. He is the one reality without a second, beyond matter and time. He is beyond the perception of our senses but can be perceived through the eyes of devotion. He is immortal and the monitor of every living being as the Supersoul in the core of everyone's heart. Knowing Him in this way can lead one to final liberation from the material energy.

The *Svetasvatara* (6.8) gives further information about the nature of God and describes the Supreme as having nothing equal to or greater than Him. Through His various potencies He manifests His parts and parcels--the individual living beings--who are all situated differently within His energy. Later on in verse thirteen of the same chapter we find it said, "The Supreme Lord is eternal and the living beings are eternal. The Supreme Lord is cognizant and the living beings are cognizant. The difference is that the Supreme Lord is supplying all the necessities of life for the many other living entities."

The point that God is one only is repeated in the *Svetasvatara Upanishad* (3.2), "Truly God is One; there can be no second. He alone governs these worlds with His powers. He stands facing beings. He, the herdsman [meaning Sri Krishna], after bringing forth all worlds, reabsorbs them at the end of time."

Herein we get an additional hint of who is this Supreme Person. We find He is called the "herdsman," which is a clear reference to His pastime of being a cowherd boy. This is none other than Lord Sri Krishna. And this manifestation of His material energy is considered to be only one of His innumerable pastimes.

The *Kurma Purana* (1.5.1-3) relates that there are innumerable names for the Supreme Person. He is named according to His qualities and activities. "Because He is not born of any prior person, he is called Svayambhu (self-born). Since He is the goal of men, he is called Narayana. Because He is the remover of *samsara* (the cycle of repeated birth and death), He is Hara. He is called Vishnu because of His all pervasiveness. He is called Bhagavan because of His perfect knowledge of everything. He is called OM because of His protectiveness of all. He is called Sarvajna (omniscient) because of His knowledge of everything. He is called Sarva because he is identical with everyone [spiritually of the same quality but infinite in quantity]." And, as we find elsewhere, the name of Krishna means the one who is attractive to everyone, who can provide the greatest pleasure.

In the Vedic classic *Bhagavad-gita* (7.6-7) Lord Krishna is quite clear about being the Absolute Truth, wherein He says, "Of all that is material and all that is spiritual in this world, know for certain that I am both its origin and dissolution. No truth is superior to Me. Everything rests on Me as pearls are strung on a thread." Also (9.5), Krishna explains that He is the maintainer of all living beings and the very source of creation.

In the four most important verses in the *Bhagavad-gita* (10.8-11), Sri Krishna explains, "I am the source of all spiritual and material worlds. Everything emanates from Me. The wise who know this perfectly engage in My devotional service and worship Me with all their hearts."

Even the *Rig-veda* (1.22.20 & 21), one of the oldest of all Vedic texts, establishes that there is no higher truth than Lord Vishnu, Krishna. "The supreme abode of Lord Vishnu, or the lotus feet of Lord Vishnu, is spread all around like the sunlight in the sky. Great demigods and saintly persons always see that supreme abode, recognizing Him as the highest truth. Spiritually awake souls learned in transcendental understanding glorify the Lord and make that abode more brilliant."

Srila Jiva Gosvami also presents a common verse that is found in three *Puranas*, namely the *Padma Purana*, *Linga Purana*, and the *Skanda Purana*, which states, *alodya sarva-shastrani / vicharya cha punah punaha / idam ekam sunishpannam / dhyeyo narayanah sada*: "By scrutinizingly reviewing all the revealed scriptures and judging them again and again, it is now concluded that Lord Narayana is the Supreme Absolute Truth, and thus He alone should be worshiped."

The *Srimad-Bhagavatam* (*Bhagavat Purana*) (10.85.4) also specifically relates how Krishna is, "the Supreme Personality of Godhead, who manifests as the Lord of both nature and the creator of nature [Maha-Vishnu]. Everything that comes into existence, however and whenever it does so, is created within You, by You, from You, for You, and in relation with You."

The *Srimad-Bhagavatam* (11.24.19) goes on to describe how the material nature, time, and Maha-Vishnu, all come from Krishna, who is the Absolute Truth. Furthermore, it is explained that the entire cosmic creation is caused by Lord Krishna, and the material manifestation is an effect of His energy.[4]

Sanatana Gosvami has also concluded, as related in the *Chaitanya-caritamrita*,[5] "Both the material and spiritual world are transformations of Krishna's internal [spiritual] and external [material] potencies. Therefore Krishna is the original source of both material and spiritual manifestations."

The three main categories of these energies of the Lord are explained in the *Vishnu Purana* (6.7.61-63). These are the spiritual potency, by which the spiritual world is manifested; the individual living beings, which belong to the marginal potency since they can enter the spiritual strata or be subject to bewilderment in the material energy; and the third energy is the material potency, which is filled with ignorance and exhibited when the living beings become godless or instilled with the desires for fruitive activities. It is this darkness which covers the living being with forgetfulness of his true spiritual position. Thus, the living beings exist in numerous forms and species while in the material creation. Through these energies, all aspects of the spiritual and material worlds are manifested. In this way, we can understand that not only does everything come from the Supreme Being, but nothing can exist without Him.

The *Vishnu Purana* (1.12.69) goes on to explain that the nature of the Supreme Being Himself is *sat-chit-ananda-vigraha*. This means the personal form of God is eternal and full of pleasure and knowledge. Thus, he is beyond all material influences. However, the living entities, being part of the Supreme in quality, can also experience this eternal pleasure and knowledge to a lesser degree once they regain their eternal spiritual position. [6]

Thus, whatever we see in this material world is but an expansion of the different energies of the Supreme Person.[7] It is He who is the Supreme Being and Creator of all. This is why the *Brahma-samhita* (5.1) explains that, "Krishna, who is known as Govinda, is the supreme controller. He has an eternal, blissful, spiritual body. He is the origin of all. He has no other origin, for He is the prime cause of all causes."

This is also why Krishnadas Kaviraja further explains in his *Chaitanya-caritamrita* (*Adi-lila*, 1.3), "What the *Upanishads* describe as the impersonal Brahman is but the effulgence of His body, and the Lord known as the Supersoul is but His localized plenary portion. He is the Supreme Personality of Godhead, Krishna Himself, full with six opulences. He is the Absolute Truth, and no other truth is greater than or equal to Him."

The *Srimad-Bhagavatam* (1.3.28) specifically relates "*krsnas tu bhagavan svayam*," which means that out of all the various incarnations of God, "Lord Sri Krishna is the Supreme Personality of Godhead in person." All other incarnations are but plenary portions or portions of the plenary expansions of the Lord.

In this way, we can understand that the ultimate philosophical conclusions, as presented in the above Vedic references, and by various spiritual authorities, is that the Absolute Truth is a person, known in the Vedic literature as Sri Krishna. It is He who manifests the material creation through His various forms and energies. Many more verses that establish this are found in the *Bhagavad-gita*, *Brahma-samhita*, as well as various *Puranas* and other Vedic texts written by many spiritual masters and teachers that verify this point, many of which will be presented in the following chapters of this book. So, we will let our present selection in this chapter be enough for now.

CHAPTER FOUR

The Supreme Being Exists Before and After the Material Creation

The point of this chapter is to understand that if the cause of the material creation is the Supreme Being, a personal God and Creator, then the attempt to find the cause of the creation by studying the elements and phenomena within it is futile. Such a study will certainly uncover additional information about the nature of the material realm, but you cannot find the cause of the creation if it is outside the universe. It is like trying to find the cause of the construction of a house by examining the interior of a house. The architect may be living many miles away, and you will never find him inside the house.

This is established by the information that has been supplied in the previous chapter, that the Creator is outside the universe and is completely transcendental to the material creation. Certainly, however, the various manifestations within the cosmic creation, or that which is created, are a reflection of the Supreme Creator, but only if we are open to perceive this fact. Otherwise, we are covered by our own limitations and inabilities to understand the nature of the Supreme Creator. The infinitesimal can hardly understand the infinite. So to perceive that the created is also a reflection or the energy of the Creator, we first need to understand that the cause of the cosmic manifestation exists before the material creation, during its manifestation, and after its annihilation. He is beyond it and outside of it, which is explained in the Vedic texts.

In the four most important verses known as the *Catuh Sloki* in the *Srimad-Bhagavatam* (2.9.33-36), Lord Krishna explains, "Brahma, it is I, the Personality of Godhead, who was existing before the creation, when there was nothing but Myself. Nor was there the material nature, the cause of this creation. That which you see now is also I, the Personality of Godhead, and after annihilation what remains will also be I, the Supreme Personality. O Brahma, whatever appears to

27

be of any value, if it is without relation to Me, has no reality. Know it as My illusory energy, that reflection which appears to be in darkness. O Brahma, please know that the universal elements enter into the cosmos and at the same time do not enter into the cosmos; similarly, I Myself also exist within everything created, and at the same time I am outside of everything. A person who is searching after the Supreme Absolute Truth, the Personality of Godhead, must certainly search for it up to this, in all circumstances, in all space and time, and both directly and indirectly."

In this same line of thought, the great sage Maitreya told Vidura, "The Personality of Godhead, the master of all living entities, existed prior to the creation as one without a second. It is by His will only that creation is made possible and again everything merges in Him." (*Bhag.* 3.5.23)

Later in the *Srimad-Bhagavatam* (6.4.47), Krishna again explains, "Before the creation of this cosmic manifestation, I alone existed with My specific spiritual potencies. Consciousness was then unmanifested, just as one's consciousness is unmanifested during the time of sleep."

The ancient *Atharva-veda* (4.2.7-8) concurs with this: "God, the master of luminous planets, existed before the creation of the world. He is the one Lord of all created objects. He sustains the earth, the sun and the created world. . . Before the creation of the world, matter fashioning the child of the universe retained the seed of its production. God was the outer covering of the world in the process of creation. May we worship with devotion, Him, the illuminator, and Giver of happiness."

The *Atharva-veda* (19.6.11) goes on to describe: "The devotees install in the very recesses of their hearts through peace-showering meditation, the Adorable and Perfect God, Who is existent even before the creation of the universe. The learned persons, the yogis with special spiritual powers, and the self-controllers get united with Him in deep meditation."

In this way, we can understand that the Supreme Being is the ultimate cause of the creation of the material manifestation, although beyond it. He exists prior to it as well as after it is annihilated. As the Supreme Creator, He is the ultimate shelter of all living beings. This is especially clarified in the prayers to Lord Krishna by the wives of Kaliya in the *Srimad-Bhagavatam* (10.16.39), in which they explain that although He is the ultimate shelter of all created material elements, He exists prior to the creation. And although He is the cause of everything, as the Supreme Soul, He is transcendental to all material cause and effects.

CHAPTER FIVE

The Spiritual Atmosphere

If the Supreme Being exists before and after the material creation, then where does He stay? What does He do? And what is the nature of His residence? From the Vedic information, we learn that the material manifestation is merely 25% of all of the Supreme Being's energy. The other 75% is His spiritual energy, which manifests as the unlimited spiritual world. Furthermore, out of all the living beings that exist, which are innumerable, only 10% of all living entities are found in the confines of the material cosmos. The other 90% are the liberated beings who belong to the eternal spiritual sky. Thus, we who are in this material creation are a definite minority. We are only a very small part of the material manifestation, and an infinitesimal part of all that is really going on when we include the immeasurable spiritual world, which is where we really belong anyway.

The spiritual world is not a myth, although it may certainly be a mystery to those without sufficient knowledge. However, this is no different than the mystery connected with many of the material planets that travel through the universe. Without sufficient knowledge, no one has any idea whether such planets have life, or if they can support life, or what their atmosphere is like. Only after gathering some bits of information can we have any idea at all. The Vedic texts, however, have many descriptions of what the spiritual world is like. So we will take a few of these to get a good idea of the conditions there. In fact, such *Puranas* as the *Bhagavata*, *Vishnu*, *Garuda*, and others explain many of the Lord's pastimes and incarnations as they are found in the spiritual world as well as the activities that He and His devotees display within this material creation.

The *Chaitanya-caritamrita* by Krishnadasa Kaviraja Gosvami has some important verses that summarize what many of the Vedic texts describe, and explain the nature of the spiritual world. In the *Adi-lila* portion of his book, Chapter Five, we find that the spiritual sky is called Vaikuntha, which means where there is no anxiety. It is all-pervading, infinite, and the supreme abode. It is filled with innumerable spiritual planets, each of which is a residence of the unlimited incarnations of the Supreme Being. The highest planet is called

Krishnaloka, which is the residence of Lord Krishna Himself, the source of all other incarnations of God. It is divided into the divisions of Dvaraka, Mathura, and Gokula. All of these divisions also appear on earth where the Supreme Being comes to display His pastimes. Gokula, also called Vraja and Vrindavana, is the highest of all. These abodes that appear on earth are expansions of the supreme spiritual atmosphere and nondifferent in quality to the places in the spiritual world.

Lord Krishna expands into many forms and incarnations, beginning with His form as Sri Baladeva, also called Balarama, who is considered Lord Krishna's brother. It is by the energy of Lord Baladeva that the spiritual world exists.

In the *Madhya-lila* section of the *Chaitanya-caritamrita* (21.55-57), the spiritual planets are described as larger than we can imagine, larger than any material universe. Each planet is also made of spiritual bliss. All of the inhabitants are associates of the Supreme Lord. And, in Chapter 20 (257-258), the spiritual world is referred to as the abode of the pastimes of the eternal spiritual energy.

There are also many verses in the *Brahma-samhita* which describe the nature and activities of the spiritual realm. In verse 29, for example, we find that the Lord engages in many playful pastimes. He is not some old man sitting high in the sky in a chair trying to manage everything while overlooking the material creation. Instead, we find that Lord Krishna is engaged in playfully tending the cows with his many friends, or engaged in dancing, having a picnic, teasing His relatives, or sporting with friends in the abodes built with spiritual gems and surrounded by millions of wish-fulfilling trees. He is served with great reverence and affection by thousands of goddesses of fortune. In verse 2, it states that Gokula, the supreme abode and planet, appears like a lotus flower with a thousand petals.

Life there is eternal, as is everything else in the spiritual world, and full of bliss and knowledge. It is full of pure devotees who have unlimited facility for their loving service to the Supreme Being. There are beautiful homes and gardens, with ample vegetables, flowers, and jewels. Each person is full with all beauty, wealth, strength, fame, knowledge, and bliss. They also wear the most beautiful of clothes, and fly in wondrous planes around the spiritual planets. All walking is a dance, and all speech is a song. The water is nectar and the land is touchstone.

The spiritual realm is not some form of nothingness, as some people may imagine. There are millions of Vaikuntha planets, each with a form or expansion of the Supreme Being who resides on it. Each resident of the spiritual world goes to whichever planet has the form of God to which he or she is most attracted. Each Vaikuntha planet is self-effulgent, and many millions of times brighter than the sun. Material time and the modes of nature have no influence in the spiritual realm. There is no birth, death, old age or disease, and no past, present, or future. Time is conspicuous by its absence. Everything, including the homes, trees, animals, and plants, are all eternal. It is full of beauty and bliss.

The Lord is like a blazing fire and the spiritual entities are like sparks of that fire who engage in unlimited varieties of service for the Lord's enjoyment. Since the Lord is also the source of all pleasure and happiness, when the living enities come into contact with the Supreme, they also feel a happiness which far supersedes any pleasure they could feel through contact with the material energy. Because the innumerable spiritual entities are engaged in serving and pleasing the Lord in this way, which is their natural, constitutional, spiritual position, they also feel a bliss that knows no bounds. They feel that there could be nothing better that they could do, or would want to do. Thus, they all feel perfectly situated.

Why does the Lord create the spiritual sparks, or the innumerable living entities? Because He is the source of both the unlimited and limited potencies. The Lord is only complete when He displays all of His energies. The spiritual potency is exhibited by the spiritual world. The limited energy is exhibited in the material cosmos. And the marginal potency, which are the living beings, can be in either the material or spiritual energy. To exhibit His omnipotency, He exhibits all of His energy. In this way, the Lord is the source of all potencies, including all pleasure potencies for which all living entities are hankering. When they come in contact with the Lord through the service attitude for pleasing Him, they are also full of all pleasure and happiness, in the same way that a spark becomes bright again when in contact with the blazing fire. Because the Lord is the reservoir of all pleasure, and He also enjoys spiritual ecstasies, there are the living beings who also give Him happiness and provide the means for many pastimes in which there are varieties of pleasurable exchanges between them. The living beings provide the means for the Lord's variegated activities. Without the spiritual entities, the Lord would remain inactive, although He is complete in Himself. However, merely by looking at all the activity within the material creation we can see that there are unlimited activities. Thus, we can get a clue as to how much more active is the spiritual realm. We can plainly see that we are not alone. So, it is illogical to think that there are no activities in the spiritual realm, or that it is merely some inactive void or Great White Light.

The spiritual world is simply for the loving relationships and recreational activities that expand the happiness and love of all, without the limitations found within material existence. Besides, what is the meaning of the word "lord" if there is no one to overlord? Similarly, a king without subjects has no meaning. Thus, the spirit souls are the complimentary side of the Supreme Being, and are His parts and parcels. So it is natural that there are reciprocal feelings of love between the infinitesimal living beings and the infinite Supreme Being. This form of love between the Supreme and His spiritual parts and parcels is the ultimate loving relationship. Every other form of love is but a dim reflection.

When the living beings display their pure spiritual tendencies to serve the Lord, they become liberated souls in the spiritual world. However, they have independence to act spiritually or materially. When they wish to pursue their limited desires for material enjoyment to satisfy themselves, then they take up existence in the material creation and acquire a physical body so they can chase after the idea of gratifying their minds and senses. The pleasure of the mind and senses is merely an idea because it is based on the mood of the mind and the level of reality that the materially conditioned soul accepts as his life and drama. The senses alone, being lumps of matter, or parts of an animated body, cannot in themselves feel happiness. Such happiness is merely an interpretation of the mind.

The Vaikuntha planets of the spiritual world float in the Brahman effulgence. Some call this the Great White Light or void. Merging into the Brahman is for those who prefer to exist in a spiritual vacuum, floating in an eternal sky without any form or activities. For this reason, it is considered an incomplete level of spiritual realization and existence.

"What the *Upanishads* describe as the impersonal Brahman is but the effulgence of His body, and the Lord known as the Supersoul is but His localized plenary portion. He is the Supreme Personality of Godhead, Krishna Himself, full with six opulences. He is the Absolute Truth, and no other truth is greater than or equal to Him." (*Chaitanya-caritamrita, Adi-Lila*, 2.5)

The *Brahma-samhita* (5.40) also describes the Brahman as being emanated from the body of Lord Krishna. "I worship Govinda [Krishna], the primeval Lord, who is endowed with great power. The glowing effulgence of His transcendental form is the impersonal Brahman, which is absolute, complete and unlimited, and which displays the varieties of countless planets, with their different opulences, in millions and millions of universes."

Herein we can understand that the Brahman effulgence, or the Great White Light in the spiritual sky, is nothing but the bodily rays coming from the Supreme Being, Sri Krishna. It is within those bodily rays that the unlimited Vaikuntha planets float, and into which the innumerable impersonalist philosophers merge who have attained liberation from material existence and who think there is no Supreme Being. However, such liberated souls who merge into the Brahman have no spiritual form or body, but remain only as a spiritual spark without any activity, floating in the Vaikuntha sky.

The *Upanishads* especially put emphasis on the great, impersonal Brahman effulgence. The *Mundaka Upanishad* (2.2.10-12) provides additional insight into the nature of the Brahman: "In the spiritual realm, beyond the material covering, is the unlimited Brahman effulgence, which is free from material contamination. That effulgent white light is understood by transcendentalists to be the light of all lights. In that realm there is no need of sunshine, moonshine, fire or electricity for illumination. Indeed, whatever illumination appears in the material world is only a reflection of that supreme illumination. That Brahman is in front and in back, in the north, south, east and west, and also overhead and below. In other words, that supreme Brahman effulgence spreads throughout both the material and spiritual skies."

The above verses mean two things. First, the very word *Brahman*, being the bodily rays of the Supreme Being, and being an effulgence which must come from a source, means that the Brahman cannot exist without its source. Therefore, by implication, the Brahman means the Supreme Personality of Godhead. Secondly, the rays and spiritual force of the Brahman also pervade the material creation. It is in a corner of this Brahman in which the material creation manifests like a cloud. Within that cloud the necessary transformations take place in order to create the material elements, planets, universes, and innumerable living beings. However, between the material universes and the brilliant effulgence of the Brahman is what is called the Virajanadi or Brahmaloka. It is like a river, also called the Viraja River, which separates the spiritual world from the material world. It is within the confines of the cloudy Viraja River that the material manifestation takes place.

The millions of universes in the material creation float on the waters of the Viraja River. On one side of this river are the material universes, and on the other are the Vaikuntha planets. The Viraja River is a marginal position between the material and spiritual realms, and is thus not under the control of the material energy. That is why those persons who merge into the Viraja River are considered to have escaped material existence, yet have still not quite entered the real spiritual worlds.

In this way, the Viraja River is also a shelter for those living beings who are disgusted with material life and who become successful in a religious or philosophical discipline that is bereft of true spiritual knowledge. For example, the goal of Buddhists is to reach *nirvana* in the Great White Light or Clear Void. This void is found in the existence in the Viraja River, which is outside of the material worlds, but still not in the spiritual realm. It is in between. Therein they deny the variegatedness of material existence as well as that of spiritual existence. Thus, if they wish to leave material life yet still have no true understanding of spiritual life, or life on the Vaikuntha planets, it is into this area in which they merge. Without knowledge or the practice of life in the spiritual world, they cannot go beyond this Viraja area.

How the creation manifests within the Viraja River will become clearer in the next few chapters. Furthermore, additional information about the personal characteristics of the Supreme Being and the nature and description of the spiritual world is provided in the first volume of this series, called *The Secret Teachings of the Vedas*. The unlimited nature of the spiritual world is such a deep topic that a number of volumes would be required to provide a more complete view and description of it, which is not our purpose here. So we will let the information that we have provided stand as it is for now.

PART TWO

THE PROCESS OF CREATION

CHAPTER SIX

The Beginning of the Creation

We have already explained in a previous chapter that the material creation is manifested because some of the living beings wish to try and serve their own mind and senses rather than serving the Lord. They wish to act outside their spiritual nature, to experience some independence from God. However, that can never be the case in the spiritual world. So another world must be created wherein the living beings can act in such a way. But when does such a world manifest?

It is explained that although the Supreme Being is happily situated in His spiritual kingdom, at various times He feels the need to manifest His material energy. The *Srimad-Bhagavatam* (3.5.24) relates that at one time when the cosmic manifestation was not present, although the internal or spiritual energy was manifest, the Lord was feeling somewhat imperfect without His separated parts and parcels, the materially inclined living beings.

The living beings who previously had been active in the material creation when it was annihilated merged within the body of the Supreme and had entered a state of dormancy. Since they are spiritual entities but have no spiritual proclivity, they do not manifest within the spiritual worlds. Therefore, there comes a time when the Lord wants to again manifest the material energy and allow the dormant living beings a means to become active again. And manifesting the material energy is the way this is done. Thus, the Lord begins to feel the inclination to create the cosmic manifestation to give another chance to the conditioned souls to regain their spiritual consciousness and return to their real home in the spiritual world. This is the very beginning of the creative process.

COMPASSION IS THE BASIS OF THE MATERIAL WORLD

Because some living beings wish to experience material existence, as explained in *Srimad-Bhagavatam* (10.87.2), the Supreme Lord manifests the

36

material intelligence, senses, mind, and vital air of the living entities so they can indulge in their desires for sense gratification. In this endeavor, they are allowed to take repeated births to engage in fruitive activities. When they finally become disappointed in their numerous attempts at material success and happiness, they can take to a genuine spiritual practice and become elevated to ultimately attain eternal freedom from material existence. Therefore, by creating the cosmos, the Supreme allows for the release of the living entities that are lying dormant within His transcendental body. Thus, it is only due to the Supreme Lord's compassion that He creates the material worlds to provide a means for the living entities to chase after their false desires and gradually realize the futility of it. In this way, we can also understand that the materially conditioned living beings are completely dependent on God to acquire what they need to pursue their desires. Nonetheless, since the basis of this universe is compassion, we should understand that this universe is set up in such a way that everything that happens to us is ultimately for our purification and upliftment, if only we can perceive the message.

This is an important point. Although material life can be full of suffering, the purpose of it is to allow those who desire it the means to pursue their attempt to serve themselves by gratifying their mind and senses. However, this is not all that it is cracked up to be. If the living being finally realizes this and asks himself why he is going through this form of existence, he has the chance to rise above the illusory nature and see his real spiritual potential.

So, as explained in the prayers of Kardama Muni,[1] although the Supreme Being has no reason to create this material manifestation, He does so not out of any will of His own, but because the conditioned souls want to enjoy it and pursue sense gratification as they like.

Thus, the Lord puts the material energy in motion which creates the many forms and species of life to accommodate the numerous levels of desires and consciousness of the living entities. When they see this, they are completely overwhelmed by the knowledge covering aspect of the illusory energy.[2] In this way, one of the main principles of the material creation is forgetfulness of one's spiritual identity, which is caused by *maya*, the illusory energy. Without this forgetfulness, the living entity could not pursue gratifying the temporary mind and body if he remembered his natural, eternal, spiritual identity.

This is also why the creation is called *shrishti* in Sanskrit, which means to send forth an imitation world. The material manifestation is like an imitation or a perverted reflection of the spiritual world. It is similar but very different. The material world is where the *jiva* souls misuse their slight independence to think or pretend that they are separate from the Lord. Thus, they can forget about their connection with God and go on pretending to be material bodies to engage in the pursuit of sense pleasure.

In some ways it is similar to someone who smokes cigarettes. Originally no one likes smoking, and they cough when they start. But they get used to it and gradually become so accustomed to it that they like it. Yet they still have to ignore the damage they are doing to their health. So they pretend they are enjoying like anything. However, if they get cancer, they suffer greatly and regret their foolish actions. And once they are addicted to smoking cigarettes, it takes a lot of endeavor to quit. Nonetheless, the health department provides so many instructions for the need to quit smoking, and companies make products to help you stop. The point being is that you never should have started. That is like material existence. Once you are in the depths of it, it can be so difficult to change your ways to get out, in spite of all the spiritual instructions that are provided.

So, to assist the living beings and provide a choice for them to either pursue material enjoyment or search out their spiritual identity, the Lord descends personally to give instructions, as found in the *Bhagavad-gita*, and sends His representatives to provide guidance for their spiritual progress. Then the living entities can make their own decision as to which direction they choose to take.

This is the plan of Lord Krishna, to give the conditioned souls a chance to return to the spiritual world by rectifying their misguided consciousness. As long as they have a domineering mentality and desire to pursue sense gratification, they are conditioned. For them to become free from this conditioning is the ultimate desire of Krishna, but it cannot be forced. To love someone is not something that you can force one into doing. It has to be developed naturally. Since the living beings are all a part of God, it is natural for them to have a loving relationship with God. But this has to be developed willingly by the living entities once they are tired of suffering in material life. So the choice is theirs to be taken in their own sweet time. This is one of the reasons for bringing forth the material creation.

As further explained in the *Chaitanya-caritamrita* (*Madhya-lila*, 20.254), there is no possibility of creation without thinking, feeling, willing, knowledge, and activity. Thinking, feeling and willing are the essence of consciousness. Wherever there is consciousness, there are these items. However, it is the combination of the thinking, feeling and willing of the Supreme Consciousness, along with His knowledge and action, which brings about the cosmic manifestation. This is the seed of origination for the material creation.

In the very beginning of the creative process, both the material nature and the dormant conditioned souls are expanded, or sent forth, from the Supreme Being. Therefore, it is the Supreme who is the ultimate efficient cause of the creation. It is the combination of the material energy, *prakriti*, the ingredient cause of creation, and the innumerable souls that together produce the many forms of material existence. This is just as air and water combine to produce so many bubbles. And when it is all over, the living beings along with the material nature again merge back into the form of the Supreme Being, similar to the way many rivers merge back into the ocean. Thus, neither the individual souls or material nature are ever born, nor do they ever die.[3]

Then, in the next stage of the creative process, the Lord expands Himself into the first incarnation, along with all of the material ingredients, and creates the necessary energies to manifest the universe.[4]

CHAPTER SEVEN

The Expansions of the Supreme

In spite of the fact that everything comes from the Supreme Being, He is still aloof from it all. He does not disengage Himself from His eternal pleasure pastimes with His devotees in the spiritual realm. So in the process of creating the material worlds, the Supreme expands Himself into various forms, which are His plenary parts. Krishna is the primeval Lord, the original Personality of Godhead, so He can expand Himself into unlimited forms with all potencies. They are no different from Him, but may exhibit differences in form.

He first expands Himself into Baladeva, or Balarama, who is considered Krishna's second body and brother. Balarama assists in Lord Krishna's innumerable spiritual pastimes in both the spiritual and material realms.

Lord Balarama is also Lord Sankarshana, the predominator of the creative energy. He creates and is the shelter of the material and spiritual worlds. By the will of Krishna and the power of the spiritual energy, Lord Balarama creates the spiritual world, which consists of the planet Goloka Vrindavana and the Vaikuntha planets.[1] Lord Balarama especially assists Lord Krishna in the creation of the material worlds. After Balarama has expanded Himself into Lord Maha-Sankarshana, He expands Himself into four different forms, including: 1) Karanadakashayi Vishnu [Maha-Vishnu], 2) Garbhodakashayi Vishnu [the expansion in each universe], 3) Ksirodakashayi Vishnu [the Supersoul in each individual], and 4) Sesha, also called Seshanaga. These first four plenary portions assist in the material cosmic manifestation. Sesha is Balarama's form who assists in the Lord's personal service. He is also called Ananta, meaning unlimited, because He assists the Lord in His unlimited variety of pastimes.[2]

* * *

To explain more clearly, all expansions of the Lord begin with Sri Krishna. For His pastimes in one of the highest levels of the spiritual realm, called Dvaraka,

Sri Krishna expands Himself into Balarama, who then expands Himself into Pradyumna and Aniruddha. These four expand into a second quadruple which is present in the unlimited Vaikuntha planets of the spiritual sky. The second quadruple is known as Vasudeva, Sankarshana, Pradyumna and Aniruddha. They are changeless, transcendental expansions of the Supreme Lord, Krishna. In this second quadruple, Vasudeva is an expansion of Krishna, and Sankarshana is a representation of Balarama.

In the Vaikuntha sky there is the pure, spiritual creative energy called *Shuddha-sattva* that sustains all of the spiritual planets with the full opulences of knowledge, wealth, power, beauty, etc., all of which pervade the entire spiritual kingdom and are fully enjoyed by the residents there. This energy is but a display of the creative potencies of Balarama, Maha-Sankarshana. It is also this Sankarshana who is the original cause of the Causal Ocean where Karanodakashayi Vishnu (Maha-Vishnu) sleeps, while breathing out the seeds of innumerable universes. When the cosmic creation is annihilated, all of the materially conditioned, although indestructible, living entities merge back into the body of Maha-Vishnu where they rest until the time of the next creation. So Balarama as Sankarshana is the origin of Maha-Vishnu, from whom originates all of the potencies of the material manifestation.[3]

So to summarize, for His spiritual pastimes in the Vaikuntha realm, Lord Krishna has four original expansions, namely Vasudeva, Sankarshana, Pradyumna and Aniruddha. Maha-Vishnu is an expansion of Sankarshana; Garbhodakashayi Vishnu is an expansion of Pradyumna; and Ksirodakashayi Vishnu is an expansion of Aniruddha.[4]

* * *

To begin explaining the purpose and function of these expansions, the *Srimad-Bhagavatam* (2.6.42) describes that, "Maha-Vishnu (Karanadakashayi Vishnu) is the first incarnation of the Supreme Lord in the process of creating the material worlds. He is the master of eternal time, space, cause and effects, mind, elements, material ego, the modes of nature, senses, the universal form of the Lord (Garbhodakashayi Vishnu) and the sum total of all living beings, both moving and nonmoving."

Then Maha-Vishnu lies down in the Viraja River, which is the border between the spiritual and material worlds.[5]

Lord Maha-Vishnu is the source of thousands of *avataras* in His thousands and thousands of subjective portions. He is the creator of countless individual souls. He is also known by the name of Narayana, meaning the shelter of all the individual *jiva* souls. From Him springs forth the vast expanse of water known as the spiritual Causal Ocean. Maha-Vishnu then reclines in the waters of the Causal Ocean in a state of divine sleep, called *yoga-nidra*. Thus, it is said that the universal creation is but the dream of Maha-Vishnu.[6]

Since the waters of the Causal Ocean, known as the Karana Ocean, come from the body of Maha-Vishnu, it is completely spiritual. The sacred Ganges is but a drop from that ocean, which can purify the fallen souls.[7]

Lord Balarama also expands into the great serpent known as Ananta, or Seshanaga. He reposes on the Causal Ocean and serves as the couch upon whom Lord Maha-Vishnu reclines.[8] That Ananta-Sesha is the devotee incarnation of God who knows nothing but service to Lord Krishna. With His thousands of mouths He always sings the endless glories of Lord Krishna. He also expands Himself to serve as Lord Krishna's paraphernalia, including such items as the umbrella, slippers, bedding, pillow, garments, resting chair, residence, sacred *gayatri* thread, and throne in the pastimes of Lord Krishna. Thus, He has attained and exhibits the ultimate end of servitude to Lord Krishna.[9]

At the time of creation, after the Supreme has been sleeping for some time, the first emanation from the breathing of Lord Maha-Vishnu are the personified *Vedas* who serve Him by waking Him from His mystic sleep. They begin to enthusiastically sing His glories, pastimes, and praises, just as a King is awaken in the morning by poets who recite his heroic deeds.[10] This shows the eternal nature of the Vedic literature. They are not merely the writings of men, but they are spiritual vibrations that exist before and after the material creation, and which emanate from the Supreme Lord.

Once the Lord is awoken, He casts His glance upon the material energy of *maya*. Then she becomes agitated. At that time the Lord injects the original seeds of all living entities. This glance is how the Supreme impregnates material nature with all the living entities. Thus, the Lord does not personally touch the material energy, but by His functional expansion He places the living entities into the material nature by His glance.[11] This functional expansion of the Lord takes the form as Shiva, which will be explained later.

After agitating material nature into three qualities, which are the modes of nature in the form of passion, goodness, and ignorance, they become active and material nature begins to give birth to the total material energy known as the *hiranya-mahat-tattva*. This is the sum total of cosmic intelligence. Thus, material nature becomes agitated by the destinations of the conditioned souls as determined by the influence of the modes of nature.[12] Simply by the glance of Maha-Vishnu consciousness is created, which is known as the *mahat-tattva*. The predominating Deity of the *mahat-tattva* is Lord Vasudeva, another expansion of Lord Krishna. This explains how the material energy is like the mother of the living beings while the Lord is the Supreme Father of everyone. Just as a woman cannot give birth without the contact of a man, or at least his seed, so material nature cannot create without the contact of the Supreme Being.

So first the total material energy is manifest, and from this arise the three types of egotism, which are the original sources of all the demigods [the minor controlling deities], the senses, and material elements. By combining the different elements, the Supreme Lord creates all of the unlimited universes. Once the material elements have been manifested, and the full potential for creating the universes has been established, the innumerable universes begin to emanate from the pores of the body of Maha-Vishnu, and from His exhalations. They appear just like atomic particles that float in sunshine and pass through a screen. When Maha-Vishnu inhales at the time of the universal annihilation, they return to His body. In this way, Maha-Vishnu is the Supersoul of all the universes.[13]

Brahma, the demigods, and each universe remain alive for the duration of one of His exhalations.[14] However, there is no limit to the exhalations of Maha-Vishnu.[15]

Once all of the universes are created, which are unlimited, Maha-Vishnu expands Himself into unlimited forms and enters each universe as Garbhodakashayi Vishnu. Once He is in each universe, He sees that there is no place to reside. Then, after some consideration, He fills half of the universe with water from His own perspiration. He then lays down on the water, again supported by the bed of Seshanaga.[16]

Garbhodakashayi Vishnu, who is known within the universe as Hiranyagarbha and Antaryami, the Supersoul, is glorified in the Vedic hymns. He is the master of each and every universe and shelter of the external or material energy. However, being transcendental, He is completely beyond the touch of the external energy.

Next is the third expansion of Vishnu, called Ksirodakashayi Vishnu, who is the incarnation of the quality of goodness. He is the universal form of the Lord and expands Himself as the Supersol within every living entity. He is known as Ksirodakashayi Vishnu because He lies on the ocean of milk on the island of Svetadvipa. These are the three expansions of Lord Vishnu who oversee and make the creation of the material world possible.[17]

CHAPTER EIGHT

The Development of Material Nature

In our last chapter we learned how the Supreme Being expands Himself into the three main Vishnu forms to create and guide the creative process for manifesting the cosmic energy. Lord Krishna has little to do with it personally, but works through His expansions. In this chapter we will begin to see how this material manifestation starts to take shape.

It is described that outside the boundaries of the unlimited spiritual Vaikuntha world is the Brahman effulgence. Beyond that is the Karana or Causal Ocean, which is also spiritual.[1] This is what surrounds the innumerable material universes. Lord Vishnu in His form as Karanadakashayi Vishnu, or Maha-Vishnu, lies on the Causal Ocean and creates the universes merely by glancing upon the material nature. Thus, Lord Krishna personally has nothing to do with the material creation, nor does He ever come in touch with the material energy. He remains absorbed and unaffected in Goloka Vrindavan, the highest planet in the spiritual sky. The material energy never comes in contact with the spiritual world, nor even the Causal Ocean, as explained in the *Srimad-Bhagavatam* (11.22.17):

"In the beginning of creation nature assumes, by the modes of goodness, passion and ignorance, its form as the embodiment of all subtle causes and gross manifestations within the universe. The Supreme Personality of Godhead does not enter the interaction of material manifestation but merely glances upon nature. As the material elements, headed by the *mahat-tattva*, are transformed, they receive their specific potencies from the glance of the Supreme Lord, and being amalgamated by the power of nature, they create the universal egg."

Before the *mahat-tattva*, however, there is the *pradhana*, which is the sum total of all material energy in its subtle and undifferentiated stage. Material nature is always existing in its subtle form as the energy of the Lord. Sometimes, under the direction of the Supreme, it manifests its temporary existence in the form of the cosmos. The Supreme Lord as Kapiladeva describes the characteristics of *pradhana* in the *Srimad-Bhagavatam* (starting at 3.26.10).

43

The unmanifested state of the eternal combinations of the three modes of material nature is called *pradhana*. It is called *prakriti*, or material nature, in its manifested state. The *pradhana* contains the five gross elements (earth, water, fire, air, and ether), the five subtle elements (smell, taste, color, touch, and sound), the four internal or subtle senses (mind, intelligence, ego, and contaminated consciousness), the five senses for gathering knowledge (the ability to smell, taste, feel, see, and hear), and the five acting senses (for speech, working, traveling, generating, and evacuating, namely the mouth, arms, legs, genitals, and anus). The twenty-fifth element is considered time, the element which causes the mixing of the *pradhana*. Time is considered to be the influence of the Supreme, and also causes the materially deluded living beings to fear death.

Therefore, the *pradhana* is the total unmanifest form of the material elements before it is glanced upon by Maha-Vishnu, and before it is agitated by the three modes of material nature, namely goodness, passion, and ignorance. It is in this state that *pradhana* is considered to be the three modes of nature in equilibrium, each one neutralizing the other. In such a state, it is unable to produce anything. It is the element of time which creates the agitation of the modes of nature, which thus brings forth the creation of all the other elements. It is also the absence of time and the modes of nature which later brings about the dissolution of the universe. (The annihilation of the universe is described in my previous book, *The Vedic Prophecies: A New Look into the Future*.)

WHEN THE PRADHANA BECOMES THE MAHAT-TATTVA

After the glance of Maha-Vishnu, the *pradhana* begins to change. This is when the *pradhana*, the unmanifest state of the ingredients of material creation, becomes the *mahat-tattva*, which is the basis of the creation when it is mixed with the time element and infused with the energy of consciousness. When the *pradhana* begins to manifest distinctions, it becomes the *mahat-tattva* because then it is affected by the time element after the glance of Lord Vishnu. This is summarized as follows:

Only after the incarnation of Karanadakashayi Vishnu [Maha-Vishnu] does the *maha-tattva*, or the principles of material creation, take place. Thereafter, time is manifested, and in due course the three modes of material nature appear. With the affect of time, it is these modes which transform into activities, which begins the evolutionary development of the various elements.[2]

The *mahat-tattva* is also described as the total consciousness because it is connected with the supreme consciousness of the Lord. A portion of it is also represented in everyone as the intellect. The *mahat-tattva* still appears as matter, and is, therefore, the shadow or a product of pure consciousness [the Lord's consciousness]. With a slight addition of the mode of passion, activity is generated and it becomes the germinating place of all creation.[3] Thus, material activities are caused by the *mahat-tattva* being agitated. At first there is transformation of the modes of goodness and passion. Later, due to the mode of ignorance, matter, its knowledge, and the different activities of material knowledge come into play.[4] Thereafter, in connection with the mode of ignorance, the *mahat-tattva* generates the false ego. It is an expansion of the Supreme Being with creative principles and time for the fructification.[5] Thus, this *mahat-tattva* is the junction of matter and spirit, *the starting point from when spiritual energy begins to manifest or transform into the material creation.* This means that matter comes from consciousness, not that life comes from a mixture of matter. And consciousness means that there must be a person, a personality. Therefore, behind everything in this material creation is the Supreme Person.

After this, the material or false ego springs up from the *mahat-tattva*. After the *mahat-tattva* transforms into the false ego, it manifests into the three phases of being the cause, effect, and the doer in the creative process. The false ego is then divided into three different modes--goodness, passion, and ignorance.[6]

To explain further: "From the agitation of the original modes within the unmanifest material nature, the *maha-tattva* arises. From the *maha-tattva* comes the element of false ego, which divides into three aspects. This threefold false ego further manifests as the subtle forms of perception, as the senses and as the gross sense objects. The generation of all these is called creation."[7]

It is this self-centered materialistic false ego, becoming divided into three divisions by the modes of goodness, passion, and ignorance, which gives way to the powers that evolve matter, knowledge of material creations, and the intelligence that guides such materialistic activities.[8]

This is the beginning of the creative process, when material nature starts to exhibit its transformations that pave the way for the solidification of elements, which then gradually combine into the forms that we see today. This is further described in this way:

After manifesting the dormant varieties in material nature, the *mahat-tattva*, which contains the ingredients of all the universes, dissipates the darkness that was there from the last universal annihilation by its reawakened activity.[9] The mode of goodness within the *mahat-tattva* then becomes manifest. This mode makes it possible for the manifestation of the mind, the eleventh sense organ, whose predominating Deity is Aniruddha. It is also this pure mode of goodness, called *shuddha-sattva*, the state of pure consciousness, which exists in the beginning, just as water is clear and sweet before it comes in contact with earth. The characteristics of this pure goodness is complete serenity, clarity and freedom. It is like the clear, white light that delivers the state of enlightenment. It is this mode which makes it possible for the living beings to realize their spiritual nature and the characteristics of the Absolute Truth. Therefore, the goal of all spiritual paths must be to bring the living individuals up to the mode of pure goodness. Without this, there is no possibility for true spiritual advancement, or the personal realization of one's spiritual identity. [10]

Another thing that happens is that after the Supreme Being impregnates the material nature with His potency, it then becomes agitated by the destinations of the conditioned souls and delivers the sum total of the cosmic intelligence, known as Hiranmaya. Then the slightest desire begins to manifest from the souls within the material nature, and the need to become physically embodied for material activities is aroused. [However, there is still quite a ways to go before nature provides them with physical forms.] This is caused by the agitation between the modes of nature, now that they have lost their equilibrium due to the glance of the Supreme Lord. Through this glance He has injected all of the materially conditioned living beings into the material nature, and the modes becoming active create the appearance of time in the form of past, present, and future.[11]

The Supreme Being in His feature as Maha-Vishnu impregnates the material nature by His glance. Through this glance, which is the impregnation of consciousness, and by the influence of the time element, the innumerable living beings appear.[12] The Supreme Being then, out of His own body, sowed the seeds of universal manifestation within the *mahat-tattva*.[13] In this way, the Lord, who is the controller of all energies, by His own potency creates eternal time, the fate of all living entities, and their particular nature. At the end of the cosmic creation He again merges them back into Him.[14]

The countless souls that appear within the material energy are all spiritual in nature, they are all spiritual beings. However, they can also become deluded by material energy. When they are thus deluded, they hanker for material activities and attractions. In order to accommodate this, the Supreme provides this material world as a playground in which they can work out their material desires. This means that regardless of species, whether it is Lord Brahma, or humans, animals, birds, or even tiny insects, material nature is the mother and the Supreme Lord is the seed-giving, universal Father.

This shows that matter cannot do anything on its own. Material nature is dull and inert, so it cannot be the cause of the material world.[15] Only after Maha-Vishnu glances from a distance over material nature and infuses His energy into it does it begin to become activated. Thus, He is the original cause of the cosmic manifestation. Thereafter, the material creation is manifested by the systematic and natural actions and reactions of the energy of the Supreme transformed through matter. In this way, material nature is merely the secondary cause of the creation. This is similar in the way the energy of the electrical powerhouse is carried through the power lines and then transformed to create all of the uses for it that we have today. The original cause is the powerhouse where the electricity is generated. The secondary cause is the power lines through which the electricity is carried, and by which all of the transformations and uses of electricity are made possible. Thus, all energies within the material creation are ultimately caused by the Supreme Being, Lord Krishna, and His expansions. This is nicely expressed in the prayers of Vasudeva to Lord Krishna in the *Srimad-Bhagavatam* (10.85.7-8):

"The glow of the moon, the brilliance of fire, the radiance of the sun, the twinkling of the stars, the flash of lightening, the permanence of mountains and the aroma and sustaining power of the earth--all these are actually You. My Lord, you are water, and also its taste and its capacities to quench thirst and sustain life. You exhibit your potencies through the manifestations of the air as bodily warmth, vitality, mental power, physical strength, endeavor and movement."

The prayers go on describing how the Supreme is everything, including all abilities that we depend on in order to exist within this material universe. It is through the expansions of Sri Krishna's energies that He is the essence of everything that makes up this universe, yet He is beyond its limitations and influence.

"Whatever potencies the life air and other elements of universal creation exhibit are actually all personal energies of the Supreme Lord, for both life and matter are subordinate to Him and dependent on Him, and also different from one another. Thus everything active in the material world is set into motion by the Supreme Lord." (*Bhagavatam* 10.85.6)

Also, "Balarama and Krishna are the original efficient and material causes of the material world. As Maha-Vishnu and the material energy, They enter into the material elements and create the diversities by multi-energies. Thus They are the cause of all causes." (*Bhagavatam* 10.46.31)

THE POTENTIALS CREATED FROM THE MIXING OF THE FALSE EGO AND MODES OF NATURE

The material element of ego is endowed with three kinds of active power, namely in accordance with the modes of goodness, passion, and ignorance. It is from these three types of material or false ego that the mind, senses of perception, the organs of action, and the material elements evolve. This material ego in the association with the mode of goodness makes way for another transformation, namely the mind, whose thoughts give rise to desires. The false ego interacting with the mode of goodness is transformed into mind. The demigods who participate in controlling various aspects of the phenomenal world are also products of this combination.[16]

The ten demigods who help control the bodily movements, who are personally manifested later, are known as the controller of directions, the controller of air (Vayu), the sun-god (Surya), the father of Daksha Prajapati (Varuna), the Ashvini-kumaras, the fire-god (Agni), the King of Heaven (Indra), Upendra, chief of the Adityas (Mitra), and Brahma.[17]

The senses are products of false ego in the mode of passion, which also provides the means for speculative knowledge and fruitive activities.[18] The means for intelligence gives rise through the combination of false ego in the mode of passion. Intelligence helps the function of the senses and the power of perception.

Intelligence has the characteristics of discerning doubt, misapprehension, correct apprehension, memory, and sleep. All of these things help with one's view and analysis of something. False ego mixed with passion also produces the senses for acquiring knowledge and the senses of action. The predominating Deity of the senses and intelligence is Lord Pradyumna.[19]

With the creation of the modes of nature, there is also the manifestation of the appearance of past, present, and future. Goodness is the cause of maintenance, which is the present. Passion is the cause of creation, which brings about the future. And the mode of ignorance is the cause of destruction, which also governs the past. Thus, under the influence of these modes of nature, we have the affect of time. Next, when false ego is mixed with the mode of ignorance, the subtle element of sound is produced, which travels through the ether. Sound is that which conveys the idea of an object or speaker. From sound also comes the potential for the creation of other senses, beginning with the ear so sound can be heard.[20] The next transformation under the influence of time comes from the element of ether, which comes from sound, which is the manifestation of form or touch. The first level of form is air. Air contains the basic principles of duration of life: sense perception, mental power, and bodily strength. Without air, strength and mental clarity are lost. Thus, air and the sense of touch become prominent. Softness and hardness, cold and heat, are the attributes of touch, characterized first in the subtle element of air. Air exhibits movement, mixing, allowing for the perception of objects through sound, and the proper functioning of other senses.[21]

Thereafter, when the air is transformed in the course of time, the powerful air interacting with the sky generates fire, the light to see the world and the ability for sense perception. When electricity or fire is surcharged in the air and is glanced upon by the Supreme, the mixture of time and external energy produces water, which makes possible the sense of taste.[22]

The next stage of evolution is in the transformation of air and touch, which manifests as fire and the ability for the eye to see forms and color. Fire has many forms, and its characteristics are in its ability to cook, digest food in the stomach and give rise to hunger and thirst, to destroy cold, and to evaporate moisture. The next transformation is by the interaction of fire, which gives rise to the ability for taste, in which water is produced under superior arrangement, along with the sense of the tongue, which perceives taste. The characteristics of water is that it moistens, softens, is refreshing, and maintains life. Now from the interaction of water and taste comes odor and the sense of smell. This manifests the earth element, which carries smell and produces the olfactory sense.[23]

So, essentially, we can see the evolutionary way the elements and senses develop. Sound is the element from which all other things develop. From sound there is ether, which carries only sound. From either there is air, which carries sound and touch. From air comes fire, which carries sound, touch and form. From fire comes water, which is created when fire warms air. Water carries sound, touch, form and taste. From water comes earth, which carries sound, touch, form, taste, and aroma. Earth, therefore, having the qualities of all the other elements, is the reservoir of all the elemental qualities.[24] In this way, the creation manifested from subtle to gross, from sound came sky, then touch and air, form and fire, taste and water, and smell and earth.

By further transformations of the mode of passion, the sense organs like the ear, skin, nose, eyes, tongue, mouth, hands, genitals, legs, and the anus, together with intelligence and living energy, are all generated. The development of the body and the variety of species cannot take place as long as these created parts of the modes of nature, the elements, senses, and mind are not assembled. Thus, when these become assembled by force of the energy of the Supreme, the universe can then come into being under the primary [from the Supreme Being] and secondary [the mixing of the modes of nature] causes of creation.[25]

Finally, as Lord Krishna teaches Uddhava in *Srimad-Bhagavatam* (11.24.9), once the potential for all of these elements and senses are created, impelled by the Supreme, all of the elements can now combine to function in an orderly and systematic way to give birth to the universal egg. Such an egg is one of innumerable universes which then appear from Maha-Vishnu's exhaling and the pores of His body. Maha-Vishnu then expands Himself and enters each universe as Garbhodakashayi Vishnu, the soul of the universe. Only then can the cosmic manifestation within each universe begin to take place.

Thus, all the universes remained in the Causal Ocean for thousands of aeons. Only after the Lord enters each of them to accept the form of Garbhodakashayi Vishnu do they become fully animated.[26]

CHAPTER NINE

The Energy of Maya and Identity of Shiva

The illusory energy, *maya*, plays an important part in the creative process of the cosmic manifestation. In the *Srimad-Bhagavatam* (3.5.25), Maitreya explains to Vidura that the external energy works as both cause and effect in the cosmic manifestation. This external energy is known as *maya* or illusion, and through her agency only is the entire material manifestation made possible.

Maya is the external energy of the Lord and is divided into two parts. *Maya* is the efficient cause, and the other part are the ingredients that create the cosmic manifestation, known as the *pradhana* or *prakriti*.[1] The *Srimad-Bhagavatam* (10.63.26) relates that in the *pradhana* aspect, *maya* is composed of time, activity, providence (the destiny of the conditioned souls) and nature. These along with the vital force or energy, the subtle material ingredients, and the material nature, known as the field of activity for the conditioned souls, and the eleven senses (the senses of perception and organs of action) and five elements (earth, air, fire, water, and ether), are the ingredients of *maya*. Thus, Lord Krishna is the creator and *maya* only helps Him as an instrument. It is this *maya*, or material nature, which the Lord glances over which becomes agitated, and into which the Lord injects the seed of life as the original living entities. Thereafter, due to the reactions of the Lord's glance and His energy which mixes with *maya*, the material energy gives birth to the myriad universes.[2]

So *maya*, or material nature, is merely the secondary cause of the creation. Nonetheless, it serves two purposes: It contains the subtle material elements, and then through the changes that take place causes the material manifestation. The *Brahma-samhita* (5.19) also explains that the primary material elements were originally separated. Then through the spiritual power of the Supreme, in His knowledge potency, *maya* was moved. It is through this combination of the efficient or spiritual potency in conjunction with the inactive material causal principles of *maya* that the elements and the different entities develop into a state of cooperation. Thus, it is by this combination of energies that the material creation can manifest, and the spiritual living beings appear as the materially

50

conditioned souls within the material elements of the creation. In a graphic description, it is explained that maya appears like a huge pot filled with the innumerable universes that are like mustard seeds within it.[3]

Another function of *maya* is to cover the living being with the material energy, and, thus, keep him in illusion as to what is his true identity. This sort of forgetfulness is one of the main principles of the material world, without which the living being could not engage in material life. After all, if it was too obvious to the living being that he is a spiritual entity, he could not be satisfied with material pursuits or the engagement of bodily sense pleasures. So to help provide a playground for the materially conditioned souls who are rebellious and want to live outside of God's kingdom, this forgetfulness must be there. This is the third function of *maya*, which covers the living entity in this way. As explained in the *Srimad-Bhagavatam* (8.14.10), "People in general are bewildered by the illusory energy [*maya*], and therefore they try to find the Absolute Truth, the Supreme Personality of Godhead, through various types of research and philosophical speculation. Nonetheless, they are unable to see the Supreme Lord."

This is further explained as follows: The internal potency of the Supreme Lord is spiritual. The marginal potency is the living beings who can lean toward the spiritual or material energy. The third potency of the Lord is the material energy, *maya*, also called nescience or darkness. It is this *maya* which makes the living entity godless and fills him with the desires for fruitive activity and sense pleasure. Thus, because of being influenced by the nescient potency, which covers his spiritual position, he suffers the threefold miseries of material existence.[4] These three kinds of miseries of material existence include those that come from the body itself, those caused by other living beings, and those problems caused by natural occurrences.

Because of being illusioned like this the living entities cannot understand the truth of the creation and, thus, they wander throughout the material world for many lifetimes. However, the living beings are independent in determining whether they want to engage in material or spiritual activities. Misusing this independence to turn toward the dark side separates the living beings to varying degrees from the spiritual light. Yet, when the living beings turn toward God and work to regain their spiritual nature, they can return to their normal spiritual state of being and be relieved of material existence.

Actually, the spiritual living beings are merely covered by this cloud of *maya*, which affects their consciousness. Therefore, the goal of any genuine spiritual path is simply to remove this cloud and the influence of the illusory energy.

The *Brahma-samhita* (5.44) also explains that *maya* is like the shadow of the Lord's *chit* or knowledge potency, and is also worshiped by people in the form of Durga, the creating, preserving, and destroying agency of this material world.

Durga is the maidservant of Lord Krishna, and conducts herself in accordance to the will of the Supreme. Her shadow is the material energy, *maya*. In this form of Durga, she is pictured as a beautiful demigoddess with ten arms, representing the ten types of material activities. She rides on her lion, indicating her heroic activities. She is also the subduer of vices, represented by the image of her trampling the demon Mahishasura. She is the mother of her sons Kartikeya and Ganesha, representing beauty and success. She is armed with twenty weapons, denoting the various pious activities enjoined by the *Vedas* for the suppression of vices. She also holds a snake, which signifies destructive time. The word *durga* also means a prison house or a fort. So the material world is like a prison from which it is hard to escape. "Dur" means difficulty and "Ga" means going. So it is very difficult to escape this material world without undergoing many hardships. But one who takes shelter of the spiritual potency can get free from the illusory nature of the material world. So when the living beings forget their spiritual nature and the service of the Supreme Being, Krishna, they are confined in the material prison of the universe. This is the aspect of the universe which is presided over by Durga. However, those who are devotees of the Lord and who are on the spiritual path to regain their real nature are free from this prison-like environment of the universe. Durga does not affect them.

The spiritual form of Durga is *Yogamaya*. The external form of Durga is *Mahamaya*, the illusory energy. The spiritual form of Durga who functions on the platform of *shuddha-sattva*, pure transcendental existence, is understood to be Krishna's sister, known as Ekanamsha or Subhadra.[5] The name Subhadra means auspicious. So Subhadra also paves the way for the devotee's spiritual progress by supplying that which is auspicious and taking away all that is inauspicious. So this is the spiritual form of Durga, the shadow of whom is the external material energy.

We should note, however, that Durga, also called Bhadra or Bhadrakali and Katyayani, works in the material world. Subhadra plays the part of Lord Krishna's sister and is the internal or spiritual energy, and does not work as Durga in the material world. So, originally their energy is one and the same, but through her expansion as Durga she works in a different capacity within the material realm.

To explain further, higher than Subhadra is Radharani, Lord Krishna's consort and the quintessence of spiritual energy. She is the personification, essence and origin of Lord Krishna's pleasure potency, *hladini-shakti*. This pleasure potency of Lord Krishna expands to become Radharani for the sake of the most intimate spiritual pastimes in Goloka Vrinadavana, the topmost spiritual planet. This potency expands further into the forms of Krishna's queens in the other Vaikuntha planets, and also as His sister, Subhadra, for other purposes and pastimes. And Durga is an expansion of this internal or spiritual energy. In this way, Durga also can be considered an expansion of Radharani. Therefore, Radharani is the source of the pleasure essence in the spiritual world, while Durga provides the means for all pleasure in the material realm.

So herein we can understand that *mahamaya* in the material world is an expansion of *yogamaya* in the spiritual world. The difference in function is that *yogamaya* manages the spiritual sky, and in her partial expansion as *mahamaya* she manages the material world. *Yogamaya* covers the devotees in the spiritual world so that they can forget the Lord's greatness and engage in loving pastimes with Him as His friends, parents, servants, and so on without being overwhelmed by His omnipotence. *Mahamaya* in the material world, on the other hand, keeps the living entities forgetful of their true eternal nature as long as they have no spiritual inclination. So *yogamaya* helps bring the devotees together with the Supreme Being in various relationships while *mahamaya* keeps them separate, or at least makes it seem they are separate.

Another way to understand this is that there are two divisions of energy, the material and spiritual. The original energy is the spiritual, in which is the *hladini-shakti* potency of Krishna, which is His pleasure potency. It is this pleasure potency from God through which all spiritual joy and happiness are felt. This is also the original form of Durga who is nondifferent from this spiritual energy, but Durga is her form in the material world. The partial expansion of the *hladini-shakti* potency is *mahamaya*, which also acts like a covering for the *hladini-shakti* potency, the pleasure of our spiritual nature. In the material world she bewilders the conditioned souls so they can think they are happy in material pursuits. In this way, the materialists remain covered over by their attraction to their desires for sense pleasure due to *mahamaya*, and the devotees and transcendentalists become absorbed in spiritual pleasure through *yogamaya*, or the *hladini-shakti*. It is through *yogamaya* that the religious become liberated from the material realm. This is the work of Subhadra who provides what is auspicious and takes away what is inauspicious for the sincere seekers on the spiritual path. Thus, the material energy is like a testing ground that must be passed before one can gain entrance into the spiritual atmosphere. It also protects the spiritual atmosphere from those who are not sincere.

The *Narada Purana* (1.3.13-15) lists many names of Durga. Since she is considered one of the energies of the Lord, she is regarded as His *shakti*, and is called Uma, Bharati, Girija, and Ambika. The great sages designate her as Durga, Bhadrakali, Chandi, Mahesvari, Kaumari, Vaishnavi (supreme potency of Lord Vishnu), Varahi (potency of Lord Varaha, and incarnation of Krishna), Aindra, Shambhavi, Brahmi (connected with Lord Brahma), Vidya (spiritual knowledge), Avidya (nescience), Maya (the illusory energy of the Lord), and Para Prakriti (the Supreme Primordial Nature).

In the *Brahma Vaivarta Purana* (*Krishna-Janma-Khanda*, 118.35) Durga talks with Shiva about how she is an expansion from the highest realms and explains herself in this way: "I am Mahalakshmi in Vaikuntha, Srimati Radha in Goloka, Shiva [connected with demigod Shiva] in the region of Shiva, and Sarasvati in the abode of god Brahma." Thus, from the highest levels of the spiritual domain she expands herself to include all other *shaktis*, or potencies.

The *Narada Purana* (1.3.27) also explains that in regard to Lord Vishnu, "His *Shakti* is the great *Maya*, the trustworthy upholder of the universe. In view of its being the material cause of the universe, it is [also] called *prakriti* by scholars."

THE APPEARANCE OF LORD SHIVA
IN THE PROCESS OF CREATION

Since it is the glance of the Supreme Being over the energy of Durga, *maya*, which sets in motion the creation of the universes, Durga is therefore known as the universal mother.[6] This is why when people speak of the material nature, it is always referred to as a female, as "she," Mother Nature, and as the goddess. And the essence of Mother Nature is represented as Durga. She is united with her husband, known as Lord Shiva, who is then considered the father of the universe.

It is explained in the *Vayu Purana* that Shiva is an expansion of Sadashiva, who is a direct expansion of Lord Krishna. Sadashiva appears in order to perform various pastimes. Sadashiva is a resident of one of the Vaikuntha planets of the spiritual world. His consort there is Ramadevi, a form of Lakshmi. She expands into *mahamaya* in the material worlds, where she is then known as Durga. Thus, the spiritual Sadashiva and Ramadevi again become related as Shiva and Durga, who are the origin of material nature.

The part that is played by Lord Shiva during the creation is more fully explained in the *Brahma-samhita* (5.6-8). Therein it states that Lord Krishna, the Lord of Gokula, the topmost planet in the spiritual sky, is the Supreme Godhead, the very Self of eternal ecstasies. He is busily engaged in the enjoyments of the transcendental realm and has no association with the mundane, illusory material energy. He does not stop His spiritual engagements. When He intends to create the material manifestation, He merely sends His glance over the deluding energy in the form of His time potency. Krishna's expansion in the form of Maha-Vishnu in the Causal Ocean carries this glance to the material energy. This glance from Maha-Vishnu is the efficient cause of the creation. The dim halo of this glance, the reflected effulgence, is Shiva in his form as Shambhu, who is the symbol of masculine mundane procreation. It is through this form of Shiva that the Supreme Lord associates with the material energy. In his role as Shambhu, he is the principle by which Maha-Vishnu impregnates the material nature with the seeds of the innumerable living entities. Otherwise, the Supreme Being has no association with the material energy.

The *Brahma-samhita* (5.10) goes on to explain that it is Shambhu, Maheshvara, who is the dim reflection of the Lord's glance, and lord of the *pradhana* who embodies the seed of all living beings. It is he who comes forth from the glance of the Lord. Shambhu is created from the space in between the two eyebrows of Maha-Vishnu. (*Bs*.5.15) Shambhu then joins with *maya* in the form of the male organ of regeneration. But he can do nothing independent of the power of Maha-Vishnu, who represents the direct spiritual power of Krishna. Therefore, the necessary changes in the material energy cannot happen unless facilitated by the will of the Supreme Lord, Krishna.

As further described (*Brahma-samhita* 5.16), the function of Shambhu in relation to the conditioned souls is that the mundane egoistic principle has originated from Shambhu. What this means, without trying to get complicated about it, is that the tendency for the individual living being to forget his spiritual identity comes from Shambhu. This forgetfulness makes the individual in this material world want to be an enjoyer of the material experience. This is because he thinks he is the material body. This false identity makes all conditioned souls want to continue with their existence in the temporary, mundane world. This is the function of Shambhu, Shiva, in relation with the Supreme Lord Krishna's creative process. This forgetfulness is then carried further by *mahamaya*, Durga, as previously explained.

However, to make it more clearly understood, Shiva is an expansion of the Supreme Lord, Krishna, as described above. He is not a second god that acts in place of Krishna. Those who think he is make an offense against the Supreme Being. Neither is he a *jiva*, a marginal spirit soul. As clearly explained in the *Brahma-samhita* (5.45), just as milk is transformed into curd by the action of acids, it is nonetheless neither the same as nor completely different from its cause, namely milk. So I adore the primeval Lord Govinda of whom the state of Shambhu is a transformation for the work of destruction.

In other words, Lord Krishna manifests His energy through Maha-Vishnu into the form of Shambhu, Shiva, in order to perform various tasks without having to give up His completely spiritual activities. It is through Shiva that the Supreme Being associates with His material energy in the form of *maya*. He does not do so directly. Thus, Shiva is not really different from Krishna, yet remains subservient to Him. The difference is like that of yogurt and milk. Yogurt is simply a changed form of milk, different in function simply by adding a certain acid. Similarly, the Supreme Being expands and changes into the distinct personality of Shambhu by the addition of a certain adulterated element to perform a particular function. It is also this form of Shambhu from whom Rudra, another form of Shiva, is created from Lord Brahma later on in the creative process. We will read about this incident later.

Another point, as previously mentioned, is that within the glance of Maha-Vishnu over *maya* is the element of time, which starts the agitation within the energy of *maya*, or the *pradhana*. This is what starts the process of creating and separating the various material elements. This element of time has been identified as Shambhu, the personality of the destructive principle. It is also this Shambu in the form of Rudra who later appears at the end of time to bring about the destruction of the universe.

So, Shiva is considered to be an expansion of the Supreme Lord Vishnu, Krishna, and is called Hara as such, and is transcendental to the material qualities. However, in his activities of destroying the world at the end of time, he is in touch with the mode of ignorance, or *tamo-guna*, and then he is considered as one of the living entities, called Rudra.

It is further explained that Lord Krishna expands a portion of His plenary portion, Lord Vishnu, who assumes the form of Rudra when it is time to dissolve the cosmic manifestation. Lord Vishnu does this for accepting the association of the material mode of ignorance. Thus, Rudra is but another expansion of the *energy* of Lord Krishna, although not a personal expansion. Rudra, Lord Shiva, has various forms, which are transformations brought about by the different degrees of association with *maya*. Although Rudra is not on the same level with the *jiva-tattvas*, the individual living beings, he still cannot be considered a personal expansion of Lord Krishna. Thus he is considered like a *jiva*.[7]

Although many people worship Lord Shiva, Shiva worships Lord Krishna. The *Shiva Purana* states that Shiva is the supreme, however, this is in regard to his power over the material world. After all, it is he who assists in the annihilation of the material creation, but no scripture ever says that Shiva is the Supreme Lord of any of the Vaikuntha planets or of Goloka Vrinadavana, or any part of the spiritual domain. Such precincts belong only to Lord Krishna and His personal expansions. That is why Lord Shiva is always pictured absorbed in meditation. He is meditating on Lord Sankarshana, who is represented by the snakes on Shiva's body. Since Shiva is the origin of the mundane egoistic principle, one who is a worshiper of Lord Shiva as a devotee of Sankarshana can be freed from the false, material ego.[8]

So here we have learned another aspect of how the spiritual energy expands to create the material energy. Thus, ultimately everything comes from Lord Krishna. It is He who expands into the forms of Maha-Vishnu and then Shiva and Durga, who are considered the indirect mother and father of the universe, and are themselves expansions of Sadashiva and Ramadevi from the Vaikuntha realm.

CHAPTER TEN

The Process of Universal Creation

As we have been describing in the previous chapters, the potential for the creation of the elements come before the actual creation of the universe, which is often referred to as the universal or cosmic egg. No universe has yet been created at this stage of the process of creation, but only the potentials for it. There are three divisions of the creative process, *maha-kalpa*, *vikalpa*, and *kalpa*. *Maha-kalpa* is that part of the creation in which the Supreme Being assumes the form of Maha-Vishnu, or Karanodakashayi Vishnu, with all the potencies of the *mahat-tattva*, or ingredients of creation. A *maha-kalpa* takes place within each exhalation of Maha-Vishnu. *Vikalpa* is the creation of the universe and Lord Brahma. And a *kalpa* is the portion of the creative process that comes from Lord Brahma, usually at the beginning of each of his days. There are thirty different *kalpas* of Brahma, of which we are presently in the Varaha-kalpa because the incarnation of Varaha appeared during this particular *kalpa*.[1]

Although all creations are basically the same, we need to understand that the creative process can vary from one creation to another. There is no difference in the creative principles, yet there are different details and order of events that may change according to the different millenniums or *kalpas* in which the creation takes place.[2] So even though I will try to describe the correct order of things, they may be described differently in other places because of these factors. Even the pattern of events within the *kalpas* can change, as pointed out in the *Linga Purana* (40.86-92), which states that these differences that occur from creation to creation in the unfolding historical patterns are limited to twenty-five. So now, doing the best I can, I will begin describing the formation and creation of the universe itself.

First, I will review some of what needs to take place in the material manifestation before the universe can finally be created.

THE MODES OF NATURE

Once the *pradhana* is in place and the creative process is ready to begin, after the glance of Maha-Vishnu, as described in the previous chapters, the modes of material nature become agitated. These are the mode of passion which effects the creation of things, the mode of goodness which maintains the universe, and the mode of ignorance or darkness which causes the destruction or deterioration of everything material. These modes are the effective causes of the creation, maintenance, and destruction of the cosmos.[3]

Within the glance of Maha-Vishnu is the time factor. Once time is produced, there is the perception of past, present, and future. It is this time factor which agitates and causes the interaction of the material modes.[4] Through the agitation of the modes of nature, the material energy manifests varieties of creation. This includes the various forms and elements made of the material energy as well as the variety of species of life. These forms of species make up the vehicles for the innumerable states of consciousness that are also manifested through this process.[5]

One point to consider is that by understanding that the source of the time element and the modes of nature, from which everything else expands, is the Supreme Being, the idea that nature goes on existing without any higher supervision, or is itself the cause of creation, is merely a product of atheism. Such an idea is an attempt by those who try to explain that the universe was created merely by a mechanistic process which requires no higher authority. In other words, they proclaim that it was an accident or a quirk of nature. However, their premise still does not explain from where this nature came.

THE FALSE EGO

From the *pradhana*, the subtle form of the material ingredients, comes the *mahat-tattva*. From this comes the element of false ego formed by the agitation of the modes of material nature. This bodily ego causes the material illusion, the false identity, and the duality that is perceived by the conditioned souls in the material creation.[6] The living beings, although above and beyond the three modes of material nature, think they are a material product and are, thus, motivated to satisfy the desires of the mind and senses. Because of this they undergo the reactions and miseries of material existence.[7]

As the false ego manifests, it takes shape in three phases according to the modes of passion, goodness, and ignorance. Within these three types of egotism are the sources of all the demigods, senses, and material elements.[8] When mixing with various portions of the material energy, false ego in the mode of ignorance is the source of the physical elements; in the mode of passion it is the source of the bodily senses; and in the mode of goodness it is the source of the demigods.[9]

Although matter and spirit are distinct and separate from each other, they become knotted by the element of false ego.[10] For example, the living entity is an eternal spiritual being, and material nature is dull, inert, and lacks self-awareness. The material body looks alive and fresh only as long as it is touched by the spirit soul within. Once the soul leaves the body, it immediately begins to get stiff and deteriorate. The living being is completely separate from material nature and this kind of decay.[11] Nonetheless, they appear to be connected because the soul exists within the body, and the false ego makes the conditioned soul within think that the material form is indeed his real identity. Thus, the diversity of the soul and the body is not easily recognized because of this false ego.[12] Real ego means to understand that you are a spiritual being. False ego is the element which causes the soul to forget its real identity and accept itself as a material body.

Once the individual misidentifies himself as a material object, the next thing that happens is that he begins to think of what he needs to satisfy his mind and senses. He becomes entrapped in the world of appearances and willingly partakes of the drama that is based on his misidentification. Through his ignorance of spiritual reality, he thinks he and everything around him is something other than it really is. He sees only the material or physical forms of identification, which are themselves temporary and illusory, being composed of different shapes and combinations of ever-changing elements and atoms. Thus, the conditioned soul remains in illusion and pursues material existence under the influence of this false ego.

Once the subtle element of false ego is manifest and begins mixing with the modes of material nature, it paves the way for the manifestation of the other separated material elements.

THE MANIFESTATION OF THE ELEMENTS

In the beginning of creation nature assumes all subtle causes and gross manifestations by the modes of goodness, passion, and ignorance, and the interactions thereof with the time element and false ego. The material creation, and especially the formation of the cosmic universe, takes place by the progressive manifestation of these elements in an orderly progression from the most subtle to gross. From the false ego proceeds the elements of ether, air, fire, water, and earth. The five knowledge acquiring senses include hearing, touch, sight, smell, and taste. The five working senses include speech, the hands, the genitals, the anus, and the legs. The mind belongs to both of these sets of senses.[13] These 16 elements along with the individual spirit souls and the Supreme Lord count as a total of 18 elements which comprise the material creation. These can be further divided into 23 elements, as they are referred to elsewhere; namely, the total material energy, false ego, sound, touch, form, taste, smell, earth, water, fire, air, either, eye, ear, nose, tongue, skin, hands, legs, evacuating organ, genitals, speech, and mind.[14]

How the material elements are evolved and transformed to create the universe and its contents is very much the same as that described previously in Chapter Six. However, now the elements are not simply manifesting their potential and functionality, but are indeed starting to manifest their being and texture, their separateness and solidification. The *Kurma Purana* (1.4.20-34) also describes this same process in a more summarized manner. We will not repeat the whole description here, but you may review Chapter Six for the details.

As the material elements are transformed, they receive from the glance of the Supreme Lord their potency to function. Then they are amalgamated by the power of nature and begin to create the universal egg.[15]

The *Vishnu Purana* (Book One, Chapter Two) also explains a little about the formation of the universe from the elements. The elements originally existed as indistinguishable. Thus, being disconnected, they could not create anything with form, including living beings. Only after the direction from the Supreme could they combine with one another into a mass of unity. Intellect and the other elements combined to form the Cosmic Egg.

As Lord Krishna explains to Uddhava in the *Srimad-Bhagavatam* (11.24.9), "Impelled by Me, all these elements combined to function in an orderly fashion and together gave birth to the universal egg, which is My excellent place of residence."

By combining all the elements, the Supreme Lord created the unlimited universes. They are floating in the breath of Maha-Vishnu as He exhales like tiny atoms floating in sunshine. When Maha-Vishnu inhales, they return within His body.[16]

As further explained in the *Srimad-Bhagavatam* (3.26.50-53), when all of the material elements were unmixed. The Supreme Being, along with time, work, and the qualities of the modes of material nature, entered into the universe with the complete material energy in seven divisions. These seven divisions are the different material elements, the *mahat-tattva* or total material energy, and the false ego. From these principles roused into activity and united by the presence of the Lord, an unintelligent egg arose, from which appeared the celebrated Cosmic Being. The universe, in the shape of an egg, is the manifestation of the total ingredients of the material energy. Around the center forms a multi-layered shell. From inside to outside, these layers are earth, water, air, fire, ether, ego, and the *mahat-tattva*, each layer ten times thicker than the previous layer. The outside of the universe is covered by the *pradhana*, or the Causal Ocean. All the universes clustered together floating in the Causal Ocean look like atoms in a huge combination of thousands of millions. The *pradhana* is the infinite, boundless, illimitable origin of material nature. Thus, each universe is like a coconut with the planetary systems inside the outer layers of material elements. Within that coconut is the universal form of Lord Hari, Krishna, in the form of Maha-Vishnu, whose body the fourteen planetary systems are but parts. Thereafter, the Supreme Being divided the universe into many departments.[17]

For over a thousand years the shiny egg lay on the waters of the Causal Ocean in a lifeless state. Then the Lord entered it as Garbhodakashayi Vishnu.[18]

So all of the universes emanate from Lord Maha-Vishnu's breathing and the pores of His unlimited body, and all the elements which compose the entire material creation also come from that expansion of Lord Krishna, Maha-Vishnu.[19] The *Brahma-samhita* (5.14) also confirms that thereafter, Lord Maha-Vishnu expands Himself and enters into each one of the innumerable universes.

When Maha-Vishnu expands Himself into Garbhodakashayi Vishnu and enters the universe, He sees that there is darkness in all directions and no place to stay. Then with perspiration from His own body, he fills half the universe with water. He then lays down on the bed of Lord Seshanaga on that water, which is the Garbhodaka Ocean.[20]

The *Narada Purana* (2.42.42-44) explains that water was first created within the universe in order to maintain and protect the living beings. Water is the very life of all living beings, and thus they grow and multiply because of it. Without it, they perish. Therefore, the whole universe is surrounded by it, which upholds and supports everything. (This is similar to the way a living entity is conceived and grown in the water of the womb or in an egg.)

The *Brahma-samhita* (5.35) goes on to describe that in spite of the fact that Lord Vishnu expands Himself to enter each and every one of the millions of universes in His work of creation, His potency remains inseparable. There is no loss in His power. All of the universes exist in Him, as Maha-Vishnu, and He is present in His fullness in each and every atom that is scattered throughout the universe, at one and the same time. This is His all-pervasiveness and inconceivable power. He is beyond human conception.

Only after the Supreme Being has entered the universe, and all the necessary elements have manifested, can there be the creation of any physical bodies in which the living entities can exist. We conclude this chapter with the explanation from *Srimad-Bhagavatam* (2.5.32-35): "The forms of the body cannot take place as long as these created parts, namely the elements, senses, mind and modes of nature, are not assembled. Thus, when these became assembled by force of the energy of the Supreme Personality of Godhead, this universe certainly came into being by accepting both the primary and secondary causes of creation. Therefore, all the universes remained thousands of aeons within the water [of the Causal Ocean], and the Lord of living beings, entering in each of them, caused them to be fully animated. The Lord [Maha-Vishnu], although living in the Causal Ocean, came out of it, and dividing Himself as Hiranyagarbha [Garbhodakashayi Vishnu], He entered into each universe and assumed the *virat-rupa* [the Supreme as the universal form], with thousands of legs, arms, mouths, heads, etc." This universal form is recognized as being composed of the planets, stars, and galaxies that spread throughout the universe.

Only now, after everything else is prepared, is the universe able to accommodate life. Now the next step is the birth of Lord Brahma, the first created living being who appears as an engineer to help in the creation of life within the universe.

CHAPTER ELEVEN

The Universal Form

In this chapter we will focus on how the Lord expands Himself and enters into each universe and then becomes the universal form. This is the form which contains everything and is the potency behind all that is. Without the manifestation of the energy and omnipotence of the Supreme Being, no one would have the sanction to possess any ability to do anything. Neither would any of the senses be able to function. It is only due to the power of the Supreme Being that the universe is a place with any activity at all, as will be described from the combined information from Chapters Six and Twenty-six of the Third Canto of *Srimad-Bhagavatam*.

THE CREATION OF THE UNIVERSAL FORM

When all of the material elements became separate and unmixed, as described in the previous chapter. The Supreme Being, the origin of creation, along with time, work, and the qualities of the modes of nature, entered into the universe with the total material energy in seven divisions. These seven divisions are the various material elements, the *mahat-tattva* or total material energy, and the false ego. It is from these seven principles, roused into activity and mixed by the presence of the Lord, that the universe in the form of an unintelligent egg arose, from which appeared the Cosmic Being, of whose body parts include the fourteen planetary systems.[1]

This is how the Supreme Being, Lord Maha-Vishnu, expands Himself to the first universal incarnation, Garbhodakashayi Vishnu, and situates Himself in the golden egg of the universe and divides it into many departments.[2]

When the Lord entered into the elements of the universe, they transformed into the gigantic form in which all the planetary systems and all movable and immovable creations rest. This form, known as Hiranmaya, lived for one thousand celestial years on the water of the universe, the Garbhodaka Ocean, and all living entities lay with Him.[3] Before the universal creation takes place and after the Lord enters the universe, there is a period of nonactivity for one thousand celestial years. All of the living entities that are injected into the *mahat-tattva* are divided among all the universes with each incarnation of Garbhodakashayi Vishnu, and all of them are as if dormant in the Lord until the birth of Lord Brahma. From Brahma all other demigods and living entities are born.[4]

It was this total energy of the *mahat-tattva* in the shape of the gigantic universal form, *virat-rupa*, that was divided by the Lord Himself into the consciousness of the innumerable living entities and the life of activity, along with self-identification.[5] The gigantic universal form of the Lord is the first incarnation or expansion of the Supersoul within the universe, Garbhodakashayi Vishnu. He is the Self of an unlimited number of living beings. In Him rests the sum total of creation, which flourishes from Him. He is the one central heart from which all other energy is generated, the dynamic force of all movements by the ten kinds of life energy.[6]

The Supreme Lord is the Supersoul of all the demigods who are entrusted with helping construct the cosmic manifestation. Then He separated Himself into the diverse forms of the demigods after the universal form was manifested.[7]

First came the manifestation of all of the senses and elements within the universe. First came a mouth and the organ of speech, and the demigod who resides over that organ, the god of fire, Agni, by which the living entities have the power to speak.[8] When the separated palate manifested, Varuna, the director of air entered therein, and thus the living beings have the power to taste with the tongue.[9] Then came the nostrils and the sense of smell. When the two nostrils manifested in the gigantic universal form, the dual Asvini-kumaras entered them by which the living beings have the facility to smell aroma.[10] *Prana*, the vital air, along with the wind-god who presides over that sense, also entered therein. Thereafter appeared eyes in the universal form and the sense of sight, along with the sun-god, Surya, who presides over it. Thus, the living entities have the power to see.[11] Next came the ears and the auditory sense and the Dig-devatas, the deities who preside over it, giving the living beings the ability to hear sound.[12]

When skin manifested, Anila, the deity directing wind entered with partial touch. Thus, the living entities have the sense of tactile knowledge.[13] When the skin manifested, the deities of sensations also entered it giving the living beings the ability to feel and have sensual happiness.[14] Upon the skin appeared hair, mustache, and beard. After this came the herbs, drugs, and then His genitals, followed by semen, the faculty to procreate.[15] When the genitals separately formed, Prajapati, or Brahma, entered into it, giving the living beings the power to enjoy sex pleasure.[16]

Next appeared the anus and organs of defecation, by which the living entities are able to evacuate stool and urine. There also appeared the god of death, Yamaraja.[17] Thereafter, the hands appeared along with Lord Indra, the ruler of heaven, and the power of grasping manifested, by which the living entities are able to transact business for livelihood.[18] Next the legs formed separately and the demigod named Vishnu [not the Supreme Being] entered with partial movement, giving the living beings power to move.[19] Then the veins of the universal body manifested, along with red corpuscles and blood. Along with them came the rivers, and then the abdomen.[20] With the abdomen came the feelings of hunger and thirst, after which came the oceans. Then a heart appeared and then the mind.[21]

When the intelligence of the universal form became manifest, Brahma entered into it, thus an object of understanding can be experienced by the living entities.[22] After that the heart formed, and the moon demigod, Chandra, entered into it giving power for the living being to conduct mental activities.[23] This is why the moon is always connected with the mind and its state of being. The materialistic ego next formed and Rudra entered into it, giving the living beings power to transact objective actions.[24] When His consciousness was brought into being, the total energy, *mahat-tattva*, entered into it, giving the living beings ability to conceive specific knowledge.[25] This is why the *mahat-tattva* is associated with cosmic or universal consciousness.

Then the heavenly planets were manifested from His head, from His legs the earthly planets, and from His abdomen the sky separated itself. With them the demigods and others were also manifested according to the modes of material nature. The demigods in the mode of goodness are situated in the heavenly planets. Human beings in the mode of passion are situated on earth. Living beings who associate with Rudra in the mode of ignorance are situated in the sky between the earthly and heavenly planets.[26]

The Vedic wisdom next manifested from the mouth of the gigantic universal form. Those who are inclined to this knowledge are called *brahmanas*, who are the natural teachers and spiritual masters of society. The power of protection was generated from the arms, from which power came the *kshatriyas* who have a nature toward protecting society from disturbance of thieves and miscreants. From the thighs came the *vaishyas*, who are the mercantile men in charge of grains and their distribution. From the legs of the universal form came the facility for service from which came *shudras* who satisfy the Lord and society by service. All these different social divisions are born with their occupational duties from the Supreme Person.[27]

When all of the demigods and presiding deities of the various senses were present, they wanted to wake their origin of appearance. Failing to do so, they reentered the body of the universal form in order to wake Him. As each one entered through the appropriate sense, the Cosmic Being still refused to be awoken. Only after the inner controller, the deity presiding over consciousness, entered the head with the ability to reason, did the Cosmic Being arise from the causal waters. Thus, only with the help of the Supersoul can any person be aroused with the ability to work and use his mind and intelligence. Without the assistance of the Lord as Supersoul in each of us, no person can function on his own.

Therefore, through spiritual knowledge acquired through concentrated devotional service, one should contemplate on the Supersoul being in the body and simultaneously apart from it.[28]

It is admitted that this next description of the universe is imaginary, but it shows how philosophers through the ages have conceived of the omnipotence of the Supreme.

Great philosophers also imagine the complete planetary systems to be displays of the upper and lower limbs of the universal body of the Lord. The *brahmanas* represent His mouth, the *kshatriyas* His arms, the *vaishyas* His thighs, and the *shudras* are born of His legs. There are fourteen planetary systems, with seven lower and seven higher. The lower planetary systems up to the earth are situated in His legs. Atala, the first planetary system is situated on the waist. Vitala, the second system, is on the thighs. The third, Sutala, on the knees. Talatala, the fourth, are on the shanks. Mahatala, the fifth, on the ankles. Rasatala, the sixth, on the upper portion of the feet. The seventh planetary system is Patala, which is situated on the soles of the feet. The middle planetary systems from Bhuvarloka are in His navel. The higher systems occupied by the demigods and advanced sages and saints are situated in His chest. The planetary systems of Janaloka and Tapaloka are situated on the front of the chest. Satyaloka, the topmost planetary system is situated on the head of the universal form. The spiritual planets are eternal. Thus, the *virat-rupa*, the universal form of the Lord, is full of planetary systems.[29]

Herein, we can understand that everything is but a display of the Lord's energy. As Krishna describes in the *Bhagavad-gita* (10.41-42), "Know that all beautiful, glorious, and mighty creations spring from but a spark of My splendor. . . With a single fragment of Myself I pervade and support this entire universe."

It is explained further in *Bhagavad-gita* (11:7-15) that everything is contained in the universal form, including all planetary systems, demigods, and all other living entities. Even the past, present, and future can be seen therein. Therefore, as pointed out in *Srimad-Bhagavatam* (10.85.10), and as we can see from the description in this chapter, Krishna is the power of the senses to reveal the sense objects. He is also the senses' presiding demigods, as well as the power the demigods give for the sanction of sensory activity. He is also the capacity of intelligent decision-making and the ability to remember. Thus, the expansions of the Supreme Being and His universal power play a much more important role in the ability for the material elements and the bodily senses to function than we realize or even think about. Without the omnipotence of the Supreme, all physical organs and senses, our thinking ability, as well as the organization and laws of the universe, would collapse.

CHAPTER TWELVE

The Creation From Lord Brahma

At this point we have to remember that the order of creation can vary in different *Puranas*. This does not meant that they contradict each other. The pattern of creation can and does change in various *kalpas* or days of Brahma. It changes depending on the different states of mind and consciousness Brahma enters as he creates the subsequent species, which may differ from one *kalpa* to the next. The descriptions also do not necessarily follow a chronological process because they are explained according to the questions given to the narrator, and are then answered accordingly, which may not follow a particular order of events. Thus, we find minor differences between the *Puranas*, or even within one *Purana*. So I am going to use the most widely accepted version. However, since the *Srimad-Bhagavatam* is considered the most ripened fruit of Vedic knowledge, and the ultimate commentary by Vyasadeva himself, the person considered the writer of the major Vedic texts, I will be following the description therein as much as possible, except when additional details are provided elsewhere.

SUMMARY OF THE CREATIVE PROCESS

There are nine types or categories of creation that are described, and they are divided into two kinds, primary and secondary. The primary creation is the *Prakrita-Sarga*, or the natural creation that comes about due to the interaction of the modes of material nature and the time element. The order of the *Prakrita-Sarga* generally begins with the manifestation of the *mahat-tattva*, or the seeds of the sum total of the material ingredients in its subtle form along with time. Due to the presence of the Supreme Lord, the modes of nature begin to interact. In the second stage of creation, the false ego is generated in which the material ingredients along with material knowledge and activities arise. In the third stage of creation, the elements, such as ether, air, fire, water, and earth, are generated, along with the objects of the senses, such as what is seen, heard, tasted, touched, and smelled. In the fourth stage is the creation of knowledge and working capacity, or the working senses.[1]

In the fifth stage of creation, by the interaction with the mode of goodness, there is the manifestation of the controlling deities, or the universal departmental managers. In the sixth stage of creation is the manifestation of ignorance or the principle of forgetfulness, which causes the conditioned souls to be bewildered as to what they really are, which is why they remain in illusion or darkness.[2] The five types of darkness are *tamasa* (ignorance), *moha* (delusion), *mahamoha* (great delusion), *andha-tamisra* (blinding darkness), and *avidya* (nescience).[3] These six kinds of creation have already been described in the previous chapters.

Now we come to the secondary creation, called the *Vaikrita-Sarga*, the creation from Lord Brahma. This is the process of creation that manifests not simply by the mixing of the modes of nature and various material ingredients, but directly by the superior power or guidance of Lord Brahma. All of the innumerable forms and types of bodies that manifest are for accommodating the different levels of consciousness of the living beings in the universe. These many forms are created out of the different levels of consciousness experienced by Lord Brahma through his creative meditation. He was able to create simply by the power of his mind. This is an example of how thoughts are actually things, they are vibrations that can produce effects. And when you have a mind as strong as Lord Brahma's, such thoughts will manifest forms. Thus, by his accepting different states of mind, material bodies were manifested that would accommodate the appropriate states of being of the innumerable living entities. This is what we will describe in this chapter.

First from Brahma is the creation of all immovable objects and entities, called the seventh stage of the creative process. The eighth stage of creation involves the manifestation of the lower species of life. The ninth creative stage is that of the humans. The creation of the varieties of demigods, and those beings living in the astral planes, are considered the tenth level of creation. Finally, the appearance of the Kumaras is considered to be part of both the natural or primary creation and the secondary creation from Lord Brahma.[4]

MAHA-VISHNU ENTERS THE UNIVERSE
AND THE MANIFESTATION OF LORD BRAHMA

When the Lord as Maha-Vishnu expands Himself and enters each and every universe, He becomes known as Garbhodakashayi Vishnu, or Hiranyagarbha and Antaryami, the Supersoul. It is this Lord who is glorified by Vedic hymns. He is the master of each universe and the shelter of the external or material energy, although He remains beyond the touch of this energy.[5]

Before the universal creation takes place and after the Lord enters the universe, there is a period of nonactivity for one thousand celestial years. All of the living entities that are injected into the *mahat-tattva* are divided among all the universes with each incarnation of Garbhodakashayi Vishnu, and all of them are as if dormant in the Lord until the birth of Lord Brahma. From Brahma all other demigods and living entities are born.[6]

Entering the universe, Lord Vishnu finds only darkness with no place to reside. Thus He considers what to do next. He then creates the waters of the Garbhodaka Ocean from the perspiration of His own body and fills half the universe. On that water He creates his own residence as an expansion of Vaikuntha and rests in the waters on the bed of the great serpent, Lord Ananta, Seshanaga.[7] Although He appears to be in slumber, enjoying transcendental bliss in his internal potency, His eyes are slightly open. When He is ready to begin the act of creation, a golden lotus springs from his navel which becomes the birthplace of Lord Brahma. Within the stem of that lotus are the fourteen planetary systems.[8]

This is similarly described elsewhere as follows: Once Lord Vishnu desires to begin the act of creation, on which the Lord's attention is fixed, the subtle form of creation pierces through His abdomen, agitated by the material mode of passion. Then a golden lotus springs from His navel as He floats on the Garbhodaka Ocean. The lotus, called Brahmaloka or Satyaloka, becomes the abode of Lord Brahma. The golden color of the lotus represents the dim reflection of pure consciousness.[9] The lotus is the gigantic universal form of the lord in the material world. This universal form becomes absorbed in Lord Vishnu at the time of dissolution and again reappears during creation. It is this lotus which contains the sum total of all fruitive activities of the conditioned living beings, the first of which is Lord Brahma who is generated in that lotus. It is also the seed from which all creation springs at the time of manifestation.

If the manifestation of this lotus is after a previous devastation, the golden lotus illuminates everything and dries up the waters of devastation. Then Lord Vishnu personally enters that universal lotus flower as the Supersoul. When it is thus impregnated with all the modes of material nature, the personality of Vedic wisdom, Lord Brahma, whom we call the self-born, is generated.[10]

The divine lotus became the birth place of Lord Brahma who is well versed in the *Vedas*. The lotus is also spiritually related with all souls in the universe, the stem of which is where the fourteen planetary systems of the universe are generated.[11]

Although generally a *jiva* soul is given the position of the demigod Lord Brahma, if there is no such being suitable to occupy the post, then the Supreme Being again expands Himself to become Lord Brahma.[12]

Lord Vishnu maintains the universe, and through His form of Brahma He creates the functional universe, and in His form of Rudra [Lord Shiva] He brings about the destruction of the cosmic creation. Thus, only by the will of the Supreme is there creation, maintenance, and dissolution of the complete cosmic creation, which are under the charge of these three personalities.[13]

The difference is that Lord Krishna expands Himself into His personal plenary form of Vishnu for the maintenance of the universe. This is like the flame of one candle being used to light another candle. However, the second candle is as powerful as the first. Being the director of the mode of goodness, He is transcendental to the material energy. However, Lord Vishnu's opulences and potencies are not quite but almost equal to Krishna's.[14]

Regarding Lord Shiva, he is an assumed form of the Supreme Being, Vishnu, just as yogurt is a changed form of milk. Lord Vishnu assumes the form of Shiva for the special purpose of material transactions.[15] Lord Shiva is an associate of the external energy, the three modes of material nature. Therefore, he is absorbed in the material quality of darkness and the element of egotism. Lord Vishnu is transcendental to *maya* and her qualities, thus He is the Supreme Personality of Godhead. The truth is that Lord Brahma and Lord Shiva are devotee incarnations who carry out orders of the Supreme.[16]

Although Brahma lives for many millions of years, he lives only within the duration of one of the breaths of Maha-Vishnu. Such a lifetime is calculated to be equal to one *nimesha*, less than a second, for the Supreme Lord Maha-Vishnu.[17]

THE DAWN OF CREATION

The *Vishnu Purana* (Book One, Chapter Two) and the *Agni Purana* (17.2) explain that at the very beginning of creation there was neither day nor night, nor sky nor earth, nor darkness, nor light, nor any other things save only the One, Supreme, unapprehensible by intellect, along with Brahma, spirit, and the subtle energy of matter and time.

Although situated in the whorl of the lotus in which he was born, Brahma could not see the world. Therefore, he circumambulated all of space, and while moving his eyes in the four directions, he achieved four heads. Brahma could not understand anything about the creation, the lotus, or himself. Then the air of devastation began to move the Garbhodaka Ocean, the water below him, and the lotus in great circles. Brahma began to wonder who he was, and how he came to be situated on top of the lotus. From where did it sprout, and what is the source that must be within the water? Brahma then entered the stem of the lotus, but try as he might he could not trace out the source. While searching in this way, Brahma realized his mortality and felt the fear of death in his mind. Then he retired to the lotus and simply contemplated on the Supreme in order to understand the ultimate cause of his existence.[18]

While thus engaged in thinking, Brahma twice heard two syllables of instruction from nearby. These syllables formed the word *tapa*, which means penance for spiritual realization. When he heard that sound, he searched all around but could find no speaker. So he thought it best to sit down and attend to the performance of penance as he was told.[19]

Brahma then engaged in meditation until finally he had the required knowledge to see what he could not see before, which was the Supreme Being in his own heart.[20]

So this is a great lesson. No one, not even the greatest of beings, can realize who they are by speculative knowledge, or by analyzing the surroundings in the universe. Only by the proper meditation and devotional surrender will the Supreme Being reveal himself to us, by which we can understand who we are and our purpose in this material world.

The *Brahma-samhita* (5.23-26) also explains how Brahma, coming out of the lotus and being guided by divine potency, turned his mind to the act of creation under the impulse of impressions he had from previous lifetimes. Thus, he began to recall his purpose. However, he could see nothing but darkness in all directions and thus still felt confused. Then the goddess of learning, Sarasvati, the divine consort to the Supreme Lord, gave Brahma the *kama-bija mantra*: *Klim krishnaya govindaya gopi-jana-vallabhaya svaha*. She told him that he should practice spiritual association by means of this *mantra* to fulfill his heart's desires. Thereafter, he meditated by using this *mantra*, and by focusing his mind in this way: "There exists a divine lotus of a thousand petals, augmented by millions of filaments, in the transcendental land of Goloka. On its whorl, there exists a great divine throne on which is seated Sri Krishna, the form of eternal effulgence of transcendental bliss, playing on His divine flute resonant with the divine sound, with His lotus mouth. He is worshiped by His amorous milkmaids with their respective subjective portions and extensions and also by His external energy [meaning Durga, who stays outside the spiritual realm] embodying all mundane qualities."

Then the Gayatri *mantra*, mother of the *Vedas*, was imparted to Brahma from the sound of Sri Krishna's flute. Having been initiated with the Gayatri from the Supreme Being Himself, Brahma attained the status of twice-born, or having a spiritual birth. This was through the realization of the transcendental pastimes of Sri Krishna through the use of the *kama-gayatri*. This is the highest Gayatri of all because it contains a meditation and prayer of the perfectly spiritual and sportive activities of Lord Krishna which are not found in other *gayatris*. The *kama-gayatri* is: *Klim kama-devaya vidmahe pushpa-banaya dhimahi tan no 'nangah prachodayat.*[21]

Enlightened by the recollection of that *gayatri*, which embodies the three *Vedas*, Brahma became acquainted with the vast ocean of Truth. Then he worshiped Lord Krishna, the essence of all Vedic knowledge, with the hymn that makes up the major portion of the *Brahma-samhita*.[22]

Being very much pleased with Lord Brahma because of his nondeceptive penance in *bhakti-yoga*, the Supreme Being, Lord Vishnu, presented His eternal and transcendental form to him.[23]

Thereafter, Brahma could see the gigantic lotus-like bedstead, which was the body of Seshanaga, on which the Personality of Lord Vishnu was lying alone. The rays of the jewels bedecking the body of Seshanaga dissipated the darkness of those regions. Lord Vishnu's unlimited spiritual body occupied the space of the upper, middle, and lower planetary systems. He was self-effulgent and beautifully dressed and ornamented. He was decorated with valuable jewels and fragrant flowers. The Lord showed His lotus feet by raising them, which are the rewards of pure devotional service. The splendor of the transcendental rays from His moonlike toenails and fingernails looked like petals of a flower. His beautiful smile vanquishes the distress of His devotees, and His face was so pleasing because it dazzled with the rays from His lips and the beauty of His nose and eyebrows. As Lord Brahma, high in the lotus flower, thus saw the Lord, he simultaneously glanced over creation. He saw the lake in Lord Vishnu's navel and the lotus, as well as the devastating water below. All became visible to him. Lord Brahma, being thus surcharged with the mode of passion and the inclination to create, began to offer prayers to the Lord to acquire the necessary energy and creative mentality.[24]

Thereafter, Lord Brahma displayed his deep realizations about the purpose of life in the many prayers he offered to Lord Vishnu. After having prayed to the Supreme as far as his mind would permit, the Lord saw that Brahma was very anxious about planning and constructing the different planetary systems. Thus, He responded to Brahma in deep, thoughtful words, which removed all of the illusion that had arisen. He told Brahma, "Situate yourself in penance and meditation and follow the principles of knowledge to receive My favor. When you are absorbed in devotional service, in the course of your creative activities, you will see Me in you and throughout the universe, and you will see that you yourself, the universe and all living entities are in Me. You will see Me in all living entities as well as all over the universe, just as fire is situated in wood. Only in that state of transcendental vision will you be able to be free from all kinds of illusion. I am the Supersoul of every individual. I am the supreme director and the dearest. People are wrongly attached to the gross and subtle bodies, but they should be attached to Me only. By following My instructions you can now generate the living entities as before, by dint of your complete Vedic wisdom and the body you have directly received from Me, the supreme cause of everything." Then the Supreme Being disappeared.[24]

BRAHMA BEGINS THE PROCESS OF CREATION

Now that Brahma had the power to create, he began the process of manifesting the various living beings and objects of the universe from his own body and mind. This is described in many places throughout the *Puranas*, and in detail in Chapter Ten of the Third Canto of *Srimad-Bhagavatam*.

At first Brahma saw that both the lotus upon which he was sitting and the water below were trembling due to a strong wind. However, due to his spiritual knowledge, Brahma was not intimidated by the illusory material energy and drank in the wind and water. This shows that from the topmost living being in this universe, Brahma, down to the most insignificant creature, all are subject to the struggle for existence with the forces of material nature.

The Creation of the Planets

Then Brahma saw that the lotus was actually spread throughout the universe, and he thought of how he could create the numerous planets, the seeds of which were merged within that lotus. Brahma then entered into the whorl of the lotus and divided it into three divisions, and later into fourteen. The lower planets are called the Patalalokas, the middle planets are called the Bhurlokas, and the upper planets are the Svarlokas. Higher than these are other planets, such as Maharloka, Tapoloka, and Satyaloka or Brahmaloka.[25]

Lord Krishna further explains that, "After Brahma, being endowed with the mode of passion, had performed great austerities, he was able to create the three planetary divisions, called Bhur, Bhuvar, and Svar, along with their presiding deities. Heaven was established as the residence of the demigods, Bhuvarloka as that of the ghostly spirits, and the earth system as the place of human beings and other mortal creatures. Those mystics who strive for liberation are promoted beyond these three divisions of planets. Lord Brahma created the region below the earth for the demons and the Naga snakes. In this way the destinations of the three worlds were arranged as the corresponding reactions for different kinds of work performed within the three modes of nature. By mystic yoga, great austerities and the renounced order of life, the pure destinations of Maharloka, Janaloka, Tapoloka, and Satyaloka are attained. By devotional yoga, one achieves My transcendental abode."[27] These three main divisions of planets were again divided into fourteen. Thus, Lord Brahma created all fourteen planetary divisions, along with their presiding deities, for habitation by the various types of living beings. The eight predominating deities of heavenly planets are known as Indra, Agni, Yamaraja, Varuna, Nirriti, Vayu, Kuvera, and Shiva.[28]

The lower planetary systems, which make up the Universal Form of the Supreme from His feet to his waist are Patala, Rasatala, Mahatala, Talatala, Sutala, Vitala, and Atala.[29] The upper planetary systems from His navel up to His head are Bhu or Bhurloka, Bhuvah, Svah, Mahah, Janaloka, Tapoloka, and Satyaloka.[30]

All the hellish planets are situated in the space between the higher planetary systems, Bhu-mandala, and the Garbhodaka Ocean. Pitriloka, the planet of the forefathers or Pitas, is also located in that region.[31]

Within these various planetary systems, there are also planets for the Gandharvas (angels or angel-like beings), Pannagas, Kinnaras, Caranas, Siddhas, and Apsaras. These are called Gandharvaloka, Siddhaloka, Caranaloka, Pannagaloka, Kinnaraloka, and Apsaraloka. Thus, various planets are created with differing atmospheres to be inhabited by many varieties of living entities.[32]

Of these numerous planets, the special nature of the sun is also described in the *Vishnu Purana* (Chapter Eleven of Book Two), which explains that the sun planet shines with such intense radiance because the energy of Vishnu presides in it. The sun thus disperses with his beams of light the darkness that spreads over the whole universe. Elsewhere it is described that the sun is but a reflection of the *brahmajyoti* effulgence, the great, self-luminous white light that exists beyond the coverings of the material creation.

The Lord's personal residence in the material creation is called Svetadvipa, which is also the polestar. Svetadvipa is the residence of the Lord's expansion as Ksirodakashayi Vishnu. The polestar is also called Dhruvaloka because the Lord sent His devotee, Dhruva, to that eternal abode. It is a Vaikuntha planet situated within the material creation, but it is not material in any way. Thus, it is also called Vishnuloka, the planet of Lord Vishnu. Naturally, no one but the devotees of Lord Vishnu can gain access to this planet by becoming spiritually perfect through the process of devotion, or *bhakti-yoga*.[33]

Furthermore, Svetadvipa, the polestar, being the residence of one of the expansions of Lord Vishnu is why all the luminaries in the universal sky, as well as all the Vaishnavas or devotees of Lord Vishnu, unceasingly circumambulate this planet, called Dhruvaloka.[34]

From this we can understand that no one can attain the higher planets by mechanical means or through the process of mystic yoga, what to speak of the spiritual planets. Great devotees of the Lord are the only ones who can gain entrance into the spiritual planets due to their spiritual devotion, love of God, and their purified consciousness. Only fools think that they can gain entrance into the higher realms of reality without adjusting their consciousness accordingly. Thus, no one who is sinful, envious, proud, lusty, greedy, or violent toward others can gain access to such regions. The beings who live there are devoid of such faults.[35]

Regardless of whether one enters the hellish planets or the heavenly planets, he returns here to this earth and the cycle of birth and death after the results of his impious acts or pious credits are exhausted. Here a person begins again with a chance to understand his or her real spiritual identity and elevate oneself to the spiritual world.[36]

The reason why this planet earth, called Bharatavarsha, is actually better than the heavenly planets is because it is neither too heavenly or too hellish, so one can have a greater chance for spiritual progress. It is also the place where Lord Krishna and His many incarnations appear in order to deliver His spiritual teachings and exhibit His divine activities. Thus, it is from this planet that one can most easily find the doorway that leads directly to the spiritual world, beyond all effects of the material creation.[37]

Even those on the heavenly planets pray that they may take birth on planet earth, even though they have accumulated great spiritual merit and attained the region of heaven. Only on earth can one engage in the meritorious acts that can provide the means of entering the kingdom of the Supreme. The residents of heaven exclaim that on earth any person who is greatly devoted to the Supreme Lord, Vishnu, is being bowed down to by those who have been born in heaven. A person who delights in the worship of Vishnu, or who utters His name, such as Narayana, Krishna, Rama, or Vasudeva, is also worthy of being saluted by the heaven-born gods, for he can attain the highest region of Vishnu.[38]

EVERYTHING IS BUT A COMBINATION OF ATOMS

These initial creations, and all others that followed, were caused by a combination of the manifestation's ultimate particle, which is the atom. Even after all material forms are dissolved, it exists as the indivisible particle of which the universe is composed. Atoms are the ultimate state of the manifest universe and are called the unlimited oneness when they remain separate, without combining into different forms. The various forms that we recognize in this world are made of different combinations of the indivisible atoms. Because of this, each form is given a name as if it has a separate and distinct identity, although it is made of the same common elements as everything else. That is why this realm is often called the world of names. Names are all that distinguish the various forms we see because when they are broken down to their most common elements and atoms, they are all made of the same things, but in different combinations.

The atom is also considered the subtle form of eternal time. Time is estimated by the movement of the atoms, or the atomic combination of bodies. All physical movement, as well as growth, maintenance, and deterioration, is an effect of the time element, which becomes a calculation on the duration or the effect of time. Various lengths of atomic time are measured according to the duration a substance takes to move through a particular space. This is similar to the difference between a certain amount of sand traveling through a small hole, like in an hour-glass, or the length of time it takes for the earth to travel around the sun. Each one establishes a standard length of time. This element of time is also the potency of the almighty Supreme Being who controls all physical movement. However, we should be able to understand that time is only an effect within the material creation. There is no influence of time in its form of past, present, and future beyond the jurisdiction of the material manifestation because in the spiritual region there are no elements or atoms that are necessary to produce the effects of time. In other words, nothing there is created or destroyed, nor does it age.[39]

Eternal time is the primeval source of the interactions of the three modes of material nature. It works as an instrument of the Supreme Being for His pastimes in the material creation. It is an impersonal feature of the Supreme. It acts as a veil to separate the material energy from the Supreme Lord and the spiritual realm.[40]

The difference in the effects of time can also be seen in the divisions known as the four millenniums, or ages, known as the ages of Satya-yuga, Treta-yuga,

Dvapara-yuga, and Kali-yuga. The aggregate number of years of these combined ages are twelve thousand years of the demigods. However, in human years they total 4,320,000 years. One year of the demigods is equal to 360 human years on earth. Satya-yuga is 4800 years of the demigods, or 1,728,000 human years. Treta-yuga is 3600 years of the demigods, and 1,296,000 human years. Dvapara-yuga is 2400 years of the demigods, or 864,000 human years. And Kali-yuga is 1200 years of the demigods, or 432,000 human years. The combined four *yugas* multiplied by 1000 comprise one day on the planet of Brahma, Satyaloka. A similar length of time comprises his night. Brahma lives for 100 years, each with 360 of such days and nights in each year. It is during Brahma's night when there is a partial annihilation of the universe, and during the day it is again manifested and brought to activity. This shows the difference the time element has in various parts of the universe.[41]

The *Vishnu Purana* (Book One, Chapter Three, p.32-34) also explains this but simply states that the ages Satya-yuga through Kali-yuga are 4000, 3000, 2000, and 1000 divine years respectively. This is because it does not include the intermediate years between the ages. This is explained as the Sandhya (before each age begins) and the Sandhyansa (the years after the age ends, but before the new one). These Sandhya and Sandhyansa periods are described as 400 each for Satya-yuga, or 800 years; 300 each for Treta-yuga, 200 each for Dvapara-yuga, and 100 each for Kali-yuga. So the calculations of the *yugas* in the *Vishnu Purana* are the same as the *Bhagavata Purana*.

THE CREATION OF THE LIVING BEINGS

After creating the worlds, Brahma began preparing for the creation of the living beings. Desirous of creating different subjects, he created them in the same forms as he had created before. As he meditated and pondered about the forthcoming creation, *avidya*, ignorance or nescience, unfolded itself into five forms. These forms were darkness, delusion, great-delusion, pitch darkness, and blind darkness. These are called *tamisra, andha-tamisra, tamas, moha*, and *maha-moha*.[42] This darkness is in regard to the lack of understanding of the living being for the purpose of life and his real identity, which is further explained as follows:

Brahma began the creation with the nescient engagements, like self-deception, the fear of death, anger after frustration, the sense of ownership of possessions, and the illusion of being the physical body and the forgetfulness of one's spiritual identity. Thus, before there was the creation of living beings and the varieties of species, Brahma first created the living conditions and the mental dispositions under which the living beings would live. In order to make it possible for the living beings to accept the various roles and parts they would play in this material world, the first principle of the universe is forgetfulness of their true spiritual identity. Only in this way would any living being be afraid of so-called death, and be motivated to pursue illusory goals and pleasures.[43]

Once the planets have been created and positioned in the universe, and all necessary conditions for material existence have been put in place, it is now time to begin manifesting the innumerable living beings that will populate the material creation. The *jiva* souls all have an eternal connection, a kinship, with the Supreme Lord just as the rays of the sun are always associated with the sun itself. Thus, they are eternal and never perishable. Though they had remained dormant within Him between manifestations of the cosmic creation, after Lord Vishnu expands Himself and enters the universes, it is time for the conditioned souls to be awakened. These spirit souls are all eternal and spiritual. However, they also have a tendency to become influenced by the material energy, which is why they are called the marginal potency. Thus, the materially conditioned souls reappear in the material world in accordance with their fruitive desires. This is done through the agency of Lord Brahma.[44]

To accommodate the various inclinations and desires of the living entities, everything is created simultaneously. All qualities and states of mind of the living entities are also created by Lord Krishna. "Intelligence, knowledge, freedom from doubt and delusion, forgiveness, truthfulness, self-control and calmness, pleasure and pain, birth, death, fear, fearlessness, nonviolence, equanimity, satisfaction, austerity, charity, fame and infamy are created by Me alone."[45] Thus, all states of being toward which the living beings are attracted are created from the start in order to give them the necessary facilities for their material experience.

In this way, there is no gradual process of evolution by which the many species of life are created. These are already pre-designed into the plan of creation so that any form of material experience can be supplied within the millions of species of life and the many planets within the universe under the guidance of the Supreme. As Lord Krishna explains in *Bhagavad-gita* (9.8), "The whole cosmic creation is under Me. By My will it is manifested again and again, and by My will it is annihilated at the end." Therefore, the conditions and suitable forms for the activities of the living beings are provided from the very beginning of creation.

Whatever activities the numerous creatures had engaged in during previous lives are again assumed when created again. Whether the temperament was violent or non-violent, gentle or cruel, righteous or unrighteous, that same tendency is awakened in this present birth. It is the creator who makes the arrangements to accommodate these many forms of mentality and consciousness in the different physical bodies and species of life.[46]

However, in each re-creation of the world, the *jiva's* sins are wiped out. Thus, he begins his existence in the newly created universe free from any past *karma*, or merits or demerits. Such *karma* gets merged and wiped out in the unmanifest nature of the last annihilation of the cosmos. The reason is because good merit merges into the mode of goodness, *sattva-guna*, while demerit merges into the mode of darkness, *tama-guna*. When the creation is annihilated, the modes of nature are brought to a stage of equilibrium, in which they no longer have any effect. Thus, all good or bad *karma* is also annihilated, and the next creation and everyone in it starts out as new.[47]

So in the beginning of the first *yuga* after the creation, called Satya-yuga, there is no *Dharma* or *Adharma*, no good or bad *karma* which the living entities inherit from their previous existence. There is a predominance of the *sattva-guna*, the mode of goodness, in which everything is beautiful and cooperation is the norm. Food is healthy, the atmosphere is clean, and there are no hindrances or clashing of opposites, and no cruelty. The subjects are happy and immune from sorrow. They are mentally so potent that even without copulation subjects can be born through mere mental conception. At that time there is truthfulness, absence of greed, longevity, and self-control. In other words, it is like paradise.[48]

Nonetheless, even though the *jiva* soul undergoes a change at the beginning of creation, and all *karma* is wiped out, the qualities of the particular modes of nature with which he was familiar in the previous existence cling to him. So this is what appeals to him in the present creation and how he begins his new activities. And this is what determines the species of life to which he is drawn.[49]

Krishna also explains in *Bhagavad-gita* (15.15) that it is He who helps the individual soul to remember his past tendencies: "I am seated in everyone's heart, and from Me come remembrance, knowledge, and forgetfulness." So as the living beings are given a new body, it is the Supersoul in the heart which helps the living beings to remember their past familiarities.

It is said that the history of when the living entity originally wanted to enjoy material nature cannot be traced, but the material creation is meant simply for the sense enjoyment of the conditioned souls. When the living being wants to enjoy the modes of material nature and falls from the spiritual strata, out of the many forms of life he will prefer to first accept the body of a human being or demigod. And this is the form he is given when he first enters material existence.[50] Then, however, due to being implicated in lower desires and degrading activities, he falls into lower forms of life. "The living entity in material nature thus follows the ways of life, enjoying the three modes of material nature. . . Thus he meets with good and evil amongst various species."[51] Then, having fallen into lower species, only through the slow process of evolution in which the consciousness of the living being can progress upward does he finally attain the human form again. Therefore, though he starts life in the new creation without any past *karma*, he may again acquire the good or bad merits which will force him to endure continued birth and death amongst many species of life, and on various planets. By using the human form properly, he can leave this world behind and enter the spiritual world, which is his natural home.

[This next order of creation is generally accepted by most *Puranas*.]

* * *

Creation of the Immovable Entities

The next stage of creation and the first living beings to manifest are the immovable living entities. These beings were without intellect or reflection, and void of perception. From Lord Brahma's bodily hairs sprang the herbs, roots, and fruits.[52] Others include the fruit trees without flowers, the trees and plants which live until the fruit is ripe, the creepers and vines, and the trees with flowers and fruits. These immovable trees and plants seek their main source of subsistence upwards, from the sun. They are almost unconscious but can feel pain within.[53]

Creation of the Lower Species of Life

Brahma, seeing that this creation was defective or incomplete, then designed another. While he meditated, from the power of his mind the *Tiryak-srotas*, or animal creation, was manifested. These were the wild beasts which were of the quality of consciousness known as *Tamasic*. These were of the quality of darkness and ignorance, being destitute of knowledge and uncontrolled in their conduct, acting only under the dictates of their nature according to their species.[54]

These lower species are of different varieties, numbering twenty-eight. They have low intellect and little memory, and subsist by recognizing their desirables by smell. These include the cow, goat, buffalo, deer, hog, lamb and camel, all of which have two hooves. The horse, mule, ass, bison, and wild cow are those with one hoof. The dog, jackal, tiger, fox, cat, rabbit, lion, monkey, elephant, tortoise, alligator, etc., are the kinds with five nails. There was also the creation of the birds, such as the heron, vulture, crane, hawk, peacock, swan, crow, owl, and others.[55] Another of these lower species were the snakes [56] as well as the aquatics.[57]

Creation of Human Beings

The next form of creation, in the ninth stage, was that of humankind, who are very much motivated by the mode of passion. They are always busy in the midst of miserable life, although they think themselves very happy.[58]

So Brahma, in his effective meditation, began to contemplate further. Then from the unmanifest appeared the downward current of creation, the *Arvak-srotas*, competent of accomplishing all goals of life. They came to be known as the human beings--illuminated with the light of knowledge, endowed with the quality of *sattva*, goodness, but contaminated and afflicted with *tamas* (the mode of ignorance) and dominated by *rajas* (the mode of passion).[59] Hence they are impelled into action to satisfy their desires.[60]

Other *Puranas* describe the creation of humans with a few more details. They explain that Brahma took up another body full of activity of mainly *rajasic* nature (mode of passion). From it humans, richly endowed with this passionate mode, were born as his sons. Brahma quickly gave up that body as well. That body became light, which is also called twilight at dawn, or the morning twilight.[61]

The *Brahmanda Purana* (1.2.8.18-21) also explains it as follows: Brahma then meditated and entered another mental disposition solely constituted of the *raja-guna*, mode of passion. Since he had meditated on creating man before the creation, they were called Manusyas, men. Since they were begotten (Prajananat) they became Prajas (subjects). After creating these subjects, Brahma also discarded that body or disposition as well, which became the moonlight. Hence, these subjects, mankind, become delighted when the moonlight appears in the evening.

Later on it is described that in the beginning of creation, Lord Brahma, the father of the living entities of the universe, saw that all the living beings were unattached. Therefore, to increase population he then created woman from the better half of man's body, for woman's behavior carries away a man's mind.[52] So, by the sexual attraction between man and woman the entire world goes on, and thus there is the increase in population.

The Creation of the Demigods and Astral Beings

The next stage of creation, as explained in the *Srimad-Bhagavatam* (3.10.27), is that of the demigods and the beings that live in the celestial and astral realms. These include, 1) the demigods, 2) the forefathers, 3) the *asuras* or demons, 4) the Gandharvas and Apsaras, or angels, 5) the Yakshas and Rakshasas, 6) the Siddhas, Charanas, and Vidyadharas, 7) the Bhutas, Pretas, and Pishachas (various ghostly beings), and 8) the superhuman beings, celestial singers, etc. All these are created by Brahma. How all of these are created is described more elaborately below.

[From here on the descriptions of the order of creation may differ somewhat from one text to another.]

* * *

Creation of Yakshas & Rakshasas & Demons & the Night

As explained previously, once Lord Brahma started the act of creation, the manifestation of the shadow coverings of the living entity came into being , which are the five different levels of ignorance that clouds the minds of the conditioned souls. These are called *tamisra, andha-tamisra, tamas, moha,* and *maha-moha.* Out of disgust, Brahma threw off that form of ignorance, which then became the night, and taking the opportunity, many Yakshas and Rakshasas, who had manifested from this state of mind, sprang for possession of that form, which continued to exist into the night. Hence the creation of the night and why demons are more powerful during that time.[63]

Other *Puranas* also agree and explain that first, when Lord Brahma was desiring to create living beings, he collected his mind into itself and was united in yogic trance. He found himself in the essence of dark traits, and the quality of darkness pervaded his body. While he thus concentrated, from his loins the *asuras* or demons were born at the outset. He cast off that wicked (mental) body full of vice and the quality of darkness, from which the night was created. Since that period is abundant in darkness, the created beings sleep at night.[64]

The *Brahmananda Purana* (1.2.8.1-7, 25) explains it this way: Even as Brahma was meditating, the mental progeny were born along with those causes and effects arising out of his body. From the cosmic body of Brahma there cropped up the individual souls. Thereafter, Brahma was desirous of creating the many thousands of beings of the four groups, namely the Devas, the *asuras*, the Pitris, and human beings. He thus engaged himself in meditation upon the creation, in which he was affected by the mode of *tamas*, darkness. So then at first the *asuras* were born from his loins. *Asu* is considered by scholars to be the vital breath, and, therefore, those born of it are *asuras*. Brahma then discarded that body, which immediately became the night. Since night has the element of *tamas* or ignorance predominating it, that is the time in which darkness prevails. Therefore, at night everyone is subjected to darkness. Since the *asuras* were created at night, they are invincible at night.

Creation of the Demigods and the Day

Brahma then created the chief demigods, shining in the mode of goodness, *sattva*. He dropped before them the effulgent form of daytime, and the demigods sportingly took possession of it. Thus, the demigods and those of the mode of goodness are stronger during the daytime.[65]

Other *Puranas* explain this in the same way but with a few more details as we can see: Then resorting to another body, Brahma desired to create. He experienced pleasure, and thence from his refulgent face proceeded the demigods who were joyful and increased in brightness, endowed with the qualities of goodness. Brahma abandoned that body too, and the day, mainly of the quality of goodness, the *sattvic* nature, was created out of it. It became the full brightness of day. This is why the demigods are stronger in the daytime and the demons are stronger at night. Also, religious minded persons worship the Devas endowed with the characteristic of *sattva* during the daytime.[66]

The *Brahmanada Purana* (1.2.8.7-12, 24) describes this in a similar manner but also explains that after Brahma had created the *asuras*, he developed another body that was unmanifest wherein the mode of goodness, *sattva-guna*, predominated. Brahma felt very happy in that body and state of consciousness. Thereafter, from his shining face arose the Devas, gods and goddesses. Since they were born from the effulgent face (Divyataha), they are glorified as Devas. After creating the Devas, Brahma discarded that body which became the day. Therefore, people worship the Devas with holy rites during the day. Since the Devas were created during the day they are stronger at that time.

Creation of Progenitors, Manes, and the Twilight

He next adopted another body or mental disposition in which the mode of goodness prevailed, and thinking himself as the father of the world, the Pitris, or progenitors, were born from his side. Then that body he also abandoned, which then became the Sandhya, twilight of evening.[67]

Other *Puranas* describe it this way: Then after creating the Devas, Brahma took up another body full of virtue, constituted by *sattva-guna*, the mode of goodness. Then Brahma meditated upon those beings, his sons, to have a fatherly nature. Thus, the manes or Pitris, the forefathers who considered Brahma like a father, were born of that body in the juncture of night and day. Therefore, that period of time is declared for them. After creating the manes, Brahma also abandoned that body. As soon as that body was cast off it became the dusk (Sandhya), the time between the end of day and the beginning of night. Hence, the day time is for Devas; the night is for the demons. In between them, the evening twilight is for the Pitris. Hence, all Devas, *asuras*, Sages, and the human beings worship with concentration in the middle period between the night and the day.[68]

Therefore, human beings are powerful when the morning light comes, and likewise the Pitris are powerful in the evening. Thus, morning twilight, day, evening twilight, and night are the four bodies of Brahma which support the three modes of nature, *sattva*, *rajas*, and *tamas*.[69]

The *Garuda Purana* (1.4.25-27) further explains that when Brahma had cast off the previous body, the twilight in between day and night was evolved, and the human beings evolved by taking up the inter-spaces of the *rajas* element. That body was also cast off and became the moonlight or the twilight of the dawn (*prak-sandhya*). Thus Brahma's bodies are four, namely the moonlight, the night, the day, and the twilight. The manes further evolved themselves by taking up the inner spaces of the mode of goodness, *sattva*.

Further Creation of Demons & Rakshasas

Now we find Lord Brahma gave birth to another set of demons from his buttocks, and they were very fond of sex. They were so drawn toward sex that they even turned to attack Brahma himself for copulation. Brahma was so distraught that he prayed to the Supreme being for help. The Lord told him to cast off his impure body, which meant changing his mental disposition in order to continue the process of creation. When he left that state of consciousness, signified by his casting off of that mental body, it took the form of twilight between day and night, which is the time which kindles passion. Thus, these particular demons took hold of the twilight as if it were a beautiful damsel.[70]

It is further explained that by taking up the *rajas* element, hunger, darkness, and anger were evolved. Then were created the giants known as Rakshasas. They were consumers of blood and emaciated with hunger and thirst. The Yakshas were created and known by their propensity for eating.[71]

So Brahma, in a form or mental disposition composed of the quality of foulness of the *tamasic* and *rajasic* nature, next produced hunger, from which anger was born. And Brahma put forth beings with hideous aspects and long beards who were overwhelmed and emaciated with hunger. Those beings hastened to Brahma, crying out, "Oh, preserve us." They were called the Rakshasas. Others who cried out, "Let us eat," were called from that expression Yakshas.[72]

The *Padma Purana* (1.3.98-102) goes on to explain how Brahma had a sneeze, which produced anger in him. Affected by it he created certain beings of darkness. These deformed beings desired to eat him and ran toward him. Those who said, "Protect him," became goblins. Those who said, "Let us eat him," became spirits. The hairs of Brahma, who was very much afraid of them, fell off and turned into serpents on account of their creeping, and snakes on account of their having fallen. Then the creator manifested fearful, angry-minded beings, who were pink in color and flesh eaters. This takes us to the manifestation of serpents.

Serpents

On seeing the ruthless Yakshas, Brahma became very displeased. His bodily hairs began to shiver and move up and down again and again. The hairs that dropped from his head moved and crawled up. They are considered as Vyala, because they were originally Vala (hairs). Since they dropped off, they are also considered as Ahis (serpents). They are also called Pannagas because they moved and wriggled, and Sarpas because they crawled. Thus, various species of snakes were created and are called according to their characteristics. Their abode is in the earth. The terrible fiery form of Brahma's anger entered those serpents in the form of venom.[73]

Gandharvas and Apsaras

Brahma then laughed at the sight of the demons infatuated with the damsel of twilight, and then evolved by his own loveliness the hosts of Gandharvas and Apsaras. These beings are the angels and beautiful damsels of the heavenly worlds. Brahma, to change his state of meditation, again cast off that level of consciousness, or mental body, which became the shining form of moonlight, and was taken by the Gandharvas and Apsaras.[74]

As Brahma was singing words, the Gandharvas were born as his sons. Since they were "drinking" the musical words, they are remembered as Gandharvas.[75] With the singing capacity of the Gandharvas, Brahma also created some of the birds as well.[76]

Goblins, Bhutas, Ghosts & Fiends

Brahma next evolved from his sloth the ghosts and fiends, but he closed his eyes when he saw them standing naked with scattered hair. The ghosts and hobgoblins took possession of the body thrown off in the form of yawning. This is known as the uncleanliness of sleep which causes drooling, and the unsteady mental state of those who are susceptible to the attack of ghosts, in which they may be called insane.[77]

It was from the mode of anger that Brahma created the Bhutas, evil spirits. These are terrible beings whose diet was flesh, and who were furious by nature. Since they were born (*Bhutatvat*) they are called Bhutas, and as they ate flesh (*Pishitashanat*) they are also called Pishachas.[78] This is how various kinds of ghostly beings became manifest. [Some *Puranas* mention the ghosts being born before the Gandharvas.]

Sadhyas & Pitas

Next Brahma recognized his own desire and energy, and evolved from the navel of his invisible form the hosts of Sadhyas and Pitas. These are the invisible realms and forms of those departed souls who have yet to receive another physical body or reappear in another human birth.[79]

Siddhas & Vidyadharas

Then Lord Brahma created the beings known as the Siddhas and Vidyadharas from his own ability to be invisible. He gave them the wonderful form known as Antardhana, which means that their presence may be felt or detected, but they remain unseen.[80] Siddhas are those deathless and perfected human beings who have no physical body yet often remain in an unseen form to give guidance to religious aspirants. Vidyadharas are greatly beautiful aerial spirits who are known for being bearers of wisdom and blessings for spiritual seekers and those in need.

Kimpurushas & Kinnaras

Then Brahma evolved the beings called Kimpurushas and Kinnaras out of the reflection he saw of himself in some water. They took possession of the shadowy reflection that was left by Brahma. That is why they and their spouses sing his praises by recounting his exploits at every daybreak during the *brahma-muhurta* hour, the time just before sunrise. This time of day is especially good for spiritual activities, thus these beings use this time of day to make spiritual advancement.[81]

More Serpents

After some time, Brahma lay down with his body stretched full length. He was concerned that the work of creation had not gone as it should have. Then he gave up that body composed of the sullen mood and from it hair dropped that formed into snakes. While the body crawled along with its hands and feet contracted, ferocious snakes and Nagas, such as the cobra species, sprang from it with their hoods expanded.[82]

* * *

In this manner, all creatures great and small proceeded from Lord Brahma. These included the gods, demons, Pitris, humans, Yakshas, Pishachas, Gandharvas, Apsaras, birds, beasts, serpents, and all things movable and immovable. These beings, now having been created, discharged the same functions as in previous creations, whether malignant, benign, gentle or cruel. The creator displayed infinite variety in the forms of bodies and level of intellect, which were from the very beginning determined by the authority of the *Vedas*, even including the offices and positions of the Devas and *rishis*. Thus, in the beginning of each *kalpa*, or day of Brahma, he creates with the power derived from the will to create, assisted by the natural tendencies of the object to be created.[83]

CREATION OF THE KUMARAS

Since Brahma could see through the illusory nature of the world, he felt it to be a sinful task to create it, and did not feel much pleasure in it, although it was necessary to allow the conditioned souls to become active again. Therefore, he engaged in the meditating on the Supreme Being and purified himself before he started another term of creation. By his mental power, he then created the four great sages known as Sanaka, Sananda, Sanatana, and Sanat-kumara. Brahma asked them, "Now my dear sons, create progeny." Although Brahma wanted them to assist him in the act of creation, because they were highly elevated in spiritual perceptiveness due to retaining their semen, they were all unwilling to adopt materialistic activities and expressed their unwillingness to participate. They did not want to become entangled in materialistic family life, for they had dedicated themselves to a higher purpose, namely the devotional service to the Supreme Lord. In fact, it was from these four sages that came one of the first spiritual lineages, or descending lines of spiritual authorities, known as the Kumara-*sampradaya*, for the advancement of *bhakti-yoga*.[84]

CREATION OF RUDRA

Brahma became terrifically angry due to his sons' refusal to assist him. Even though he tried not to express his anger, it was generated from between his eyebrows and came out in the form of a child of mixed blue and red color. The child immediately began to cry and asked what was his name and place. Brahma pacified him with gentle words, telling him that he would be chief of the demigods and be called Rudra by all people because he had so anxiously cried.[85] In this way, Rudra was created out of anger from the mode of passion, partly touched by ignorance. Then Brahma told him he could reside in the heart, the senses, the life-air in the body, the sky, the air, fire, water, earth, sun, moon, and in austerity.

The esoteric meaning of this is that the egocentric attitude of thinking oneself to be the body is the Rudra principle in the heart. Earlier in the process of creation it was also Shiva or Shambhu who carried the egocentric principle into the creation when he carried the unlimited number of souls into the mixture of the material energy in the glance of Maha-Vishnu. Now he is also carrying the same principle into the heart of each individual that would be manifested in the material creation. What happens is that anger develops in the heart because of the false identity and desires that accumulate. From there, the anger extends through the senses, exhibiting itself through the angry eyes or clenching hands or kicking legs, or even fast breathing. This is the exhibition of the Rudra principle. This same principle can be observed in angry or stormy clouds in the sky, fiercely blowing winds and ocean waves in the water, or in a blazing fire, and so on. Sages and yogis who have accumulated mystic powers through austerity and then use those powers under the influence of anger or passion is also this Rudra principle. These are all manifestations of this form of Rudra.

Brahma then designated Rudra's other names, including Shiva, along with the names of his eleven wives, such as Uma, Ila, Ambika, Iravati, etc. Then Brahma asked Rudra, being one of the masters of the living beings, to increase the population on a large scale.[86]

The *Vishnu Purana* (Book One, Chapter Seven, p.72-74), *Padma Purana* (1.3.170-175) and other *Puranas*, explain that Rudra originally appeared as half male and half female. Upon being ordered to generate other beings, he separated his male and female natures and again divided his male being into eleven persons, some of whom were agreeable, some hideous, some fierce, and some mild. He then multiplied his female nature in the same way, of black and white complexions, being various energies or *shaktis* of Rudra.

We have to understand, however, that these descriptions of Rudra can relate to his activities in different *kalpas*, or days of Brahma, which change in actions from time to time. So if the descriptions have certain variations, it is not that they are contradicting each other. As I mentioned before, there are occasional differences in the pattern of creation from one *kalpa* to another.

The *Kurma Purana* (1.7.25-32) explains that after Shiva had manifested from the anger of Brahma, Brahma asked Shiva to create various entities. Shiva, the incarnation of anger, then mentally created sons that were similar to him, all with matted hair, three eyes, of dark blue complexion, and free from fear and death. However, Brahma was fearful of the situation and asked Shiva to create beings that were subject to death, but Shiva refused. He told Brahma that if he wanted, he could create such subjects himself.

The *Srimad-Bhagavatam* (3.12.15-20) goes on to describe how the sons of Shiva were unlimited, but when they assembled together they attempted to destroy the universe with the fiery flames from their eyes, and they even tried to attack Lord Brahma. Upon seeing this, Brahma became afraid of the situation. He then requested Rudra not to generate living beings of this nature, and to engage in penance which would bring all benediction and allow Rudra to create the universe as it was before. Thus, Rudra agreed and entered the forest to perform austere penances. In this way, Brahma prevented Shiva from creating any more beings and again began to create them himself.

CREATION OF BRAHMA'S MIND-BORN SONS

So after Brahma's episode with Rudra, he created the original sages, his mind-born sons.

Having equipped himself with austere penance, mental concentration, and absorption in adoration and devotion, along with his dispassion and control of his senses, Brahma evolved great sages as his beloved sons. To each of them Brahma gave a part of his own body, characterized by deep meditation, mental concentration, supernatural power, austerity, adoration, and renunciation.[87]

Brahma, who was empowered by the Supreme Lord, thought of creating living beings and generated ten sons for the expansion of generations. Thus, his mind-born sons named Marici, Atri, Angira, Pulastya, Pulaha, Kratu, Bhrigu, Vashishtha, Daksha, and Narada were born. In some places they are called the nine Brahmas, excluding Narada, because in many qualities they were just like Brahma. Since Shiva in the form of Rudra and his sons began to devour the universe, Brahma created new sons who were in favor of worldly activities. Narada, however, was dedicated to devotional service to the Lord, and became the spiritual master for all those who are spiritually inclined. Narada was born from the deliberation of Brahma, while Vashishtha was born from his breathing, Daksha from a thumb, Bhrigu from his touch, Kratu from his hand, Pulastya from the ears, Angira from the mouth, Atri from the eyes, Marici from the mind, and Pulaha from the navel.[88] Thus, these householder sages were created by Brahma. Assuming human form, activities of piety and religion were initiated by them.[89]

Thereafter, Brahma created religion from his breast where the Supreme Lord is found, and irreligion from his back, where horrible death takes place for the living beings. Lust and desire manifested from Brahma's heart, anger from between his eyebrows, greed from between his lips, the power of speaking from his mouth, the ocean from his penis, and low and abominable activities from his anus, the source of all sins. The great sage Kardama Muni, husband of Devahuti, was manifested from the shadow of Brahma. Thus, everything became manifested from Brahma's body or mind.[90]

MANIFESTATION OF THE VEDAS

Thereafter, once when Brahma was thinking of how to continue the creation of the worlds, the four *Vedas*, which contain all varieties of knowledge, became manifested from his four mouths. There also came knowledge of the form of worship of the fire ritual as provided in the supplementary *Vedas*.[91] Gradually, the four *Vedas*--Rig, Yajur, Sama, and Atharva--became manifest, along with other Vedic hymns, including the Gayatri *mantra*, which had not been pronounced before. He also created the medical science, military art for social order, musical art, architectural science, and so on, all from the *Vedas*. They all emanated one after another from the mouths of Brahma. Then he created the fifth *Veda*, the *Puranas* and the histories, since he could see all of the past, present and future. Also, priestly rituals, subject matter of recitation, and all spiritual activities were all established.[92]

CREATION OF THE FOUR SOCIAL ORDERS

There also came the four principles of religiosity, namely truth, austerity, mercy, and cleanliness. Education, charity, penance, and truth are said to be the four pillars of religion, and to learn this Brahma manifested the four social orders of life with different classifications according to vocation. The duties of the four social orders also became manifest.[93]

When this took place, the *brahmanas* manifested from Brahma's mouth, the *kshatriyas* came from his chest, *vaishyas* came from his thighs or legs, and *shudras* came from his feet.[94]

The sacred thread ceremony, for *brahmanas*, was also inaugurated, as were the rules to be followed after accepting the Vedic injunctions, rules for celibacy, vocations in terms of the Vedic injunctions, various professional duties for household life, and methods of maintaining a livelihood. The four divisions of retired life and the renounced order of life were also established. Thereafter, the science of logical argument, the Vedic goals of life, the moral codes of law and order, the celebrated hymns, and the *pranava omkara* [the *om mantra*] was manifested from his heart. Then the art of literary expression was generated, as was the principle Vedic hymn, the Gayatri, was manifest. The art of writing verse, along with the alphabets and vowels, and the seven notes of music were all manifest.[95]

The *Vishnu Purana* goes on to explain in relation to the four social divisions, called *varnas*, that Brahma also created the various sacrifices or rituals by which one can understand the truth and that also please the demigods. Through such sacrifices there would also be rain, by which mankind is supported. Thus, this path to happiness is followed by pious men, walking in the way of virtue. Such men will acquire the heavenly abodes and go, after death, to whatever sphere for which they aspire.[96] Later, the *Vishnu Purana* explains that the heaven of the forefathers, Pitris, is the destination of the devout *brahmanas*. The heaven of Indra is for the *kshatriyas*, warriors who do not flee battle. *Vaishyas* who are diligent in their occupations and submissive are assigned to the region of Vayu, the wind god. And pious *shudras* are elevated to the sphere of the Gandharvas, angels.[97]

The *Padma Purana* (1.3.137-138) explains the same thing but with a few more details. It states that when Lord Hari is well settled in the hearts of people, and they are very mindful of Him, then by such pure minds they can see that place in the spiritual world which is the abode of the Supreme Spirit and of pure knowledge. Later it explains that the faithful *brahmanas* attain the abode of

Satyaloka, the highest abode in the material universe of Lord Brahma. *Kshatriyas*, *vaishyas*, and *shudras* reach the heavens of Indra, Vayu, and the Gandharvas respectively. The place for the anchorites is the realm of the Seven Sages. Pious householders will reach the place of Prajapati, and the ascetics go to Brahma. Staunch yogis who are in constant meditation will reach the Brahman. However, though the heavens may come and go, those who are intent on Narayana, Lord Vishnu, will never return to the material world. But for those who condemn the Vedic path and create obstacles, they will reach the lowest levels of ignorance and hellish existence.[98]

One thing we have to put into focus is that the Supreme Creator is actually the Supreme Being, Lord Krishna, not Lord Brahma. Brahma, through his great mystic abilities, manifested what was already there in its potential. He is like a gardener in the sense that the seeds of the innumerable living beings were already there, but he merely manifested them to a physical reality. That is why Lord Krishna says in *Bhagavad-gita* (4.13), "According to the three modes of material nature and the work ascribed to them, the four divisions of human society were created by Me." Thus, such living beings and their divisions were already there before Lord Brahma brought them into being.

CREATION OF SVAYAMBHUVA AND SHATARUPA

When Brahma saw that in spite of greatly potent sages there was no sufficient increase in population, he again began to consider how the population could be increased. Just then two other forms were generated from his body. One of them was male, Svayambhuva Manu, and the other female, Shatarupa, the queen of the great Manu. Now through sexual indulgence they gradually increased the population through generations. Before this time sexual indulgence was not necessary for producing offspring since the creation and expansion of the population could be achieved through the power of the concentrated mind. That is how powerful the mental creative force once was in the people of that time. Manu and Shatarupa begot two sons, Priyavrata and Uttanapada, and three daughters, Akuti, Devahuti, and Prasuti. Manu handed over his daughter Akuti to the sage Ruci, Devahuti to Kardama, and Prasuti to Daksha. From them many generations filled the world.[99]

From Akuti and Ruci was born one son, Yajna, who was an incarnation of the Supreme, and one daughter, Dakshina, who was a partial incarnation of Lakshmi, the Lord's internal potency and eternal consort. Later, they married and twelve sons were born to them who were demigods called the Tushitas or Yama-devas. From Daksha and Prasuti came 16 [some *Puranas* say 24] daughters. From these daughters and their husbands came many more great personalities, the names of whom are given in the *Puranas*.[100]

The two great sons of Manu, Priyavrata and Uttanapada, ruled the world, which consisted of seven great islands or continents.[101] Kardama Muni and Devahuti produced nine daughters and Kapila Muni, an incarnation of the Lord. Kardama handed these daughters over to the great sages at the request of Lord Brahma. Kala went to Marici, Anasuya to Atri, Shraddha to the sage Angira, Havirbhu to Pulastya, Gati to Pulaha, Kriya to Kratu, Khyati to Bhrigu, Arundhati to Vashistha, and Shanti to Atharva.[102] It is from these descendants of Manu, collectively called the Prajapatis or progenitors, consisting of the greatly powerful sages and their qualified wives, that filled the world with many more varieties of population. More complete details about the genealogy of Svayambhuva Manu and the daughters of Daksha are provided in the Fourth Canto, First Chapter, and the Sixth Canto, Sixth Chapter of the *Srimad-Bhagavatam*.

Further descriptions of the descendants of the sages, the daughters of Daksha, and the descendants of Manu are found in the *Garuda Purana* (First Book, Chapters Five & Six), as well as the *Brahmanda Purana* (1.2.8.42-80) and the *Agni Purana* (Chapter 18). It is this description of Manu and Shatarupa that is often referred to in other traditions as the creation of the first man and woman, along with their descendants, who then populated the world.

THE ORDER OF THE CREATIVE PROCESS

Prakrita-sarga
(This is the primary creation that naturally occurs
due to the interaction of the material modes
with the time element)

1st creation:
Mahat-sarga, which produces the *mahat-tattva*.

2nd creation:
This produces the false ego, which gives rise to the material ingredients, material
knowledge, and material activities.

3rd creation:
Bhuta-sarga, the creation of matter, including the material elements and sense
perception.

4th creation:
Aindriyah-sarga, the creation sense organs, the knowledge acquiring and working
senses and sense objects.

5th creation:
Vaikarikah-sarga, creation of the mode of goodness from which the appearance
of the controlling deities, demigods, and the mind is made possible.

6th creation:
Tamasah-sarga, creation of the mode of *tamas*, the darkness of ignorance which
causes forgetfulness for the living beings.

Vaikrita-sarga
(The secondary creation
from Lord Brahma.

7th creation:
Mukhya-sarga, the creation of the immovable entities.

8th creation:
Tiryak-srotas, creation of the lower species of life--animals, birds, etc.

9th creation:
Arvak-srotas, creation of human beings.

10th creation:
Deva-sargah, or *Urdhvasrotas*, creation of the demigods and super-human entities, including eight varieties of forefathers or progenitors, asuras, Yakshas, Rakshasas, Gandharvas, Apsaras, Bhutas, ghosts, Sadhyas, Siddhas, Vidyadharas, etc.

11th creation:
The Kumara brothers, which are considered a combination of belonging to both the *Prakrita-sarga* and *Vaikrita-sarga* types of creation.

These that follow are not necessarily classified in a particular type of creation, such as *Prakrita* or *Vaikrita-sarga*, but they do take place in the creative process nonetheless.

12th creation:
The manifestation of Rudra.

13th creation:
Manifestation of the great universal sages who are the mind-born sons of Brahma.

14th creation:
The manifestation of the Vedic texts--the four *Vedas* and the main *Puranas*.

15th creation:
The creation of the four social orders or *varnas*.

16th creation:
Manifestation of Svayambhuva Manu and his numerous descendants.

CHAPTER THIRTEEN

Continued Transformations

Aside from the initial process of creation, the material cosmos goes through constant transformations. This is also explained in the *Bhagavad-gita* (9.10) by Lord Krishna, "This material nature is working under My direction, O son of Kunti, and it is producing all moving and unmoving beings. By its rule this manifestation is created and annihilated again and again."

The material manifestation undergoes these transformations due to the fact that it is founded upon the three modes of material nature. Like the original process of creation, the continued changes are caused by the agitation of these modes, which affect the many levels of ongoing creation, maintenance, and destruction.[1] Not only does the environment around us change with the seasons, but the material body in which we are situated also goes through various transformations. This, as we shall see, is for the unfoldment of the living beings in their evolutionary development. It is all part of the process by which they experience every aspect of material existence so they can learn whatever is necessary for them, while getting closer to reaching full enlightenment.

As previously explained, Lord Brahma is active during his day, which is equal to the length of time of one thousand cycles of the four *yugas*, Satya-yuga through Kali-yuga. Then he sleeps during his night, which is of the same duration. When he sleeps, there is a partial annihilation of the lower planetary systems below Brahmaloka, which get submerged in the waters of devastation. Under the influence of the mode of darkness, the powerful manifestation of the universe merges into the darkness of night. The innumerable living entities stay merged in that darkness while everything remains silent. All three levels of planetary systems are out of sight, and the sun and moon are also dark. The process of the annihilation is caused by the flames emanating from Lord Sankarshana, which produces the intense changes that cause the worlds to come to an end. Brahma then dreams about Lord Vishnu who gives him instructions about the recreation. When Brahma awakes, he reconstructs the devastated areas of the universe to start anew.[2] (The complete details of the annihilation of the universe are supplied in my previous book, *The Vedic Prophecies: A New Look into the Future*.)

The new cycle of the secondary creation then begins to manifest. It exists by the mercy of the Lord and is the amalgamation of the desires of the living entities. The activities of the living beings in the former manifestation that promoted material desires again produce various moving and nonmoving forms of life to accommodate those innumerable desires.[3] Thus, the material creation is manifested and goes on in a similar fashion as it had before, as described in the previous chapters.

As Lord Krishna explains, "At the end of the millennium every material manifestation enters into My nature, and at the beginning of another millennium, by My potency I again create. The whole cosmic order is under Me. By My will it is manifested again and again, and by My will it is annihilated at the end."[4]

Therefore, it is Madhusudana, Krishna, the Supreme Being, who is the origin and foundation of all the cycles of creation, preservation, and destruction of all cosmic manifestations. As the material energy is the result of the transformation of spiritual energy, so also the non-existence of the world is the absorption of material nature back into the spiritual energy from whence it derived. It is the Supreme Being whose energy is the elements, and who abides in all bodies as the Paramatma, the Supersoul, who not only arranges the creation and annihilation of the universes, but also the constant production, existence, and dissolution of all forms of material life, in all seasons. He who frees himself from the perpetual cycle of birth and death of the physical body, and the creations and annihilations of the universe, goes to the supreme sphere, the spiritual strata, from where he never returns again to material existence.[5]

THE MAINTENANCE OF THE UNIVERSE

Not only do the creations and annihilations of the cosmos go on continually, but the maintenance of the universe also takes constant supervision. It is explained that as long as the Supreme Being continues to glance upon nature, the material world continues to exist. Thus, the variegated flow of universal creation perpetually manifests through procreation.[6] So, we can see that time and nature have no power to act independently, but are under the supervision of the Supreme.

However, it is not only the material nature that is maintained, everyone in it is also given the ability to act and function through the power of the Supreme in His form as the Supersoul. He creates the entire variegated universe and then enters into it as the Supersoul. Through this means He provides the life force and consciousness of everyone, and, thus, maintains the creation.[7] As Sri Krishna further explains, "As the mighty wind, blowing everywhere, always rests in ethereal space, know that in the same manner all beings rest in Me."[8] As the Supersoul, He also enters into each planet, and by His energy they maintain their orbits.[9] Thus, the Lord's energy enters each planet, every living being, and even each atom, by which everything is appropriately manifested and maintained. Without this, everything would revert back to chaos and deterioration.

Another way that the Lord maintains the universe is by personally appearing within it, or by manifesting His plenary expansions. The scriptures proclaim that Lord Krishna descends to take away the burden of the earth. However, it is Krishna's expansion as Lord Vishnu who primarily engages in maintaining this universe. It is Lord Vishnu who makes the adjustments for the proper administration of the cosmic creation. When Lord Krishna personally appears, His primary mission is to simply display His transcendental pastimes and attract the conditioned souls for going back to the spiritual domain. However, since Lord Krishna is the source of all incarnations of the Supreme, all other incarnations and expansions meet together within Him when He descends. In this way, all other *lila* or pastime incarnations, the *yuga-avataras*, the *manvantara* incarnations, and as many other incarnations as there are, all descend in the body of Sri Krishna when He appears. Thus, He is the complete Supreme Personality and can do whatever He likes to exhibit His power and maintain the universe when He descends.[10]

The Supreme Being also sets up the universal demigods to continue overseeing the maintenance of the universe. For example, it is explained that Indra, after receiving benediction from the Supreme Lord, maintains the living beings by pouring sufficient rains all over the planets. Furthermore, in every *yuga*, the Supreme Lord assumes the form of Siddhas, such as Sanaka-kumara, to preach transcendental knowledge. He assumes the form of great saintly persons such as Yajnavalkya to teach the way of *karma*. He assumes the form of great souls, such as Dattatreya, to teach the system of mystic yoga. In the form of Prajapati Marici, the Supreme creates progeny; becoming the king, He kills rogues and thieves; and in the form of time, He annihilates everything. All of the different qualities of material existence are aspects of the Supreme Absolute Truth.[11]

So because of the benediction and power given by the Supreme to the demigods, they can provide the living beings with all necessities. However, Lord Krishna explains in the *Bhagavad-gita* (3.14-15) that all living entities subsist on food grains, which are produced from rains, which is manifest through the performance of spiritual activities prescribed in the spiritual writings of the Vedic scripture and the teachings of the Lord and great sages. Consequently, the all-pervading Transcendence is eternally situated in acts of sacrifice.

This is all a part of the process of maintaining the world. As mankind engages in acts of sacrifice, which simply means the worship of the Supreme, He and the demigods are automatically satisfied to supply everyone with all necessities of life. In this way, there can be proper cooperation between man, nature, and God so that everyone can be peaceful and content with the facilities for living in this world.

CHAPTER FOURTEEN

The Incarnations of God

As mentioned in the previous chapter, the Supreme Being also descends in various forms and incarnations. Each incarnation has a specific mission, but primarily they help maintain the world and guide the living beings in life, and to attract them back to the spiritual domain.

To dispel the power of the illusory energy, the Lord maintains all of the planets in the universe and assumes roles or incarnations to perform pastimes to reclaim those in the mode of goodness.[1] In this way, throughout the many millions of universes in which the Supreme Being appears, the purpose is to bring society to its senses, at least those who are in the higher grades of consciousness and are receptive to understanding their spiritual relation with Him. He also sends His pure representative and instructions in the authorized scripture to guide people. In either case, the purpose is the same, to point the suffering living beings back toward the spiritual world. Only there can the living beings find the true happiness for which they are hankering. That kind of happiness is not found in any part of the material universe.

The source of the various incarnations within this universe is the Lord of the universe, namely Garbhodakashayi Vishnu.[2] The form of the Lord that descends to the material world to create is called an *avatara*. All expansions of Lord Krishna are residents of the spiritual world who are also called *avataras* when they descend into the material world.[3]

There are six kinds of incarnations of Krishna, which include those of Vishnu (*purusha-avataras*), pastime incarnations (*lila-avataras*), incarnations that control the modes of nature (*guna-avataras*), incarnations of Manu (*manvantara-avataras*), incarnations in different millenniums (*yuga-avataras*), and the empowered individuals (*shatyavesha-avataras*).[4] However, Lord Krishna Himself descends to this world once in a day of Brahma to manifest His transcendental pastimes.[5] All other incarnations are potentially situated in the body of the primeval Lord Krishna. Thus, according to one's opinion, one may address Him as any one of the incarnations.[6] This is because all of the plenary expansions of the Supreme exist within the body of the original person. Thus, He can expand Himself as one flame from a candle lights another, but all such flames come from the original. Some say that Krishna is directly Nara-Narayana. Others say that He is Vamana, or the incarnation of Ksirodakashayi Vishnu, the Supersoul. None of these statements is impossible. Everything is possible in Krishna, for He is the primeval Lord.[7]

From Krishna comes innumerable incarnations, the most prominent of which are the *lila-avatars*, such as Matsya, Kurma, Varaha, Rama, etc. I will describe most of these later. There are also the qualitative incarnations who are in charge of the modes of material nature, such as Brahma, Vishnu, and Shiva, along with the Manus and the *yuga-avatars.*[8]

The time and reason for these incarnations is that whenever and wherever there is a decline of religion and a rise in irreligion, at that time Lord Krishna manifests Himself. In this way, in order to protect the *sadhus* (the pious), destroy the envious, and reestablish the principles of religion, He advents Himself millennium after millennium.[9]

Let us remember that Lord Maha-Vishnu is resting in His *yoga-nidra* trance, in which He manifests the material energy. He is also the seed of the other incarnations of the Supreme who appear in the material world. So you could say that the Lord is like a sleeping person who creates a separate world in His imagination and then enters His own dream and sees Himself within it.[10]

THE LORD INCARNATES IN EACH UNIVERSE

Even though there are so many incarnations of the Supreme Being and plenary expansions of Him who appear in this world, we have to be aware of how to distinguish who is and who is not an incarnation. As in other ages, an incarnation is accepted according to the directions in the scriptures.[11] In all descriptions of an incarnation the scripture will provide the name of the father and the name of the place of birth in which the incarnation will appear.[12] Such descriptions will also elaborate on His bodily symptoms and activities. Therefore, we must be able to recognize the characteristics of an incarnation of God by the descriptions and must not be whimsical about accepting someone as an incarnation, or even a representative of the Supreme.[13] An actual incarnation of God never proclaims that He is God or an incarnation. The great Vedic texts have already recorded the characteristics of all the *avataras.*[14]

Whenever the Lord Sri Krishna desires to manifest His incarnation on earth, He first sends His respectable predecessors. These take the form of the incarnations of His father, mother, and spiritual master. They appear first in order to prepare the way for the Supreme Being's appearance.[15] These people, however, are the Lord's great devotees who serve Him by participating in His pastimes. Thus, though the Lord personally has nothing to do with this material existence,

He comes to earth and imitates material life just to expand the varieties of ecstatic enjoyment for His devotees.[16] In this way, Krishna, the original Soul of all living beings, has appeared as an ordinary human being for the benefit of the whole universe and out of His causeless mercy. This He has done by the strength of His own spiritual potency.[17] Not only do the devotees enjoy Krishna's pastimes, but He also enjoys His transcendental activities in various forms in this material world, which cleanse away all the unhappiness of those who joyfully chant His glories.[18]

In this way, Lord Krishna appears in each universe. When His activities are finished in one universe, He begins His pastimes in another. Thus, His eternal pastimes go on like this in the universes as long as the material manifestation continues. Furthermore, His eternally liberated devotees also follow Him from one universe to another to accompany Him in His blissful pastimes.[19]

The Supreme is also joined by those devotees who are nearly perfect in their spiritual consciousness. By joining the Lord's pastimes in another universe, and by their personal association with the Lord and His pure devotees, they can complete the necessary qualifications for entering directly into the spiritual atmosphere. This is how the Supreme Being displays the eternal pastimes of the spiritual domain within the material creation and attracts the materially conditioned souls.

In this way, the consecutive pastimes of Krishna are manifest in one of the innumerable universes moment after moment. There is no possibility of counting the universes, but in any case some pastime of the Lord is being manifest at every moment in one universe or another.[20]

THE MAIN INCARNATIONS OF THE SUPREME BEING

There are 22 main *lila-avataras* of the Supreme Being who appear throughout the ages. They all have specific forms or bodily features, and particular purposes for appearing. These are listed in the varius Vedic texts, especially the *Puranas*, and their many pastimes are explained in detail therein.

The first listed of these incarnations are the four sons of Brahma, the Kumaras. They took a vow of celibacy and underwent severe austerities for realization of the Absolute Truth. They are considered empowered incarnations, or *shaktyavesha-avataras*, whose mission was to teach the process of spiritual development.[21] Knowledge of spiritual truth had disappeared from the previous universal devastation and they helped re-establish it.[22]

Lord Varaha was the second incarnation who appeared in the form of a huge boar. He lifted the earth out of the nether regions of the filthy waters of the universe, which was a suitable activity for a boar. He did this to counter the nefarious activities of the demons who had put the earth planet into jeopardy.[23]

The third incarnation was the empowered *avatara* known as the sage among the demigods, Devarshi Narada Muni. He collected expositions of the *Vedas* which dealt with the process of devotional service to Lord Krishna, and authored the great classic *Narada-pancaratna*. He also traveled throughout the universe singing His praises and giving instruction on *bhakti-yoga* and how to attain real happiness. Thus, he has many disciples all over the creation.[24] Narada Muni had once been taught the science of loving service to the Supreme during the Lord's Hamsavatara incarnation, the swan-like form of the Supreme, who had been very much pleased by Narada.[25]

In the fourth incarnation, the Lord became the twin sons known as Nara and Narayana. They were born of Murti, the wife of King Dharma. They underwent severe austerities in the area of Badarikashrama in the Himalayas to demonstrate the process of controlling the senses for spiritual advancement.[26] The celestial beauties who were the companions of Cupid went to distract Narayana from His vows, but were unsuccessful when they could see many other beautiful women like them emanating from the Supreme Being. Everything comes from the Supreme, who remains unattached to all His manifestations.[27]

The fifth incarnation was Lord Kapila, the foremost among perfected beings. He explained for the first time the system of the Sankhya philosophy and the way of understanding the Truth by the analysis of material elements.[28] He was the son of the sage Kardama Muni and his wife Devahuti. He also gave great expositions to his mother on the science of devotional service to the Supreme Lord. By that means she became cleansed of all material tendencies and achieved liberation.[29] This information is provided in detail in the *Srimad-Bhagavatam*.

The sixth incarnation was born as Dattatreya, the son of the sage Atri and his wife Anasuya, both of whom had prayed for an incarnation to be their son. He had spoken on the subject of transcendence to Alarka, Prahlada, Yadu, Haihaya, and others.[30]

The seventh incarnation was Yajna, the son of Ruci and his wife Akuti. During the time of Svayambhuva Manu there was no living entity qualified to take the post of Indra, the King of Heaven, Indraloka. So Yajna took up the post of Indra and was assisted by His own sons, such as Yama, the lord of death, and other demigods to rule the administration over universal affairs.[31]

King Rishabha was the eighth incarnation, who appeared as the son of King Nabhi and his wife Merudevi. Again He demonstrated the path of spiritual perfection by performing yoga and instructing His sons in the process of *tapasya*, austerities for spiritual development. This path sanctifies one's existence and leads to eternal spiritual happiness. This is followed by those who have fully controlled their senses and are honored by all orders of life.[32]

The Lord also appeared as the Hayagriva incarnation in a golden color during a sacrifice performed by Brahma. When He breathed, all of the sweet sounds of the *Vedas* came out of His nostrils.[33]

The ninth incarnation was Prithu, who accepted the body of a king. He had been prayed for by the *brahmana* priests to counteract the problems that had been brought on by impious activities of the previous king, Vena. Prithu made various arrangements to cultivate the land to yield various forms of produce.[34] Although King Vena was bound for hell due to the reactions of his misdeeds and the curse of the *brahmanas*, he was delivered by Prithu.[35]

After the time of the Chakshusha Manu there was a complete inundation over the whole world by water. Manu had been warned about this flood and built a ship in which he and his family survived. The Lord accepted the form of a huge fish to protect Vaivashvata Manu and guide the ship to safety on a huge mountain peak. This was the Matsya *avatara*. After the period of each Manu there is a devastation by water over the earth. The Lord then appears to show special favor to His devotees and protect them from the devastation and allow society to start anew. In this way, He protects all of the living entities as well as the *Vedas* from destruction.[36] After the last flood, Manu and his family and the surviving living creatures again repopulated the earth. Local people of Uttarakhand in Northern India identify the Nanda Devi mountain as the one in the story of the flood.

The eleventh incarnation of the Supreme was in the form of a huge tortoise, Kurma, whose main mission was to act as a pivot for the Mandara Hill, which was being used as a churning rod between the demons and demigods. The scheme was that the demons and demigods wanted to produce a nectar from the ocean by this churning action which would make them immortal. Each side wanted to be the first to get it, and the back of Lord Kurma was the resting place for the hill.[37] As the mountain moved back and forth on the back of Matsya while He was partially asleep, He felt it as an itching sensation.[38]

In the twelfth incarnation the Lord appeared as Dhanvantari who produced the nectar that came from the churning action. He is considered the lord of good health. It is He who inaugurated the medical science in the universe.[39] The Lord accepted the thirteenth incarnation by becoming Rohini, the most beautiful woman who allured the demons away from the pot of nectar and gave it to the demigods. Thus, the Lord prevented the havoc that would have taken place if the demons had gotten the nectar and became immortal.[40]

In the fourteenth incarnation the Lord appeared as Narashimhadeva, the half-man half-lion form that displayed the anger and power of the Supreme Being when one of His devotees was in peril. The Lord placed the demon Hiranyakashipu on His lap and with His long fingernails tore apart the body of the atheist who had threatened the life of his son, Prahlada, who was a staunch devotee of the Lord.[41] This is one of the most popular stories described in the *Puranas*.

In the fifteenth incarnation, the Lord as Vamana assumed the form of a *dwarf-brahmana*. He appeared as the youngest son of His mother, Aditi. He visited the sacrificial arena of Bali Maharaja on the pretense of asking for a measly three steps of land. Bali quickly agreed, thinking that this dwarf could not take up much land. However, when Vamana took two steps, His body became so gigantic that it covered the whole universe. There was no where else to place His third step, so

Bali, understanding that this was the Supreme Being, offered his own head. Thus, Vamana humbled Bali, who then became qualified to attain his own planet.[42]

In the sixteenth incarnation, the Lord accepted the mighty form of Parashurama and annihilated the wicked class of warrior kings twenty-one times in order to free the earth of the burden of these nefarious rulers. In this way, He could establish a noble administration.[43]

The seventeenth incarnation was Srila Vyasadeva, who appeared as the son of Parashara Muni and his wife Satyavati. His mission was to divide the one *Veda* into various branches and sub-branches so the people who are less intelligent can more easily understand them.[44] He then composed the more important Vedic texts, culminating in his own commentary of the Vedic writing in the form of the *Srimad-Bhagavata*. In this way, the one *Veda* became the four main *samhitas*, namely the *Rig*, *Yajur*, *Sama*, and *Atharva Vedas*. Then came the *Brahmana* texts, the *Vedanta Sutras*, the *Mahabharata*, and then the *Puranas*, of which Vyasadeva considered the *Bhagavat Purana* the most important and complete.

It is also explained that the *Bhagavat Purana* is the literary incarnation of God, which is meant for the ultimate good of all people, and is all-blissful and all-perfect. Sri Vyasadeva offered it to his son after extracting the cream of all Vedic literature. This *Bhagavat Purana* is as brilliant as the sun, and has arisen just after the departure of Lord Krishna to His own abode. Persons who have lost their vision due to the dense darkness of this age of Kali can get light from this *Purana*.[45]

To explain further about Srila Vyasadeva, Jiva Gosvami quotes the *Vishnu Purana* (3.4.2-5) in his *Tattva-sandarbha* (16.2) that a different empowered *jiva* soul takes the position of Vyasadeva in each incarnation as a *shaktyavesha-avatara*. However, in this particular *divya-yuga*, or cycle of the four ages, Lord Narayana Himself appears as Srila Krishna-Dvaipayana Vyasa to divide the Vedic literature into various branches, and is not simply an empowered living entity.

In the eighteenth incarnation, the Lord appeared as King Rama. In order to please the demigods and mankind, He displayed His superhuman powers as the ideal king and killed the demon King Ravana.[46] This is one of the most popular stories in all of India that make up the great Vedic epic known as the *Ramayana*. Lord Rama appeared in the family of Maharaja Ikshvaku as the son of Maharaja Dasaratha, with His internal potency and wife, Sita. Under the order of Dasaratha, Lord Rama had gone to the forest to live with Sita and His brother Laxmana. While in the forest, Sita was kidnaped by the demon Ravana, which made way for the telling of the *Ramayana*. Being aggrieved, Rama went to search for Sita. With red-hot eyes, He looked all over India and on to the city of Ravana, which was on present day Sri Lanka. All of the aquatics in the ocean were being burnt by the heat in His angry eyes, so the ocean gave way to Him. During the course of battle, proud Ravana was killed by the arrow from Lord Rama, who was then reunited with Sita.[47]

In the nineteenth and twentieth incarnations, the Lord advented Himself as

Lord Krishna and His brother Lord Balarama in the Yadu dynasty near the end of Dvapara-yuga. He displayed wonderful pastimes to invoke the attraction of the people and, again, to relieve the burden of the world of numerous demons and atheists.[48] Lord Krishna is directly the original Personality of Godhead, and Balarama is the first plenary expansion of the Lord. From Balarama comes all the other expansions of the Divine.

The next incarnation of the Lord appeared in the beginning of Kali-yuga as Lord Buddha, the son of Anjana, for the purpose of deluding the envious who had misused the Vedic path, and to preach a simple system of nonviolence.[49] At the time people in general were falling away from the proper execution of the Vedic system and had misused the Vedic recommendation of sacrifice and began offering and consuming animals. Buddha denounced all such actions and taught people simply to follow him and his teachings. Thus, he fooled the faithless people who then believed in Lord Buddha. [I have explained more about the real purpose of Buddha and his philosophy in my book, *The Universal Path to Enlightenment*.]

The twenty-second and final incarnation of the Supreme will appear at the end of Kali-yuga, at the conjunction of the next *yuga*. He will take His birth as the Kalki incarnation, the son of Yasha, when the rulers of earth will have degenerated into common thieves and plunderers.[50] At the time there will be no topics on the subject of God, nor any knowledge of religion. Then, rather than trying to teach or show the way of progress when people will be too retarded and slow minded to understand philosophy, He will simply slaughter the foolish rogues who wander the earth. This will take place about 427,000 years from now. [Details about Lord Kalki and His activities are provided in my previous book, *The Vedic Prophecies: A New Look into the Future*.]

As is summarized in the *Srimad-Bhagavatam* (1.3.28), all of these incarnations are either plenary portions or portions of the plenary portions of the Lord. However, as explained, *krishnas tu bhagavan svayam*, Lord Sri Krishna is the original Supreme Personality of Godhead.

Although learned men discuss the birth and activities of the Supreme unborn, Lord of the heart, the foolish who have a poor fund of knowledge cannot understand the transcendental nature of the forms, names, and activities of the Supreme Being, who is playing like an actor in a drama.[51] However, only those who render favorable service to Lord Krishna can know the creator of the universe in His full glory, power, and transcendence.[52]

THE MANU INCARNATIONS

The Manus appear for certain durations during a day of Brahma. Brahma's day is calculated as 4,300,000 years (the time of one cycle of the four *yugas*) times 1,000. Within one day of Brahma there are 14 Manus. The list of the 14 Manus in this universe are as follows: Yajna is Svayambhuva Manu, Vibhu is Svarocisha

Manu, Satyasena is Uttama Manu, Hari is Tamasa Manu, Vaikuntha is Raivata Manu, Ajita is Ckakshusha Manu, Vamana is Vaivasvata Manu (the Manu of the present age), Sarvabhauma is Savarni Manu, Rishabha is Daksha-savarni Manu, Vishvaksena is Brahma-savarni Manu, Dharmasetu is Dharma-savarni Manu, Sudhama is Rudra-savarni Manu, Yogesvara is Deva-savarni Manu, and Brihadbhanu is Indra-savarni Manu. These fourteen Manus cover the 4,320,000,000 solar years of one day of Brahma.[53]

To understand more completely how long these Manus reign we can consider the following information. For example, there are four ages, namely Satya-yuga, Treta-yuga, Dvapara-yuga, and Kali-yuga, which comprise a *divya-yuga*, one set of the four *yugas*. Let's remember that Satya-yuga lasts 1,728,000 years, Treta-yuga 1,296,000 years, Dvapara-yuga 864,000 years, and Kali-yuga 432,000 years. That is a total of 4,320,000 years. A day of Brahma, called a *kalpa*, lasts for 1,000 of these cycles, and is thus 4,320,000,000 solar years. There are 14 Manus in each day of Brahma. Each Manu is said to exist for one *manvantara*, which is a period of time lasting 71 *divya-yugas*. Therefore, each Manu exists for roughly 306,720,000 years. Additionally, Brahma lives for 100 years, composed of 365 of such days in a year.[54]

From further analysis we can also discover the age of the earth from these Vedic calculations. The present Manu is the seventh in line, called Vaivasvata Manu, the son of Vivasvan. Twenty-seven *divya-yugas*, or cycles of the four *yugas*, of his age have now passed. So 27 *divya-yugas* means 116,640,000 years. It is scheduled that at the end of the Dvapara-yuga of the twenty-eighth *divya-yuga* of the seventh Manu, Lord Krishna appears on earth with the full paraphernalia of His eternal spiritual abode, named Vrajadhama or Goloka Vrindavana. Brahma's day consists of 4,320,000,000 years. Six of these Manus appear and disappear before Lord Krishna takes birth. This means that 1,975,320,000 years of the day of Brahma have gone by before the appearance of Lord Krishna.[55] Therefore, this is also the age of the earth in this particular day of Brahma by these Vedic calculations. Science is sometimes surprised that such lengths of time were part of the ancient Vedic conception of the universe.

THE YUGAVATARAS

Getting back to the various incarnations of the Supreme, we now come to the *yugavataras*. The *yugavataras* are divided by the millenniums in which they appear. They appear in a particular color according to the *yuga*. In Satya-yuga the color is white, in Treta-yuga the color is red, in Dvapara-yuga it is black, and in Kali-yuga the color is yellow or golden. For an example, in Dvapara-yuga Lord Krishna was a blackish color while in Kali-yuga Lord Chaitanya had a golden complexion.[56]

In Satya-yuga the people were generally quite advanced in spiritual knowledge and could meditate upon Krishna very easily. During the time in the white incarnation, the Lord taught religion and meditation, and in this way showed His mercy to the people of that era. In the Lord's reddish incarnation during the Treta-yuga, He taught the process of performing great rituals and religious sacrifices. In Dvapara-yuga, the Lord appeared in His blackish form as Krishna and induced people to worship Him directly. Then in Kali-yuga the Lord appears in a golden color as His own devotee, showing others the spiritual process for this age. Accompanied by His personal associates, He introduces the process of *hari-nama-sankirtan*, or the congregational singing and chanting of the Lord's holy names, specifically in the form of the Hare Krishna *mantra*. He personally chants and dances in ecstatic love of God. Through this process He delivers this love of God to all. Whatever spiritual results are attained through the other processes in the previous three *yugas* can easily be achieved in Kali-yuga by the chanting of the holy names of Krishna. It is the easiest process for becoming freed from material existence and reaching the transcendental kingdom.[57]

THE SHAKTYAVESHA-AVATARAS

The last kind of *avataras* are what is called the *shaktyavesha-avataras*. These are the living beings who are empowered by the Supreme to act in certain ways or accomplish a particular mission. Such *avataras* include the four Kumaras, Narada Muni, Lord Parashuram, and Lord Brahma. Lord Seshanaga in the spiritual Vaikuntha worlds and His expansion as Lord Ananta in the material world are also empowered incarnations. The power of knowledge was given to the Kumaras. The power of devotion to the Lord was given to Narada. Brahma was, of course, empowered with the ability to create. Parashuram was given the power to kill the many rogues and thieves who were on the planet at His time. Whenever the Lord is present in someone by a portion of His various potencies, that living entity is considered a *shaktyavesha-avatara*--a living being invested with special power.[58]

Another example of a *shaktyavesha-avatara*, as described by Bhaktisiddhanta Sarasvati Gosvami, one of the spiritual masters in the Brahma-Madhava-Gaudiya disciplic succession, is Jesus Christ. He said Jesus Christ was such an empowered person to preach the glories of God.

It is through these many incarnations that the Lord maintains the universe and provides guidance to the living beings within it. To understand this knowledge is an important part in perceiving the plan behind the universe and our purpose in it, and it provides great benefits for all who hear it. As it is explained in the *Srimad-Bhagavatam* (8.23.30), "If one hears about the uncommon activities of the Supreme Personality of Godhead in His various incarnations, he is certainly elevated to the higher planetary systems or even brought directly back to Godhead, the spiritual domain."

CHAPTER FIFTEEN

Clearing Confusion About the Creation

It is no surprise that when it comes to the creation of the world, there are so many theories to consider. Some theories come from the many cultures and traditions from around the world, while others come from the hypothesis of scientists. This is because we want to find out the source and cause of the creation, but have yet to agree on how it came to be. Some philosophers feel that the seven elements, such as earth, water, fire, air, either, mind, intelligence, and false ego, as well as the spirit soul and Supreme Soul, are the basis of the material and spiritual energies. In this way, everything else, such as the body, senses, life air, and all material phenomena, are but products of these seven elements. Others feel that there are five material elements which come from the Supreme Being who creates the universe and then personally enters within it. Others consider that from the Self comes the three main elements, namely fire, water, and earth, which produce the cosmic manifestation. Still other philosophers make additional perspectives on the number of elements and identify the soul with the mind. This shows how great philosophers throughout the ages have analyzed the material elements and the cause of creation in many different ways.[1]

So the questions that we find today about the cause of the creation are not new. Did the material manifestation come from a Supreme Creator? Did it come from a Big Bang? Or did it come from a miracle of nature and just naturally evolve? Or was it always here? Many people have their own opinions.

However, Lord Krishna explains that whenever philosophers argue that one does not analyze or perceive this topic in the same way as another, it is simply the insurmountable energies that are motivating their disagreements. By the interactions of the Lord's energies in the form of the modes of material nature, different opinions arise. Therefore, while one is influenced by the interactions of these modes, he is affected the same way as a person who is standing in thick smoke from a fire. As long as he is affected by the heavy smoke, he cannot clearly see the cause or source of the fire, and, thus, various opinions on it will arise. That is why it is explained in *Srimad-Bhagavatam* (11.22.5-6), "Only for those who have fixed their intelligence on Me [Krishna] and have controlled their senses, differences of perception disappear, and thus the cause for argument is removed."

As we have related previously in this volume, the modes of material nature are always at competition with each other to produce various effects and by-products. Even in one's intellect, the modes are active, especially in one who has not been able to control the mind or senses. In such a person, he is controlled by his perceptions and what he distinguishes through his senses. The senses are already faulty in many ways. So the conclusions at which one arrives through such perceptions are also likely to be subject to these kinds of faults and misjudgments.

For example, if we look at the sun from this planet with our ordinary eyes, we may conclude that it looks like its size is equal to that of a silver half-dollar. We may even think we can prove that idea by holding a silver dollar in our hand at arm's length and conclude, "Yep, it's the same size." But actually that is not reality.

In the same way, we may discuss how it is that we get hungry and what we should do about it. However, once we have eaten a nice meal, there is no longer any argument about how we can satisfy our hunger. Being satisfied in such a way is a universal experience. No one argues about it any further. Similarly, when one attains the Absolute Truth beyond the ever-changing modes of material nature, the answers are automatically revealed. This is the difference between those philosophers or scientists who try to acquire knowledge through their imperfect sense perception, and those who try to understand things through the process of acquiring knowledge from the Absolute Truth.

Those people who do understand the universe from beyond the simple perceptions of their senses and the interpretation by the mind recognize that everything, whether stationary or moving, is but a manifestation of the Supreme Being. This creation is but a display of His energy. Thus, there is no reality apart from the Lord. It is explained that Krishna is the source of even the subtle and unmanifested form of material energy. So what in this world is separate from Him?[2]

In this way, we can understand that the material universe is but a testimony to the unlimited power and glory of the Supreme Lord. Even while engaging one's senses in contact with the material elements, one who sees this whole world as the energy of the Supreme is indeed the greatest among seers.[3] Similarly, seeing a world separate from Krishna is an illusion. A person being freed from such illusion opens the gateway to a state of complete fearlessness, for he knows that the whole universe is founded on the Supreme Personality, of whom we are an eternal part.[4]

PART THREE

OUR PURPOSE IN THE UNIVERSE AND HOW TO GET OUT

CHAPTER SIXTEEN

How and Where the Spirit Souls are Manifested

In understanding the creation and purpose of the universe, it would also be beneficial to understand how the living beings, the innumerable *jivas*, spirit souls, are manifested and why. "Why are we here and from where have we come?" is a question that at some point many people ask. Some people may think this question cannot be answered. Others may feel that it does not matter because we are still often overwhelmed with the day to day problems to which we must attend. Nonetheless, if we are to increase our understanding of why we are here and what to do now that we find ourselves within this cosmic manifestation, then it would also be to our advantage to know how we have come into being in the first place.

So, the following is my construction of the explanations and evidence as I have been able to find and piece them together in order to provide a preliminary clarification of this subject. This, of course, is a weighty topic, and some people may feel that there are differences of opinion on the matter. However, the accurate evidence as I have found it can speak for itself, and I am sure that this will nonetheless provide the majority of readers with deeper insights into the subject and new information that they may not have had before. Furthermore, the fact of the matter is that no where else but in the Vedic context is any such explanation for the origin of the souls found. Therefore, I stand behind the fact that this chapter will open the eyes and further the understanding of anyone who has ever wondered from where we originate. It will also help in the realization that everything is but a manifestation of the Supreme Being.

THE ORIGINS OF THE JIVAS

To begin with, it is explained in the *Brihadaranyaka Upanishad* (2.2.20) that, "As tiny sparks fly from a fire, so all the individual souls have come from the

Supreme." Thus, the individual souls come from the Supreme Being as sparks come from a fire, or as rays of light come from the sun. However, as the rays of light are both different and the same as their source, so the individual souls are different in power and size, yet the same in quality with the Supreme.

In this line of thought, learned scholars of the Vedic spiritual topics, such as the Gosvamis of Vrindavana, have analyzed that the Supreme Personality has sixty-four principle attributes. Sri Krishna is the possessor of all these attributes, while His incarnations and the *avataras* possess up to 93 percent of these spiritual characteristics. Lord Shiva possesses up to 84 percent of these transcendental qualities. The *jiva* souls possess only up to the limit of 78 percent of these spiritual attributes, in minute degrees, varying in terms to the level of piety in which the living being exists.[1] This is how *jiva* souls are similar in quality to the Lord but different in quantity and power.

One of the big differences is that the Lord is the controller of all energies, including the illusory potency, *maya*, while the individual souls can come under the influence of this illusory energy.[2]

We can also explain it this way: The Supreme Being, Sri Krishna, is like the blazing fire or sun. The *chit-shakti*, or the thinking potency, or power of complete knowledge, is present in the center of that sun. A great expanse is illuminated by the sunlight. The rays of this light, or the effulgence of the Supreme, are manifested by the *chit-shakti*. The rays that come from that effulgence are the particles of His internal potency, the *svarupa-shakti*. Those atomic particles that make up the rays of His potency are the individual spirit souls. It is the internal or spiritual potency, the *svarupa-shakti*, that is the core or cause of this blazing fire of the Supreme Being. The individual souls or particles of light that are manifested from that fire, or in the rays of the effulgence, are manifested by the Lord's potency known as the *jiva-shakti*. This is how the Lord's spiritual potencies work together to manifest the *jiva-shakti* sunlight. This sunlight, or illumination, shines on the borderline, or *tata*, in between the spiritual and material worlds. In this way, the spirit souls are generated in the region between the spiritual and material energies, known as the *tatastha-shakti*, which will be explained further a little later in the chapter.[3]

So herein we can also understand that the *jivas* are not created like something we produce in the material world. They are manifested from the eternal Lord and co-exist in the same way as the sunshine co-exists with the sun. However, the sunshine is dependent on the sun the same as the individual souls are dependent on the Supreme Soul. Thus, as we do not say the sun creates the rays of the sun because there is no beginning to the process, the *jiva* souls are also said to be eternal as is the Supreme Being. We are emanated from the Lord, and just as the Lord is eternal, so are His emanations, the *jiva* souls. So, the spirit souls are originally from beyond time and, thus, eternal.

Not only are the living beings eternal, but so is the material nature. This means that they both existed before the material creation. Both the material energy and the living beings within it are of the superior energy of the Lord and existed within the Supreme Being in His form of Maha-Vishnu. From Maha-Vishnu came both the material energy and the living entities to form the cosmic creation.[4]

This is also confirmed in the *Aitareya Upanishad* (1.1.1) which describes things in this way: Before the creation of the universe, verily the Brahman (the Supreme Personality of Godhead in the form of Lord Vishnu) along with His own potency was existent and nothing else remained separately. Thereby it is to be known that His *tatastha-shakti* (the potency that encompasses the individual *jiva* souls), and *maya*, His external potency, were not separately existing but they were within Him.

It is further explained that Maha-Vishnu, who appears in the Karana Ocean and is an incarnation of Lord Sankarshana, becomes the resting place of the *jiva-shakti*.[5] "There is one marginal potency, known as the *jiva*. Maha-Sankarshana is the shelter of all *jivas*."[6] It is this Sankarshana who is the original source of all living entities because they are expansions of His marginal potency. Some become conditioned by the material energy while others are under the protection of the spiritual nature.[7]

It is further related that Sankarshana, Maha-Vishnu, is Vasudeva's [Krishna's] personal expansion for pastimes. Not only is Sankarshana the reservoir and original source of all living entities, but when the cosmic creation is annihilated, the indestructible living entities return to His body and rest until the next creation.[8]

To continue this line of thought, it is explained that when Maha-Vishnu glances at *maya* in the process of creation, He sends numberless atomic souls into the material energy. However, now that they are on the side of *maya*, the *jivas* become affected and entrapped by the illusory attractions of the material energy. It is because they are atomic in size and appear from the *tatastha-shakti* region, the border between the material and spiritual energies, that they must glance on either the spiritual or material energies. It is explained that since they have not engaged in the service of the Lord before, or have already become materially conditioned souls, they are swayed by the influence of *maya* and desire to enjoy the temporary pleasures that *maya* has to offer. Once these same souls turn toward spiritual life and the service of the Lord, they can attain their original transcendental nature and enter the spiritual world.[9]

Regarding how Maha-Vishnu fills the universe with conditioned souls, the great sage Markandeya explains in the *Vishnudharmottara Purana* (1.18.12-14) that even if someone or even thousands of people become liberated from the material worlds, as when those who have achieved Brahmaloka are liberated with Brahma, the inconceivable Supreme Lord manifests additional living beings [from the unlimited stock of unmanifested or sleeping souls] in the next *maha kalpa* and thus keeps the material worlds full.

This is similar to the statement of Sri Haridasa Thakura to Sri Chaitanya Mahaprabhu, in the *Chaitanya-caritamrita* (*Antya-lila*, 3.78-79), that even if the

Lord sends to the spiritual world all the developed living entities in different species, still He will awaken the living beings who are not yet developed and engage them in activities. Thus, the universe will again become filled as before.

* * *

In explaining the *tatastha-shakti*, Srila Bhaktisiddhanta writes in his book, *Sri Caitanya's Teachings* (Part Two, Chapter One, p. 365-6, 391-2, Third edition), that all human souls are emanations from the Lord's *tatastha-shakti*, which is the region found between the eternal (spiritual) and temporal (material) worlds. It is by this potency that He manifests human souls. . . The *tatastha* has the power to associate with both the material or eternal spiritual planes of existence. Souls coming from this region have free will, which they can use properly or improperly. In the *tatastha* region, souls do not show any activity, but are in an indolent stage until they choose which direction they wish to go. However, with this independence, the *jiva* may choose to engage in one of two fields of activity. When he feels like enjoying, or that he is the predominating Lord of the energy he surveys, the *jiva* soul is in a fallen condition and enters the field of *maya*. When the soul shows the aptitude for serving the Supreme, he is freed from the illusory influence of *maya* and can engage in the eternal service of the Supreme Being.

This is further confirmed by His Divine Grace A. C. Bhaktivedanta Swami in his purport to *Srimad-Bhagavatam* (3.7.9) in which he states: "According to *Vishnu Purana*, *Bhagavad-gita*, and all other Vedic literatures, the living entities are generated from the *tatastha* energy of the Lord, and thus they are always the energy of the Lord. . ."

So the *tatastha* region is in between the spiritual and material worlds, and is where the living beings are manifested. The *Brihadaranyaka Upanishad* (4.3.9 & 18) describes it like so: "A person has two places: the spiritual world and the place where the spiritual world meets another world. There is also a third place, a place of dreams [the material domain]. Standing between them, the soul sees on one side the spiritual world and on the other the place of dreaming. . . As a large fish in a river may go to one shore or the other, so a person may go to one world or another. He may go to a world where he is awake, or may go to a world made of dreams."

The *tatastha* region is further explained by Srila Bhaktivinoda Thakur in his *Jaiva Dharma* (Volume Three, Chapter 15, page 70-1) as follows:

> The place where a river's waters meet with the land of the shore is called the "*tata*." The "*tata*" is then the place where the water meets land. What is the nature of this "*tata*"? It is like the thinnest of threads that runs along the boundary of land and water. A "*tata*" is like the finest of lines, so small that the gross material eyes cannot even see it. In this example the spiritual world is like the water and the material world is like the land. The thin line that separates them is the "*tata*." That

boundary place is the abode of the individual spirit souls. The individual souls are like the atomic particles of sunlight. The souls can see both the spiritual world and the material world created by *maya*. The Lord's spiritual potency, *chit-shakti*, is limitless, and the Lord's material potency, *maya-shakti*, is gigantic. Standing between them, the individual spirit soul is very tiny. The individual spirit souls are manifested from the *tatastha-shakti* of Lord Krishna. Therefore the souls are naturally situated on the boundary (*tatastha*) of matter and spirit.

The "*tatastha*" nature of the souls refers to the fact that they must be under the control of one of these two potencies. The actual place of the "*tata*" (shore) may change. What was once dry land may be covered with water, and what was once covered by water may again become dry land. If he [the *jiva* soul] turns his gaze upon Lord Krishna, the soul comes under the shelter of Lord Krishna's spiritual potency. But if he turns away from Krishna and turns his gaze to the material potency, *maya*, then the soul is caught in *maya's* trap. That is what is meant by "the soul's *tatastha* nature."

The spirit souls are completely spiritual. However, because they are atomic in size, the souls are not very strong. That is why *maya* can dominate them. However, in the soul's nature there is not the slightest scent of *maya*.

From this description we can understand that the *tatastha* region is also a tendency or freedom of the individual spirit soul to independently choose the plane of existence in which he wishes to associate. Thus, as the spirit souls manifest from Lord Vishnu, they can choose to go to the spiritual or material domain. However, it is the natural sentiment of the living being to serve God. This is why it is also described above that there is no *maya* whatsoever in the nature of the soul. This is further explained by Bhaktivinoda Thakura in his *Sri Caitanya Shikshamrita* (pp.156-7), in which he relates that just as God has His *svarupa-vigraha*, or essential and eternal form, so the *jiva* also has his *chit-vigraha*, or eternal form with complete knowledge. That *chit* body is manifested in Vaikuntha, the spiritual domain, not in the material realm. However, while in the material worlds, the *jiva's chit* body is hidden under the two coverings of the subtle and gross physical bodies. The *chit* body of the soul, in which is the natural mood of serving the Lord, was in existence prior to its contact with matter. However, due to its contact with *maya*, the consciousness of the soul becomes transformed to consider itself a servant of matter, meaning the mind, senses, and the physical body. In this way, the *jiva* soul becomes entrapped in *maya*, and its spiritual nature and identity becomes hidden.

Ramanujacharya explains the hidden identity of the soul while in the material realm in his commentary on the *Vedanta-sutra* (4.4.3). He describes the soul's pure qualities as being shrunk while in the material world, and then being expanded into pure knowledge, bliss, etc., upon liberation when the karmic bondage is destroyed. Thus, the soul was always pure from the start. Only from the contamination of consciousness while in association with matter does the soul appear to be misdirected.

Therefore, *maya* has nothing to do with the creation nor the identity of the spirit souls. The individual souls are small and weak, and can be influenced by *maya*, but they are superior to it.[10] Srila Bhaktisiddhanta Sarasvati Thakur also explains in his book, *Brahmana and Vaishnava* (Chapter Two, p. 86), that before acquiring any material designations, the living entity is supremely pure.

This leads to the point that the *jiva* soul is eternal and ever-existing, and so is his function, or *dharma*, which is to love and serve God in the form of Sri Krishna. When the soul becomes purified from its association with matter, his spiritual identity and devotion to God become revived and expanded.

THE NATURE AND INDEPENDENCE OF THE SPIRIT SOULS

Although the *jiva* souls are spiritual in nature, why do some souls turn toward *maya* after being manifested? This was the question asked by Vrajanatha in Srila Bhaktivinoda Thakur's *Jaiva Dharma* (Volume Three, Chapter 16, page 91). In the book, Bhaktivinoda Thakur explains the answer by way of the reply from Babaji, another character in the book. He explains that the qualities of the Lord are present in a very small degree in the spirit souls. Because the Lord has independence and free will, the *jiva* souls also have a small quantity of eternal free will. However, although the *jivas* are independent, they cannot do everything they want like Krishna can. For the *jivas*, proper use of free will is seen when the soul favorably serves Krishna, while a misuse of free will is recognized when the soul turns away from Him. Then the soul tries to enjoy *maya*. Then the pure spirit soul becomes covered over by five kinds of ignorance so that he can pretend to be something other than what he really is.

Vrajanatha then asks why the Lord made the tiny souls so weak that they fall into *maya*. Babaji responds, saying that Krishna is merciful and also playful. He desires many kinds of pastimes with the individual souls in a variety of conditions. So He creates many exalted conditions, such as those in the spiritual world, as well as many degraded situations as found in the material worlds. In this way, by the influence of *maya*, there is a descent into the lower depths of consciousness. And on the higher level, by the help of Sri Radha, the personification of the *hladini-shakti*, Krishna's bliss potency, there is the attainment of unlimited spiritual bliss. And. The souls that enter *maya's* depths lose interest in serving God and in understanding their spiritual nature. They are only interested in their own selfish pleasure. Nonetheless, the Lord sends His own personal representatives from the spiritual world to make these souls favorable to Him and turn them toward the spiritual atmosphere.

When Krishna sees how the *jiva* souls enter the material worlds, He weeps to see how they are suffering. He even follows them into the material world, which He does out of His causeless mercy. He does this in two ways; through His numerous incarnations, and by expanding Himself into the Supersoul to accompany each and every *jiva* through material existence. In order to give them the chance to witness His spiritual pastimes, He brings His liberated devotees into this world to exhibit His nectarean pastimes in His various incarnations for the world to see. This helps awaken those who are receptive to their dormant devotion to the Lord, and brings them to the spiritual dimension.

Which way the independent *jiva* souls turn is never forced. It is up to their own free will. This free will, however, is a precious gift. It is one of the eternal qualities of the spirit. It is what allows them to choose whatever way they wish to exist. This is further described in a very enlightening way by Srila Bhaktisiddhanta Sarasvati Thakur in his book, *Brahmana and Vaishnava* (Second Chapter, p. 86):

Before acquiring material designations, the living entity is supremely pure. Even though he is not engaged in serving the Supreme Lord, he remains situated in the neutral position of *santa-rasa* due to his marginal nature. Though the living entity, born from the marginal potency, does not at that time exhibit a taste for serving the Lord due to a lack of knowledge of self-realization, his direct propensity of serving the Supreme Lord nevertheless remains within him in a dormant state. Though the indirect propensity of material enjoyment, which is contrary to the service of the Lord, is not found in him at that time, indifference to the service of Hari and the seed of material enjoyment, which follows that state of indifference, are nevertheless present within him.

The living entity, who belongs to the marginal potency, cannot remain indifferent forever by subduing both devotional and nondevotional propensities. He therefore contemplates unconstitutional activities from his marginal position. As a sleeping person dreams that he is active in the physical world without actually being involved in activities, when the dormant, indifferent living entity of the marginal potency exhibits even a little apathy to the service of the Supreme Lord and situates himself in a neutral, unchanging condition for even a little time, he is infected by impersonalism. That is why the conditioned soul desires to merge in the impersonal Brahman, thus exhibiting his mind's fickle nature. But due to neglecting the eternal service of the Lord and thereby developing the quality of aversion to the Lord, he cannot remain fixed in that position. In this way, aversion to the Lord breaks his concentration of mind and establishes him as the master of this world of enjoyment.

Maya, the external energy of the Supreme Lord, then induces the marginal living entity to enjoy this world through her covering and throwing potencies, and, thus, shows the living entity the reality of being averse to the Lord's service.

So this description explains that due to the living being remaining in a neutral position, he does not exhibit a taste for serving Krishna, which is in a dormant state. He also exhibits indifference to the material world and its enjoyment at first. However, since he cannot remain in a state of inactivity and indifference for long, he contemplates material activities and the enjoyment they might offer. Then *maya* induces the living entity to try to enjoy the world.

It is explained that *maya* is the reflection of the Lord's internal potency. She is a perverted manifestation of the Lord's pure, spiritual potency. The purpose of *maya* is to purify the rebellious souls who are averse to service to the Lord. She provides a way they can reform, and keeps the defiant away from the spiritual domain by keeping them pre-occupied with material activities. Troublesome concerns and worries are their punishment. The world of *maya* is their prison, from which there is no escape. They simply remain chasing after the illusory pleasures lifetime after lifetime. Nonetheless, as it is out of kindness that a king sends a criminal to prison, not only for the criminal but also for the law abiding citizens, it is out of kindness that the Lord sends the materially inclined living beings to the world of *maya* so they may work out their desires and one day realize that true happiness lies in the spiritual domain in the association of the Supreme Being.[11]

As further described by Srila Bhaktisiddhanta Sarasvati Thakur in his book, *Brahmana and Vaishnava* (Second Chapter, p. 86), when the living being first enters the material worlds, he often appears in the form of Lord Brahma:

> At that time the living entity considers himself the king of enjoyers, and being situated in the mode of passion, he takes the position of Brahma and creates progeny. The living entities who are born from Brahma, the grandfather of everyone, expand themselves in families of Aryans and *brahmanas*. In this world of duality, however, living entities who are covered and thrown under the control of the external energy naturally become envious. This enviousness further creates pride, illusion, greed, anger, and lust, and induces the living entities to dance frantically in aversion to the Lord. At that time they forget both that they were born from Grandfather Brahma and the Lord's instructions in the *Vedas*.

One thing we need to understand is that both God and the living beings are full of desires. This is another way they are similar to each other. This explained more completely by Srila Bhaktivinoda Thakur in his *Jaiva Dharma* (Volume 3, Chapter 15, p.80):

The Supreme Personality of Godhead is consciousness, a knower, an enjoyer, a thinker, self-manifested, and visible to others. He is also the knower of all fields of activity and He is full of [spiritual] desires. The individual spirit soul is also consciousness, a knower, an enjoyer, a thinker, self-manifested, and visible to others. He is also the knower of a field of activity [his or her own body] and he is also full of desires. Because He is the master of all potencies, the Supreme Personality of Godhead has these qualities to the highest degree. On the other hand, the individual spirit soul, possessing only very slight power, has these qualities in a very slight degree. Although they are different in the sense that one is perfect and complete and the other is very small and atomic, the Supreme and the individual spirit soul are alike in that they both possess these qualities. The Supreme Personality of Godhead is the master of all potencies. He is the controller of the *svarupa-shakti* (internal potency), *jiva-shakti* (the marginal potency), and *maya-shakti* (the energy of the material nature). These potencies are all His obedient maidservants. He is their master. Whatever He wishes, they do. That is the nature of the Supreme Being. The individual spirit soul has a very tiny drop of these qualities. He is subordinate to the Lord's other potencies.

This shows the difference and similarity between the Lord and the small *jiva* souls. However, the point is that we all long for pleasure, as high a pleasure as we can reach. The reason for that is because the source from which we have emanated is fully powerful in all pleasure. The individual soul is originally a part of the pleasure potency. It is our right to acquire that pleasure and be happy. And the highest pleasure is found in loving relationships. We simply have to realize that real love is in association with the Supreme Being in the eternal, spiritual world. Whatever love we usually encounter in the material world is often but a limited or perverted reflection of what we wish to find. Therefore, it lacks continuity and fulfillment, and leaves us wishing and searching for something more substantial. Such deep love is only found on the spiritual platform.

At this point we should further understand that although the individual *jiva* souls are manifested from the *jiva-shakti* of Lord Krishna, the *jiva-shakti* is counted among Lord Krishna's incomplete potencies, or the *apurna-shakti*. From this incomplete potency all the individual souls, the atomic fragments of consciousness, are manifested. Thus, the individual spirit souls are not eternally perfect, but they can become perfect (*sadhana-siddha*) by engaging in the activities of devotional service (*sadhana*). Afterwards they can enjoy spiritual bliss like that enjoyed by the eternally perfect (*nitya-siddha*) beings.[12]

In the *Srimad-Bhagavatam* (3.3.26,pur.), His Divine Grace A. C. Bhaktivedanta Swami describes the differences between the *nitya-siddha* and the *sadhana-siddha* devotees. He explains that the *nitya-siddha* devotees never fall down into the material atmosphere, even though they may sometimes appear in the material worlds in order to carry out the mission of the Lord. The *sadhana-siddha* devotees are the perfected souls from among the conditioned beings. Even amongst these there are pure and mixed devotees. Pure devotees are free from all materialistic tendencies, and the mixed devotees sometimes are eager for fruitive activities or philosophical speculation.

It is further explained that *nitya-siddha* devotees may also come from Vaikuntha to this material world to teach by their personal example and allow conditioned souls the means to advance spiritually. Such a devotee comes to the material world upon the order of the Supreme Being, and are never allured by whatever temporary pleasures this world has to offer.[13]

An example of this is found in the *Srimad-Bhagavatam* (10.8.49) wherein the devotees who play the part of Lord Krishna's eternal father and mother are praying to appear on planet earth knowing that after they appear, Krishna will also soon descend in order to display His pastimes with His devotees. This means that devotees who play such intimate parts in the activities of Lord Krishna are already designated. Therefore, those living entities who have perfected themselves to become *sadhana-siddhas* can never become Krishna's father or mother, or His consort or most special friends, but they can attain the same affection for the Lord. Thus, they can also participate in similar pastimes to which they are most attracted. In this way, the conditioned souls in the prison of *maya* can rectify themselves and return to the spiritual dimension where there is plenty of room for everyone. Through such affectionate reciprocation between the Lord and His devotees, the Lord's pleasure is increased, and, likewise, the pleasure of the devotees is expanded millions of times more. Thus, there is no limit to the transcendental bliss that exists in the spiritual world.

A FALL FROM THE SPIRITUAL WORLD

Those who have a direct and eternal relationship with the Lord, whose numbers are limitless, either in Goloka or in the Vaikuntha planets, do not even know that a potency called *maya-shakti* exists. They are eternally liberated and know nothing of the suffering and material or selfish pleasure that goes on within the material worlds. They only taste the nectar of worshiping and serving the Lord. They have no inclination except toward spiritual things and seek nothing but the happiness of serving the Lord. They are always protected by their spiritual strength and never touch *maya*.[14] This is the condition and sentiment of the *nitya-siddhas*, or eternally liberated devotees. Thus, they never have any connections with *maya*.

Although many Vedic texts explain that upon reaching the spiritual world no one ever falls down into *maya*, there is evidence that such is a possibility, although extremely rare. It is explicitly related that even when one is liberated, the soul is capable of coming under *maya's* control.[15] So how is this possible?

One point to which we may want to refer is made by Srila Bhaktisiddhanta Sarasvati Thakur in his book, *Brahmana and Vaishnava* (Second Chapter, p. 86), wherein he states: "Before acquiring material designations, the living entity is supremely pure. Even though he is not engaged in serving the Supreme Lord, he remains situated in the neutral position of *santa-rasa* due to his marginal nature."

Although this is in reference to the origin of the spirit soul, nonetheless, it does provide a hint of the condition of the soul that may indeed fall from the spiritual world. The pure state of the living being would be in reference to only two conditions; when the soul is manifested without the karmic contamination from associating with the material worlds of *maya*, and that found in the purely transcendental atmosphere within the spiritual worlds. Nonetheless, the point about being in the neutral state of *santa-rasa* could be worth noticing, since it is this platform, which he mentions, from which the living being can fall into the world of *maya*. This would indicate that only those souls within the *santa-rasa*, or relationship of neutrality, are at all capable of falling from the spiritual world.

This explanation also seems to concur with that given by Srila A. C. Bhaktivedanta Prabhupada in the *Srimad-Bhagavatam* (3.25.29,pur.). "Sometimes it is asked how the living entity falls down from the spiritual world to the material world. Here is the answer. Unless one is elevated to the Vaikuntha planets, directly in touch with the Supreme Personality of Godhead, he is prone to fall down, either from the impersonal Brahman realization or from an ecstatic trance of meditation."

So how can such a fall take place? One example is the servant of Lord Chaitanya, Kala Krishadasa, who was allured from the direct association of the Lord by the female Bhattatharis during the Lord's tour of South India. Some people may feel that this is only a pastime, but Srila A. C. Bhaktivedanta Swami mentions in his purport in the *Chaitanya-caritamrita* (*Madhya-lila*, 10.65): "This is factual evidence showing that it is possible at any time to fall down from the Lord's association. One need only misuse his little independence. Once fallen and separated from the Supreme Personality of Godhead's association, one becomes a candidate for suffering in the material world."

Another example is that of Jaya and Vijaya as described in the *Srimad-Bhagavatam* (3.16.2). Therein, when the Kumara brothers wanted entrance into the Vaikuntha region, they were denied entrance by the guards, Jaya and Vijaya. The Kumaras then cursed the guards to take birth in the material world because the guards could not tell who was a qualified devotee and who was not. Lord Vishnu later pointed out that it was because they had ignored Him that this had happened. It was further revealed that they had previously detained the Goddess of Fortune herself at the doors to Vaikuntha when she was returning once after having left the spiritual kingdom. Thus, at that instance Jaya and Vijay committed a grave offense and became affected by duality in the same way as they did with the Kumaras. When the spirit soul is affected by duality, it must then go to the realm of duality, which is the material world. Later, it became evident that the Lord wanted to use Jaya and Vijaya in His pastimes in the material world and arranged a situation in which they would enter the material domain to participate. Nonetheless, it is an example of how the independence can be misused, forcing one to leave the spiritual world.

The point is that in the spiritual world everyone has a spiritual body, and there is no conception of material existence. There is only spiritual service given by the *jiva* souls and the receiving of service by the Supreme Being. There is only *sevya*, *seva*, and *sevaka*–the person served, the process of service, and the servant.[16] If there is any disturbance or change of attitude in any *jiva* soul, the Lord gives that being all facility for his own particular preferences or pursuits by allowing him to enter the land of duality and imagination, which is the material creation. However, such occurrences among the innumerable *jivas* in the spiritual worlds are almost non-existent.

When beginning to fall from their spiritual position, the *jiva* souls exhibit an extremely subtle change of disposition. They are first attracted to their independence, their free will to decide to do something or not to do something. They begin to think in terms that one service is favorable and something else may be less favorable, or what is likeable and unlikeable. In other words, they begin to think in terms of their own enjoyment. It is this subtle diversion in which the living being begins to display the symptoms of wanting to enjoy according to one's own preferences, or outside of the association with God. In the spiritual strata this is most unusual and a form of duality. It is a type of rebellion against the eternal service of the Lord, which is the purpose of their existence and situation in the spiritual world. Once that service is interrupted, then they are no longer engaged in their natural tendency. Not only does it disrupt their own spiritual life, but also that of others around them. Therefore, rather than have such *jivas* cause disturbances in the natural flow of spiritual and loving exchanges between the Lord and His devotees, the Lord allows the nonconformist to enter the material realm where all of the other rebellious beings can play and act out their desires to their heart's content, or at least try.

When this happens, it is not that *maya* has entered the spiritual world to affect this particular entity, but it is more like his consciousness has gone to the realm of duality, the realm of *maya*. This is where the illusory energy provides the playground for those who think they can find their own form of enjoyment or pleasure outside of the spiritual strata, outside of the association of God. And it is that consciousness which, thus, immediately takes the person to *maya's* realm. It is automatic and immediate, based on the free will of the living entity.

In any case, it is the marginal nature of the *jiva* to be pure or impure through the proper use or misuse of his independence, in whatever situation he is found. When there is a distortion in his proper functional nature, the *jiva* becomes impure, and thus qualified to be brought to the material plane, devoid of spiritual shelter. Through such association with the material energy, the *jiva* forgets his service to Krishna. When this happens he begins to imagine his pursuits and identity in any number of personas. In this way, the process of repeated birth and death open up for him.

* * *

It is often said that the original nature and identity of the living being is spiritual, and that our original home is also in the spiritual domain. For example, the *Srimad-Bhagavatam* (4.28.54) states: "My dear gentle friend, both you and I are exactly like two swans. We live together in the same heart, which is just like the Manasa Lake. Although we have been living together for many thousands of years, we are still far away from our original home."

In the purport to this verse, His Divine Grace A. C. Bhaktivedanta Swami explains that this verse refers to the spiritual world as the original home of the living beings and the Supreme Lord. While there, they all share a very peaceful and blissful life. However, when the living being wants to enjoy himself in something other than service, or separate from the Lord, which is not his nature anymore than a fish living outside of water, then he falls into the material world. As soon as one feels a little envy of the Lord, then he must leave the spiritual kingdom because no envy of the Lord exists in the spiritual world. The choice to love God or not always exists within each of us. And without such love, the living being becomes conditioned and may go on like that for millenniums.

So this is the key to a misuse of independence and free will. When the living beings desire to enjoy themselves separate from the Supreme, they develop duality in their consciousness, as described above. Then they tend to disregard the devotional service of the Lord. Thus, the living beings fall from the spiritual strata.

The natural function of the living entity, and his purpose in the spiritual world with the Lord, is to serve and enjoy the loving relationship with the Supreme. Krishna is the Supreme Enjoyer, and the living being is meant to be enjoyed by the Lord. In that way there is an intense exchange of love and happiness between the *jiva* and the Lord. However, when the *jiva* soul begins to feel that something else is more important, or worse, feels that he would like the same attention as the Lord, or even wants to compete with, imitate, or be the Lord, then this is not possible, except in one's imagination. And the freedom to imagine such things is provided only on the material platform. This is also the mercy of the Lord to allow the living being the freedom to pursue his imaginations and desires. Thus, the Lord also accompanies the living being as the Supersoul. By this means, the living being may one day regain his senses and turn back toward the spiritual strata and service to God.[17]

So due to free will and independence, the tendency to fall may always be there, but the relationship with Krishna is never lost. So in one sense, the fall is superficial because one's relationship with God is never broken, although it may seem to be while one is in the material worlds, affected by forgetfulness and covered by the subtle and gross bodies. However, such a fall of a devotee who is in a direct relationship with Krishna is practically impossible. Usually anyone who has developed his relationship with Krishna never falls down in any circumstance. It is always more blissful to be enjoyed by God for the love and service that you do than trying to enjoy the dull material mind and senses.

* * *

While in the material world, if the living being gives up the material embodiment and by the practice of devotional service enters back into the spiritual dimension, he will revive his spiritual body. In his spiritual form he can see the Supreme Lord face to face. He will be able to hear and speak to Him and understand Him as He is.[18] As it is explained, "Just as gold when smelted by fire, gives up its impurity and again takes on its own form, similarly the soul, shaking off the contamination of *karma* by the practice of *bhakti-yoga*, attains to Me."[19]

As further described by Srila Bhaktisiddhanta Sarasvati Thakur in his book, *Brahmana and Vaishnava* (Second Chapter, p. 86), "On that platform of progress, if a living entity cultivates transcendental sound vibration [the chanting of Krishna's holy names] and revives the process of remembering the lotus feet of Sri Krishna, he then achieves scientific, spiritual knowledge. By this process, all *anarthas* [unwanted obstacles to devotional service] are destroyed and he becomes situated in a supremely auspicious position."

In this way, by the practice of the spiritual process, one can become purified to return to the spiritual world. Even though *maya* ensnares the insincere and conditioned souls, when the *jiva* devotes himself to serving the Lord, *maya* manifests her mode of goodness, the *sattva-guna*, to help him on his way back to the spiritual world and gives him knowledge about Krishna.

Then, as explained in *Krishna Book* (Chapter Twenty-Eight) by Srila A. C. Bhaktivedanta Swami, for those who become perfect in their practice of *bhakti-yoga*, in their next life they are immediately transferred to the universe where Krishna is appearing. Thus, they get their first chance to associate with Krishna directly, just before returning to their activities in the spiritual world.

When one returns to the spiritual world, he hardly remembers his experience in the material realm. It is like a vague, bad dream noted mostly for being separated from and forgetful of God. You can't have the kingdom of God without Him. Thus, upon returning, no one ever falls back down from the spiritual world. Just as once a child experiences the pain of putting his hand in a fire, he would have to be quite retarded to try it again to see if it still causes pain. In the same way, once attaining the spiritual world, no one returns to the material domain.

KARMA AND MATERIAL EXISTENCE

It is understood that the material nature and the living beings are beginningless[20] because both of them are from the energy of the Supreme and exist before the cosmic manifestation. However, it is the material creation that gives the sleeping or dormant conditioned souls a chance to be active again. They are absorbed within the body of Maha-Vishnu, and when it is time they are manifested through the agency of the *mahat-tattva*.

The materially inclined living beings must have a physical body because the subtle body alone is not enough for them to perform actions. The subtle body is where the desires and consciousness reside, while the physical body allows the conditioned souls to act out those longings. This is the purpose of the material creation.

However, because of the gross physical body, the living beings undergo the six stages of existence, namely birth, growth, maintenance, production of by-products such as children, and then dwindling and death. The body also feels the pangs of hunger, thirst, heat and cold, and other bodily conditions, and the desires to solve such problems along with the wishes for more pleasure. Thus, pushed by these desires, the soul within the body becomes the obedient servant of the needs of the body. The living entity also becomes the servant of the longings for the association of members of the opposite sex, and other material activities. In this way, he may perform all kinds of pious activities with the hope of attaining heaven, if he is religious. Otherwise, if he is impious, he may simply engage in any activity he chooses with thoughts of nothing but his own selfish pleasure, which will take one farther downward into darkness. In either case, once a person has attained the reactions to his activities and, for example, lived in heaven to use up his good *karma*, or gone through hell to rectify himself of his bad acts, he again eventually returns to accept a human birth to try again.

In this way, the person is stuck on the wheel of *karma* for many lifetimes, directed by his desires for material facility and pleasure. Caught in this trap, the living being suffers and works to reduce his miseries. He works hard to acquire food and drink, to collect money, to attain clothing, and drive away the cold. He may also become married for companionship and then must work hard to increase the happiness of his new family and descendants. He must find doctors and medicines when he and his family are attacked by disease, and he must pay taxes and protect his property, and so on. In such endeavors, the soul becomes tossed around by such feelings as lust, anger, greed, pride, envy, and bewilderment. Thus, the materially inclined living being thinks he is enjoying while working so hard.[21] This sort of pleasure is compared to the camel who loves the taste it gets from eating the branches of the thorny bush, not realizing that what he is relishing is the taste of his own blood.

The main reason for these sorts of activities and the suffering of the conditioned soul is due to the forgetfulness of one's spiritual identity as an eternally blissful servant of God.[22] Because of this, the conditioned living being engages in activities meant to solve his problems that only lead him deeper into karmic bondage in material existence.

The whole trouble for the living beings while in the material world is that he is attached to the concept of being independent and free from the influence of any controller above him. This is actually illusion because the living being is subjected to many influences around him which keep him under control. Thus, he continues to be entangled in material existence because he does not know how to get free.[23]

The *karma* of fruitive activities is also considered without a beginning because it is manifested simultaneously from the *mahat-tattva*, the ingredients of the material creation, as when time agitates *avidya* (ignorance) and *jnana* (knowledge of the impersonal). From *karma*, the modes of goodness and passion are manifested, which then produces knowledge and action, and then all other aspects of the creation begin to manifest. Thus, *karma* is a key ingredient in material nature which has existed within Maha-Vishnu with all the other aspects of material nature.[24]

Another consideration for how *karma* is without a beginning, and how the *jiva's* aversion to God is also beyond the scope of time, is explained by Srila Bhaktivinoda Thakur in his *Sri Caitanya Sikshamrita* (p. 185): ". . . many cannot understand distinctly how *karma* has no beginning. Time pertaining to matter is only material reflection of [spiritual] *chit*-time and is a material thing suited to the performance of *karma*. [The] *jiva* takes recourse to *chit* i.e., transcendental everlasting time in Vaikuntha, where there is no past and future; only the present exists. When the *jiva* in bondage enters in material time, [he] becomes subject to past, future, and present, and being server of *tri-kala* [material time] suffers pleasure and pain. Material time operating from *chit-kala* [spiritual time] and *chit-kala* having no beginning, the origin of the *jiva's karma* i.e., aversion to God, is coming even prior to material time. Therefore, judged impartially with regard to *jada-kala*, the root of *karma* lies prior to this time and therefore *karma* has been designated as *anadi* i.e., without any beginning."

Regarding time in the spiritual world, we should make one comment for clarification, that understanding spiritual time is beyond material logic and cannot be understood because it is outside our experience. At best we can say that time and space in the spiritual world is different from that found in the material worlds. Material time is divided by past, present, and future due to the agitation of the modes of nature. In the spiritual world time is not broken up like that. There time is in an ever-present state. There is only the eternal now. In the spiritual realm things do not come into being, nor do they end. Everything exists in an eternal present. While living in the material realm, we try to describe the manifestation of the *jiva* souls as, "The spirit souls were created," or "the individual souls were imprisoned by *maya*," and so on. This only shows how much we are influenced by our material conditioning. And we will continue to talk in this way while remaining influenced by the limiting factors of our existence in *maya*. We have to understand things from beyond the limits of material logic. Only then we may get a glimpse of understanding that the spiritual world is eternal and we also are eternal beings. By taking to the spiritual process seriously, it can prepare our consciousness for perceiving higher realms and loftier states of being. The more we understand the Truth that exists beyond the limitations of the illusory world, the more we will perceive our own spiritual identity, which is beyond all time and matter.[25]

WHY THE LORD CREATES THE JIVA SOULS

Finally, we could ask why the Lord bothers to create the small *jiva* souls at all. One reason is that the Lord performs various pastimes, and displaying His material energy for the materially conditioned souls is one of them. He is Lord of all, within both the eternal spiritual potency as well as the temporary material energy. However, as explained in another portion of this book, the individual soul being in the material energy is not the fault of God, but it is the choice of the *jiva* soul who wants such an existence.

Another explanation why the Lord creates the *jiva* sparks is that the Lord is omnipotent and displays both His limited and unlimited potencies. To be omnipotent, He must display both potencies, not merely one. The living beings have only limited potency, although they are part of the Lord and of the same quality. Furthermore, He is the Lord of all beings. If there were no one to control, the concept of the supreme controller, or God, would have no meaning, just as a king without subjects has no significance. Thus, for the Lord to be the supreme controller there must be a creation to control. Such creation is displayed in the manifestation of both the spiritual and material worlds. The basic purpose of life is for the spiritual pleasure of both God and the living beings. The Lord displays His pleasure potency as the innumerable living entities. In this way, He is the reservoir of all pleasures and all forms of enjoyment, both spiritual and material. Everything comes from Him. Because He wants to enjoy pleasure, there must be energies to give Him pleasure or supply the impetus for pleasure. This is why there is the manifestation of the *jivas*. This is the understanding of the Absolute Truth.[26]

A further explanation is that the Supreme Absolute Truth is complete when He is both infinite and infinitesimal. If He is infinite only, then he is not complete. The infinite portion of the Supreme is the Lord Himself, the *Vishnu-tattva*, while the infinitesimal portion is the living entity, the *jiva*.

Because the Lord has infinite desires for transcendental activities and pleasure, there is existence in the spiritual world. And due to the tiny desires of the living entities, there is existence within the material energy. In this way, the infinitesimal *jiva* souls are simply a complimentary portion of the Supreme. Thus, it is essential that the Infinite have infinitesimal portions which are His parts and parcels, and between which there is an eternal relationship. That relationship manifests in many levels of spiritual loving reciprocation. Without the Lord's parts and parcels, the Supreme Being would have been inactive, and there would be no variegatedness in spiritual life, and no need for a material creation for the desires of the conditioned living beings, which we see all around us right now. So if there was no God, or if He was inactive with no *jiva* souls, there would be no material manifestation. However, as we can see, all life is full of activity. God is not merely some impersonal force or Brahman effulgence. And the living beings are not meant simply for merging into a white light or nothingness. Everything is meant for reaching eternal, spiritual, loving relationships and blissful activities. This is the meaning and purpose of the material creation. Thus, everything we see is but an emanation of the Supreme Absolute Truth. The living beings are but expansions of the active energy of the Supreme Being. And the Supreme Lord is the energetic, or source from which everything else manifests. [27]

Without His devotees, the Lord does not desire to enjoy spiritual pastimes and activities, although the Supreme Being is self-sufficient. Those devotees, such as the devotee cowherd boys of Vrindavana, increase His transcendental bliss and are most dear to Him. And such friends also increase in their own spiritual pleasure by serving the Lord. Thus, there is a continued increase in the state of transcendental pleasure that goes on like a competition between the Lord and his devotees. As the devotees increase in the transcendental pleasure they feel in serving the Lord, the Supreme also feels an increase in His own spiritual happiness, which is then reflected back to the devotees. This continues back and forth unlimitedly. Because the Lord is unlimited and wants to increase His devotees unlimitedly, He descends into the material worlds in order to attract the nondevotees and rebellious living beings to regain their spiritual state and return back to their constitutional nature and original home in the spiritual strata. [28]

CONCLUSION

So who am I and where did I come from? This question should be much easier to answer after reading this chapter. We are all atomic particles of the supreme spiritual sun of the Lord. We possess consciousness and a spiritual identity, which contains a drop of the highest spiritual bliss. Our spiritual form is made of a tiny fragment of spirit and is somewhat like the form of Lord Krishna. Our misfortune is that we cannot see our spiritual form. However, because we are now aware of it and want to see it means that we have become fortunate. Understanding this is the primary purpose of human existence. [29]

By understanding our spiritual identity, as summarily described above, we can also perceive that we are actually beyond the labels of being liberated or in material bondage, as explained in the *Srimad-Bhagavatam* (11.11.1): "The Supreme Lord said: The terms 'bound' and 'liberated' are an explanation from the modes of nature, not from real substance. Because *maya* is the root of the modes [and I am the Lord of *maya*], there is no liberation or bondage for Me."

These may be the words of the Supreme as they apply to Him, but they also apply to the individual souls as well. If we are spiritual beings, then, ultimately, bondage and liberation have no substantiality. The soul is not bound or liberated in substance, but only by the temporary association with the material modes, which means that such designations are also impermanent. Since the modes of nature are based on *maya*, there is no actual bondage. It is only a perception, not an actuality. Thus, there is also no liberation. The soul is never penetrated by the modes, or *maya*. It is purely spiritual. It is only the individual consciousness that surrounds the soul, so to speak, which is affected like one in a dream. Therefore, the goal of life is to become spiritually awakened, purify our consciousness to become free from our false perceptions, and return to the spiritual strata and the association of, and service to, the Supreme Being. In this way, material existence comes to an end after attaining love of God.

As is summarily concluded: This material creation is like a dream. Having been created by the external energy of the Lord, it is like an imaginary town visualized in a forest. Every conditioned soul has a natural attraction and attachment for material things, but one must give up this attachment and surrender unto the Supreme Personality of Godhead.[30]

CHAPTER SEVENTEEN

The Nature of Material Life

When we come into this material realm, as when we are born, we often do not understand what is happening and what we are meant to do. We are basically just becoming aware of everything around us. Either it gives us pleasure, pain, joy, or fear. With a little development, we become aware of when we are hungry, tired, or when something is bothering us. When such is the case, we may not even know what it is, or how to describe it, but we know something is not right. So, as babies we simply cry. Later, we learn how to express such happiness or sadness with language, and we become more aware of our own thoughts and feelings. In the meantime, we hardly know where we came from, or where we are going, or what the purpose is of anything. We have to figure it out as best we can as we go along, depending on what level of knowledge with which we acquaint ourselves.

Unfortunately, we have no idea how many times we have previously gone through this cycle of events. We go through life until finally we pass from the present body into the life beyond and enter the next body, which is created by our *karma*. Total forgetfulness of one's past material identity is called death. Birth is simply a person's total identification with a new body. A person then immediately becomes absorbed in the pleasure and pains of the new body and completely forgets the experience of any previous lives. Thus, one accepts a new body like a new dress in a dream.[1]

A person coming into a new body forgets all previous forms and thinks he is just now coming into being for the first time. It is only by illusion that the living being appears to be born and die. And although the material body is different from the soul, because of ignorance one falsely identifies oneself with the conditions of the body, such as being beautiful, ugly, fat, skinny, rich or poor. Sometimes a fortunate person can give up and see beyond such mental interpretation of things.[2]

Without any spiritual knowledge, we embrace the most foolish way of perceiving life, by accepting the temporary and ever-changing material body as our real identity. From this premise we think that the goal of life is material happiness, which is thus accomplished by catering to the desires of the mind and senses. From there we begin to see so many attachments and possessions that we think we need in order to acquire and maintain our happiness. So many relations to "my body," "my property," "my family," "my community," and on and on. In this way, the living being actually becomes increasingly entangled and bewildered in material life. Thus, he becomes absorbed in activities and topics for the development of his bodily existence while forgetting that time is continually shortening his temporary life and he still has no idea of who he really is. Therefore, we should not unnecessarily waste our short duration of life on topics that do not enhance our spiritual awareness.

When the living entity is associated with matter, the soul also appears to be a material substance, just as the moon appears to tremble when viewed as a reflection on water.[3] This is the unsteady nature of the living entity in contact with matter. This unsteady nature relates to the way the conditioned souls in the material realm involve themselves with the temporary visible objects around them. These objects are in the form of wife, children, community, property, and possessions. These are all temporary, but he identifies with them as extensions of who he is and what he needs for his mental and physical happiness. Thus, they become part of the basis of his self-imposed identity and duties or drama in life. He becomes so fixed in thinking that this is all part of what he is that, by his mental concoctions and without a spiritual foundation, this life becomes completely real to him, although it is compared to a temporary dream in the night.[4] At night one may imagine either heavenly, delightful dancing girls, or maybe fearful, ferocious, man-eating tigers, and we are affected by what we envision. But these things are not actually present because they disappear when we awake from the dream. So they are not real.

While in these bodies, which are but a variety of machines made up of different combinations of atoms and the five basic elements, the living beings suffer three kinds of misery, 1) that which is caused by the body itself in the form of diseases and bodily troubles, 2) that which is caused by other entities, like insects, animals, or hot tempered people, war, etc., and 3) problems caused by nature, like hot summers, cold winters, lack of rain, storms, and so on. In this way, the body is the cause of the numerous tribulations we encounter in material existence. Spiritually, the living being is not affected by such miseries, but because he identifies with the body, the mind then accepts these miseries as reality and he becomes affected by them.[5]

The next thing that happens is that as the spiritual living being becomes absorbed in his attachments because of his search for happiness and pleasure, and his actions in attempting to be rid of suffering, he forgets his real identity. Thus, he tries to enjoy the material world according to his own ideas. Then he becomes covered over by *maya*, illusion, and he becomes ever more attracted to materialistic life, such as house, home, wife, children, friends, and society.

Once a person descends to this level of consciousness, his identity and happiness are based so much on the surrounding paraphernalia that he also suffers fear and anxiety at the thought of losing what he has. He is forced to make so many arrangements in order to provide what he thinks is security. However, one who believes in security in a world which imposes constant change believes an illusion. There is no real security. And the ultimate change, death, is getting increasingly closer with every breath we take. This concern is also a form of suffering in this world. As soon as we awaken from this material dream to our spiritual identity, we become free from this illusory suffering. That is why it is considered that the material world, having been created by the temporary external energy of the Supreme, is like an imaginary town in a dream.[6] However, as in a dream, all material lamentation, happiness, and distress have no essential reality. It is as if the living being suffers the consequences of his own imagination. It is as if he projects his own conception of life out into the world around him. Thus, he takes things very seriously that actually cause little affect on him, if he only realized that he was a transcendental living being, above this material nature. However, when he forgets this, so many things that are not directly related to him will agitate his mind and consciousness in the same way the flame of a candle flickers and goes dim at the slightest breeze.

In such a material condition, no matter what facilities one has, the living being goes through continual ups and downs, and his consciousness carries him through higher and lower forms of births, planets, species, and states of mind.[7]

On the absolute level, however, the living being is always spiritual, so there is no real bondage of the soul to the material energy, and no liberation from it. It is only a matter of reawakening to one's normal spiritual consciousness, which can be done right here, in this body, in this lifetime. Until that happens, however, it is as if the living being is covered over by this illusion, which is merely the forgetfulness of the materially conditioned soul. Such forgetfulness and influence by the illusory nature is also considered a false situation. It is as unnatural as fish being out of water. It is simply not the constitutional position of the spiritual being, who is eternally a minute particle of the blissful spiritual energy of the Supreme Being. Therefore, regaining that awareness is the best thing one can do in the human form of life. Only in the human form can the living entity have the intellectual capability to rise above the influence of the illusory nature and the bodily concept of life and understand one's spiritual identity.

To explain further, considering the many millions of species of life, to be born in a human body is a most rare achievement. However, the temporary nature of life means that this rare opportunity can also be lost at any moment. Therefore, we must keep in mind not to misuse this human form.[8] The human body is the best of bodies and is compared to a boat. A proper spiritual teacher is the expert captain of the boat, and the Vedic teachings are the favorable winds that will power the boat for crossing over the ocean of material existence and reach the spiritual sky. Any human being who does not use this life for such a purpose is described as a killer of his own self.[9] This simply means that instead of preparing for his spiritual freedom, he has engaged in activities that will keep him bound in material life.

So, in this chapter we can understand that the soul's bodily life of gratifying the temporary material senses is false, like a fantasy world. However, for one who is absorbed in the material conception and focuses on sense gratification, such a life does not go away but continues just as a dream continues as long as one is not awakened.[10] However, a person can be freed from this dream when one becomes spiritually situated. Then he or she can at once realize his or her true identity and relationship with the Supreme. In that consciousness, one never laments nor desires for anything; he is equally disposed to every living being. In that state he attains his constitutional position of pure devotional service to the Lord.[11] In this way, he is thus relieved from the bodily concept and the influence of *maya*, illusion.

CHAPTER EIGHTEEN

The Purpose of Life

In the last chapter we understood some of the difficulties and illusory nature of material life. So now that we find ourselves in this human form, and in this material world, what are we really supposed to do with it? Everybody at some point in their life wonders why God created this world and how they got here, and what they are meant to do. The world is obviously meant for those who have a taste for bodily existence in which they can try to enjoy the pleasure of the senses. So the material creation is manifested for the sense enjoyment of the conditioned soul. It is the playground for those who want this form of existence. What this means is that the infinitesimal living being has the limited free will to think of himself as he likes. That is also one purpose of the illusory energy, that the tiny spirit soul has the independence to pretend to be something other than what he really is. Then he projects his beliefs and his self image out into the world around him. Thus, it is as if he becomes a world unto himself. And this is the world of *maya*, illusion. One cannot trace out the history of when some of the living beings first wanted to enjoy material nature, but the cause is there. So to fulfill that desire, out of compassion the Lord provided the material creation.[1]

However, we often find that the pleasure of the mind and senses only goes so far; it is limited, temporary, and does not really satisfy the soul, which is the real identity of the living being. So, with compassion, the Supreme Lord also creates the material manifestation in a way that can give the living beings a chance to work out their material desires and understand their real spiritual position. By following the proper instructions that the Supreme provides, the living being can be delivered from the repeated cycle of birth, death, and the suffering in materialistic life by regaining his original spiritual consciousness and eternal position.[2] So whenever you don't know what you are supposed to do in life, or whenever you do not remember who you are, you simply read the instructions that have been provided by the Supreme Being. Don't think the Lord created this world without giving us the means to get out of our confusion, or get out of this world altogether.

So the basis of the material creation is to give the living beings the chance either to follow their material and bodily desires and cultivate more gratification of the temporary senses, or progress toward ultimate liberation through spiritual progress.[3] Everyone has the independence to make that choice. No one is forced to do one or the other. However, short-lived sense gratification can be achieved even in the animal species. Therefore, the topmost use of human life is to engage in the advancement of Self-realization. This is also explained in *Srimad-Bhagavatam* (11.9.29), which says that after many lifetimes one finally achieves a human birth. Although a human lifetime is temporary and can be short, usually only 60, 70, or maybe 100 years, it affords one the opportunity to reach the highest perfection in spiritual life. One lifetime is all it takes to make the necessary spiritual advancement to enter the higher realm. This is the way a sober person should act in order to prevent falling back into the cycle of repeated births and deaths by chasing after his sensual desires.

One point to consider is that if we need to get back to our original spiritual position, this means that we were completely spiritual beings before entering the material world. Thus, our conditioned state of existence is caused, in essence, by our swaying away from the Supreme Being.[4] Once we again engage in genuine spiritual practices, which are the natural activities of the pure living being, our normal state of being can be reawakened in which we are fully satisfied in spiritual bliss. It is simply a matter of making the connection and linking ourselves to the Supreme again. This state of being is attained when one reaches the pure activities of the soul, which is devotional service to the Supreme Being.[5] However, when we are covered over by the physical body with a materialistic consciousness, our desires become polluted with lust, anger, greed, and foolishness. We think that making the mind and body happy is the ultimate goal of life. We think if we supply ourselves with all of the demands of the mind and body, then how much happier can we be? Thus, the soul inside is forgotten, and we are unable to experience the supremely blissful state found in regaining our spiritual consciousness. Then, we go through life somehow feeling empty and unfulfilled and having no clue as to why, even if we have everything we think we want. Therefore, engaging in the practices that allow us to regain our spiritual consciousness is the ultimate goal of human life.

Naturally, everyone wants to be happy. This is because happiness is the genuine state of the living being. We want to be happy because the spirit soul is *sat-chit-ananda*: eternal, and full of knowledge and bliss. So that is what everyone naturally wants to feel. Even while covered by a material form, one will automatically try to reach this normal state of consciousness through varieties of enjoyment, even if they are misdirected in the aim of life. However, in order to accept living in the material world and various levels of material or bodily enjoyment, the living entity must forget his real identity and natural state of spiritual bliss. If we could fully remember our spiritual happiness, all forms of pleasure of the body would immediately become insignificant. They would have no practical meaning. Therefore, one of the first conditions of the materialistically inclined living being is that he forgets his real identity. Such a person does not realize that matter is an inferior energy and is incompatible for his true happiness. He may think that working hard to take care of this body and all of its demands is the normal state of affairs. However, he forgets that spirit is a finer state of existence and full of bliss, and the strata in which exists the real consciousness of the living entity. It is his natural state of being. Therefore, whether one realizes it or not, this is the level of happiness for which everyone is always hankering, which exists in the spiritual atmosphere.

One of the first things to understand about the difference between matter and spirit is that the material world is not false, it is real but temporary. This is the same with the material body. It is not false but is subject to change and is temporary, and in that sense not real because it may be here today but gone tomorrow. Being subject to change also means that whatever happiness one derives from the material energy is fluctuating, meaning that it is interrupted, usually by different forms of misery. What is real and eternal is the spirit soul within the body. It is changeless and belongs to the spiritual world. Identifying with the material energy is a matter of misidentification. So the first point in realizing your spiritual identity is to understand that you are not this body, you are a pure spiritual being who belongs to the eternal, blissful, spiritual atmosphere. Therefore, for a living being to accept the cosmic manifestation as his real home, or the inferior material energy as his field of happiness, is illusory.[6]

Therefore, people should take to discussing and learning about the eternal spiritual world and the Vaikuntha planets. Unfortunate people do not engage in such topics but take to conversations of the material world. Thus, they become more forgetful of their spiritual nature. This only perpetuates the continued cycle of birth and death amidst many lifetimes in the material realm.[7]

So the purpose of life in the material realm is, 1) To work out our material desires, or rise above them, 2) To experience all aspects of material existence, which is done automatically as we travel through the many forms and species of life, 3) Once we reach the human form, to balance our karma and the lessons we need to learn to reach a point where we ask who we are and why we are here, 4) To begin seeking the answers to these questions by reading the instructions provided by the Maker of all that is, 5) To reach a point in which we see that every aspect of life, whether it's our challenges or reversals, misfortunes or successes, joys or sorrows, are all avenues of discovering who we are and which contribute to our wisdom, understanding, and our purpose for being here and helping others. That is the task--to realign our consciousness to see the unity between us all and regain our intimate love for God. When our lives become meaningful by serving others and God, then you are also serving yourSelf. That is when you really become spiritual, when you see God in all others and all others as a manifestation or reflection of God. Then you will automatically know how to be a better person, how to be a better mother, father, husband, wife, or friend. There will not be any confusion about what you need to do. You will just need to do it.

You will know that the universe (life) has a purpose for you. And when you truly realize this, you will know that you can trust that God will take care of you to accomplish that purpose, whatever it may be, whether you know what it is or not. And be open to discover what it is. Ask for guidance. Let go and let God show the way. Let go of your ego and be open to learn and receive the lessons that God has in store for you. And it's OK if you feel a little scared. It's been said that if you do not feel a little scared, a little challenged, you are not progressing. You are not moving forward. But you have to remember that the more you move forward on the spiritual path, the closer you are getting to God, to putting on the robes of immortality. And don't think that God is going to reject you. He is waiting for you. It's been said that for every step we take toward God, He takes ten steps towards us. So we just have to keep going. And don't worry about feeling unqualified, or undeserving, and all that. Why complain about how dirty you may be if you are already standing in the shower? Just stay in the shower of the spiritual path and you will become clean. You may have to use a little soap, however, in the form of more prayers, spiritual activities, chanting your *mantras*, etc. Yet, when the tiny soul connects with the Supreme Soul, it is the most blissful experience.

In this way, if a living being can come to his senses about the true purpose of this universe and material life, then by the Lord's mercy he may attain to the spiritual process of devotional service, which is the natural inclination of the soul. Thus, you become saved from the world of *maya*, illusion. Then you can become free from all lamentation and material desires.[8] It is your attachment to temporary things that cause you to become upset, angry, sorrowful, or out of balance. If you let go, that is when you can regain your link with God. That is when you are free. Freedom in this sense means freedom from bodily concepts that limit your potential and spiritual possibilities. It means freedom from the attachment to the material conception of life and temporary possessions that keep you bound to that consciousness. Once you enter into that freedom, that is where the unbounded love and unlimited bliss that we all look for can be found.

As a result of understanding this spiritual knowledge and our real identity through the process of *sadhana*, or the practice of religion and *yoga*, one's dormant love for God reawakens. When such a person awakes to his real identity, he can taste the association with the Supreme Being, and he loses all interest in material existence. Thereafter, his material life and the repetition of birth and death come to an end.[9] There is no higher purpose than that.

CHAPTER NINETEEN

The Vedic Texts and Their Source

In a previous chapter we read how the Lord supplies the Vedic spiritual teachings in this cosmic creation as the winds that help propel us across the ocean of material existence to the shores of the spiritual world. However, from where does this Vedic knowledge come, what does it consist of, and how is it developed?

Although the Vedic sound vibration is eternal, how this begins to manifest in the universe is explained by Lord Krishna Himself to Uddhava in the *Srimad-Bhagavatam* (11.21.37-40). He says that as the unlimited, unchanging, and omnipotent Personality of Godhead within all living beings, He personally establishes the spiritual *omkara* (*om*) sound vibration within all. Then He manifests Himself as the primeval vital air which exhibits the sounds of the alphabet of all sacred Vedic meters, full of transcendental bliss. Thus, the Lord creates the limitless Vedic vibration through the power of His mind. From there the Vedic sound spreads out in all directions, expanded from the syllable *om*. The *Veda* is then elaborated in many varieties. Then, at the end of time, the Lord again withdraws His manifestation of Vedic sound within Himself.

From this we can understand that all Vedic knowledge and this cosmic manifestation are produced from the sound representation of the Lord in the transcendental vibration of *omkara*.[1] It was also from that *omkara* that Lord Brahma created all the sounds of the alphabet, including the vowels, consonants, semivowels, and so on.[2]

Thereafter, from this collection of sounds, Brahma produced from his four faces the four *Vedas*, along with the sacred *omkara* and seven invocations for the planetary systems. Brahma taught these to his sons, who were the great sages among the *brahmanas*. They in turn imparted the *Vedas* to their own sons. In this way, generation after generation of disciples have received the Vedic knowledge. At the end of each Dvapara-yuga they are composed into separate divisions by Srila Vyasadeva and eminent sages.[3]

135

How this happens is explained as follows: At one time the demigod leaders of the universe requested the Supreme Personality of Godhead to save the principles of religion. Thereafter, the Supreme Being manifested a spark of His plenary portion in the womb of Satyavati as the son of Parashara. Thus, He took the form of Krishna Dvaipayana Vyasa (Vyasadeva) and divided the one *Veda* into four. He separated the verses or *mantras* of the *Rig, Atharva, Yajur,* and *Sama Vedas* into four divisions, and four distinct Vedic texts. Upon calling four of his most trusted disciples, he gave each one of them one of the Vedic texts. From there they became further divided and were passed down the disciplic succession, which is further described in the *Bhagavatam* (12.6.48-51).

Of the *Puranas,* there were six masters. Each of them studied one of the six anthologies of the *Puranas* from Romaharshana, a disciple of Vyasadeva. Suta Gosvami became the disciple of these six authorities and learned all of their presentations of Puranic wisdom. Authorities understand that a *Purana* contains ten characteristics, namely descriptions of the creation and subsequent creations of the universe, the maintenance of all living beings, their sustenance, the Manus, the dynasties and activities of the great kings, the annihilation and motivation of the universe, and knowledge of the Supreme Lord. Expert sages in the ancient histories have declared that the *Puranas* can be divided into 18 major *Puranas* and 18 minor *Puranas,* according to their characteristics. The eighteen major *Puranas* are known as the *Brahma, Padma, Vishnu, Shiva, Linga, Garuda, Narada, Bhagavata, Agni, Skanda, Bhavisya, Brahma-vaivarta, Markandeya, Vamana, Varaha, Matsya, Kurma,* and *Brahmanda Puranas.*[4]

Before the creation of the universe, Lord Krishna had enlightened Brahma in his heart with the full *Srimad-Bhagavatam.* This was while Brahma was sitting on the huge lotus flower, frightened by the material existence before the process of creation had begun.[5] Only after having received this knowledge did Brahma realize how to proceed with the creation of the universe. Even afterwards, when it came time to manifest the Vedic sound vibration, the Supreme Lord had directly spoken the *Srimad-Bhagavatam* in summary to Brahma, who in turn then gave it to Narada.[6] It was Narada who had played the role of spiritual master to Vyasadeva and gave the same *Bhagavatam* to him.

From Brahma, we also get the disciplic succession of the Brahma-*sampradaya.*[7] This *sampradaya,* or chain of spiritual masters and disciples, descends through the following personalities: Brahma, Narada, Vyasadeva, Madhva Muni (Purnaprajna), Padmanabha, Nrihari, Madhava, Akshobhya, Jayatirtha, Jnanasindhu, Dayanidhi, Vidyanidhi, Rajendra, Jayadharma, Purushottama, Brahmanyatirtha, Vyasatirtha, Lakshmipati, Madhavendra Puri, Ishvara Puri, Sri Caitanya Mahaprabhu, Svarupa Damodara and Sri Rupa Gosvami, Sri Raghunatha dasa Gosvami, Krishnadasa Gosvami, Narottama dasa Thakura, Vishvanatha Chakravarti, Jagannatha dasa Babaji, Bhaktivinoda Thakura, Gaurakishora dasa Babaji, Srimad Bhaktisiddhanta Sarasvati, and A. C. Bhaktivedanta Swami Prabhupada.

Out of all the *Puranas*, the *Srimad-Bhagavatam* (*Bhagavat Purana*) is considered super excellent. Since it is Srila Vyasadeva's own commentary on the Vedic texts, it is said to be the most ripened and mature fruit of the tree of Vedic literature.[8]

The *Bhagavatam* is also considered the essence of all Vedanta philosophy because it discusses the Absolute Truth, the ultimate reality, with the exclusive goal of devotional service unto that Supreme Truth. All other Puranic scriptures shine forth as long as this great ocean of nectar, *Srimad-Bhagavatam*, is not heard. Thus, *Srimad-Bhagavatam* is the greatest of all *Puranas*. Anyone who seriously tries to understand this *Srimad-Bhagavatam*, who properly hears and chants it with devotion, becomes completely liberated.[9]

In the *Srimad-Bhagavatam* (12.4.42), Shukadeva Gosvami explains to King Pariksit that the great personality Srila Vyasadeva taught him this scripture, *Srimad-Bhagavatam,* which is equal in stature to the four original *Vedas.*

"This *Bhagavat Purana* is as brilliant as the sun, and it has arisen just after the departure of Lord Krishna to His own abode [around 3102 B.C.]. Persons who have lost their vision due to the dense darkness of ignorance in the age of Kali shall get light from this *Purana*."[10] Because of the potency of the *Bhagavat Purana*, to understand the highest levels of spiritual topics, one should seriously immerse oneself in it.

Much further analysis and explanation of the contents and development of the Vedic literature is provided in my book, *The Universal Path to Enlightenment.*

CHAPTER TWENTY

The Purpose of the Vedic Literature

The word *veda* means knowledge. The purpose of the Vedic literature is for guiding humanity about the purpose of life and how to utilize it for the utmost benefit. In some ways it is like the instruction manual you get when you buy a new appliance. The manual will explain how to use it, what it's functions are, what to do if something goes wrong, and things like that. The Vedic literature serves the same purpose in explaining the material creation and how to use it and the life we have properly.

In this way, Krishna gave the ancient religious path of the *Vedas* for the benefit of the whole universe. However, whenever that path becomes obstructed by wicked persons who follow the path of atheism, the Supreme Being will take the form of one of His incarnations.[1] By appearing as an incarnation, or sending one of His representatives, the Lord makes sure that humanity always has a source of spiritual knowledge which they can use for attaining the ultimate purpose in human life. However, this becomes more difficult in the age of Kali when atheists and misdirected persons become widely prominent in society.

Nonetheless, it is explained that no matter who or what a person is, even if one is a demigod, the Vedic literature is the best means to understand things that are beyond our direct sense perception, which include the way to attain heaven or even complete spiritual liberation. The Vedic literature constitutes the highest levels of revelation.[2] Therefore, the *Vedas*, being the word of God, is the excellent eye through which we can see and obtain the purpose of life.

After all, as it is further explained, the conditioned soul cannot revive his own spiritual or Krishna consciousness by his own effort. That is why, out of His causeless mercy for the materially conditioned souls, Lord Krishna, through Srila Vyasadeva, compiled the Vedic literature and its supplements, the *Puranas*. It is through these Vedic texts that the Lord provides the forgetful spirit souls with an education of spiritual topics. Through this means, the living being can understand the most important factors in life, namely who or what is the Supreme Being, how to become free from the clutches of *maya*, how to regain our forgotten loving relationship with God, and how to return home to the eternally blissful spiritual world, which is the ultimate goal of life.[3]

So the Vedic literature is primarily for knowing the Lord. And, as the *Garuda Purana* (3.12.17-18) mentions, special traits of the Supreme Being that are described in the Vedic literature are known only to the aspirants who are on the Vedic path. The *Vedas* are so-called because they know the Lord, but so do the *Puranas*, *Mahabharata*, and *Pancharatna* texts.

As further explained by Krishnadasa Kaviraja Gosvami in his *Chaitanya-caritamrita* (*Madhya-lila* 20, 146-8), directly or indirectly the ultimate declaration of Vedic knowledge points to Lord Krishna as the Supreme Being. This is further verified in the *Srimad-Bhagavatam* (11.21.42-43) that out of all the injunctions, rituals, formulas for worship, and levels of knowledge, it is ultimately Krishna who is established as the essential meaning and goal of all Vedic knowledge. When one reaches this conclusion he becomes satisfied. And as Krishna explains in the *Bhagavad-gita* (10.41), "Know that all beautiful, glorious and mighty creations spring from but a spark of My splendor."

In this way, the culmination of all Vedanta philosophy is to reawaken one's loving relationship with the Supreme Personality of Godhead, and to understand how to engage in activities that are based on that relationship.[4] Thus, one begins to see and act in this Truth, always doing good to others, tolerating all worldly conditions while maintaining one's faith and connection with the Supreme, and growing ever deeper in one's love of God. That is the essence of regaining one's spiritual identity and attaining freedom from material existence and returning to the spiritual abode.

CHAPTER TWENTY-ONE

Getting Back to Our Spiritual Nature

Once we realize the nature of the material world and our purpose in it, and the assistance we have in getting out of it by using the Vedic literature, then we will begin to see the importance of bringing our existence in this world to an end. Living in this world is kind of like going to school: When you have learned enough and had all the experiences you need to graduate, you should not have to come back. It will be time to move on. And there are plenty of other planes of existence out there to keep you busy.

So you could say that we "graduate" from this material plane by taking the spiritual path that will help us attain our spiritual nature and reawaken our relationship with the Supreme Being. This is the ultimate aim of religion: To see beyond the clutches of illusion, *maya*, and release oneself from the bondage of a physical body, and to regain our life of freedom in the spiritual world.

Religion, or *dharma*, means to follow the laws of God. However, there may seem to be so many religions that claim to have the exclusive law given by God. Yet, it is explained that, "The religion which is best is that which causes its followers to become ecstatic in love of God which is unmotivated and free from material impediments, for this only can completely satisfy the self."[1]

The *Narada Purana* (1.3.80-83) even points out that real *dharma*, or religion, has the Supreme Being, Vasudeva (Krishna), as the highest object and ultimate goal. Everything, including all mobile and immobile beings, from Brahma and Shiva down to the blade of grass, are but expansions of Krishna's energy. Nothing exists separate from Him. There is nothing else greater, nor smaller, nor more immense than He. The whole universe is pervaded by Him.

For this reason, it is also explained that all of the demigods, such as Brahma, Shiva, and others, along with the Siddhas (perfected beings) and prominent leaders of the sages, all prefer to stay permanently at the residence of a person who is engaged in devotion to the Lord, Hari.[2]

In *Bhagavad-gita* (11.55), Sri Krishna further describes how one can easily return to Him by such devotion. "One who is engaged in My pure devotional service, free from the contaminations of previous activities and from mental speculation, who is friendly to all, certainly comes to Me."

We can get a broader view of this opportunity of returning to the spiritual world when we consider that the materially conditioned soul is wandering throughout the universe, from one body to another, according to his material desires. However, when the living being finally wakes up to his real spiritual position, he accepts the path of devotional service, *bhakti-yoga*, to the Supreme Being. Thus, he is released from the grip of *maya* and the suffering therein. Upon awakening his spiritual consciousness, he can experience the bliss for which he was searching throughout the material universe.

The process of this path is not to negate all loving propensities that exist in our consciousness, but to merely redirect them toward the Supreme Lovable Object, namely God. When our desires are focused on satisfying our mind and body, they keep us bound in materialism. However, when those desires become redirected toward serving the Supreme, those same desires become purified and are then a cause for our liberation from further material entanglement. Affection for the temporary body and basing our relations on nothing more than that is the path of *maya*, part of the temporary external energy. However, when such relations become based on the eternal Truth, the science of the soul, they are transformed into factual relations.

We can further explain it this way: When we understand that we are all parts of God and act and treat each other in that way, then those same relations that were once based on our temporary, bodily identity, become changed into something real. They are no longer merely temporary interactions between bodies that are based on the flickering mood of the mind. Acting in and basing our relations and friendships on that Truth is the way we all become the cause of each other's spiritual progress. It is the way we become the cause of each other's liberation from the temporary illusory world. It is the way we help ourselves enter the eternal realm of complete knowledge and bliss. That is when we see each other for who we really are, and recognize the true spiritual potential of which each one of us is capable. It's already there, we simply have to reawaken ourselves to it. Then we are each other's true and best friends, for not only are we helping each other reawaken to this, but we are friends in God.

As explained in the *Bhagavatam* (4.20.32), only by such purity of purpose through devotional service can one cross over the insurmountable illusory energy of *maya*. It's all quite simply really. As Sri Krishna explains in *Bhagavad-gita* (7.14), "This divine energy of Mine, consisting of the three modes of material nature, is difficult to overcome. But those who have surrendered unto Me can easily cross beyond it." Therefore, one's real occupation is service to the Supreme, and by adopting that lifestyle one attains his real position. Simply by sticking to that position, one can overcome the need to take another physical birth.

Of all the different spiritual paths, the specific process of *bhakti-yoga*, loving devotion, is said to be the highest, especially by Lord Krishna Himself in the *Bhagavad-gita* (6.47): "And of all yogis, he who abides in Me with great faith, worshiping Me in transcendental loving service, is most intimately united with Me in yoga and is the highest of all."

Why is that the case? The word *yoga* comes from the root word *yuj*, which means to "link up" or "to bind." The word *religion*, coming from the Latin *religio*, means nearly the same thing, which is to "bring back" or "to bind." What is to unite with or to bind to is the individual soul to the Supreme Soul. The highest form of binding oneself to the Supreme is with love, devotion. That is the strongest tie there is, as we can see here in this world. However, spiritual love is stronger than material love and is eternal, being based on the Truth of the soul, not the temporary body. That love is called *bhakti*, and through the process of *bhakti-yoga*, one can naturally awaken one's love of God. This form of *bhakti*, devotion, is seen to varying degrees in all forms of religion, no matter whether Christian, Judaism, Islam, Jainism, Sikhism, or Buddhism. They all have varying levels of *bhakti*. In fact, it is the essence of each religion. However, in the Vedic form of *bhakti-yoga*, it is described and developed to the highest degree, to a personal loving relationship with the Lord.

Although other spiritual paths share the same process of devotional love within it, there is a warning about other forms of religion that carry the divisive concept of "I and Mine," or "Yours and Mine," which gives way to the idea of "Us and Them." Once we see these divisions drawn, we also see those who contemplate or actually carry out the killing of their enemies for the glory of their culture or beliefs. Such religions continue to produce the quality of envy and anger between various factions, which paves the way for quarrels and divisiveness between people, as well as the performance of irreligious practices and detrimental activities. What is the benefit of such a system? All forms of religion which are full of passion and jealousy are impure and temporary, producing a minimum of spiritual merit. Therefore, we find that the path of *dharma* which leads to the Supreme and full spiritual consciousness is the best.[3]

Another reason why *bhakti-yoga*, the path of devotion to God, is the highest process is that there are but three things which are eternal: 1) the individual soul, 2) the Supreme Being, and 3) the relationship between them, which is pure spiritual love. That is all that is eternal. Everything else is temporary. The eternally blissful spiritual world is where that preeminent spiritual love can develop and manifest to its fullest degree. And those who practice this method will naturally have a high regard for all beings, seeing that we are all spiritual in nature. That is also why we are all hankering after loving relationships while wandering throughout this material creation. It is a natural condition that we want, but we just don't know where to find it. We don't know where to find the real thing that lasts forever, which is also why we often settle for what is merely a dim reflection of what we hope for. It is like finding a few drops of water while in a desert: It's not quite enough to really satisfy us. That is because only in the spiritual atmosphere does it exist on a non-temporary basis and to its fullest extent. That is what we are all looking to find. Furthermore, in the spiritual world this is all anyone is engaged in--assisting each other in pure loving devotional activities to the Supreme Being, which naturally includes spiritual relations with each other.

Thus, "*Bhakti-yoga* is the ultimate goal of life. By rendering devotional service to the Supreme Personality of Godhead, one transcends the modes of material nature and attains the spiritual position on the platform of direct devotional service."[4]

It is further explained that it is only by devotional service, beginning with hearing about the Supreme Being, that one can approach the Supreme Personality. This is the only means to approach Him. This sort of devotional service must be practiced under the guidance of a proper spiritual master. Then one can awaken his dormant love of God.[5]

The reason why this process is so exalted is that there is no need to make a separate endeavor to see God, as some people say you must, but you simply act in such a way that God will see you. Then He will reveal Himself to you. This is further explained by Krishnadasa Kaviraja Gosvami in his *Chaitanya-caritamrita* (*Adi-lila* 7.145), that the Supreme Lord, who is greater than the greatest, becomes submissive to the insignificant devotee because of his devotional service. This is the beauty of the process, that the infinite Lord becomes submissive to the living entity because of it. In such reciprocal devotional exchanges with the Lord, the devotee enjoys the spiritual bliss of the devotional service.

Lord Krishna Himself further explains in *Srimad-Bhagavatam* (11.14.20-21) that through no other process can one satisfy Him as much as one can by developing unalloyed devotional service to Him. Even such processes as *astanga-yoga*, analytical study of the Absolute, study of the *Vedas*, austerities, charity, or accepting the renounced order do not have the effect of *bhakti-yoga*, devotional service, in pleasing the Supreme. Krishna is attained only through unflinching faith and devotional service. This process of *bhakti-yoga* is so powerful that even those of the lowest of births can be elevated to the highest spiritual platform.

Furthermore, one of the easiest and most powerful items to use in this process is the holy name of the Lord. As it is described, simply by sincerely uttering the holy name of the Lord even once, anyone in any condition can be relieved of the bondage of material existence. He or she can transcend the six material whips that effect everyone in this bodily existence, namely hunger, thirst, lamentation, illusion, old age, and death, as well as conquer the mind and senses.[6]

The reason why this is so powerful is that in this age of Kali-yuga, the most difficult age for spiritual practices, the holy name of the Lord, especially in the form of the Hare Krishna *mantra*, is the incarnation of Lord Krishna Himself in the form of sound vibration. Therefore, simply by chanting the holy name, one associates with the Lord directly. In this way, by chanting the holy name as much as possible, one overcomes all obstacles.[7]

Therefore, if one is especially serious about attaining the spiritual strata, it is advised to engage in the process of *bhakti-yoga* under the guidance of a great devotee who is also perfectly engaged in the devotional process. It is said that there are no other processes for understanding the Absolute Truth. The Absolute is only revealed to one who has attained the mercy of a great devotee.[8]

The pure devotee may live in his body which appears to be on this planet, but he lives in his consciousness, which is fixed on the spiritual platform, absorbed in the pastimes of the Lord, Krishna. Thus, he is like a via media between this material realm and that of the spiritual strata, so he can guide one to reach the same platform as himself.[9]

This, therefore, is the way for assuring ourselves of becoming free from any further material entanglement and all the problems that go with it, and reaching the eternal spiritual strata. This is the ultimate achievement in the human form of life.

* * *

One of the things that many people do on the spiritual path is visit great holy places and temples, and spiritual sites of great significance where occurrences of historical importance took place. Although doing this is not required, it can be a lot of fun to dovetail our desires for travel into something for spiritual merit. Furthermore, to see such holy places and important temples can not only bring great spiritual experiences to you, and the opportunity to meet and associate with those of great wisdom who have also attained spiritual accomplishments, but it can give ourselves a blissful, spiritual charge. This can help relieve ourselves of negative *karma* and uplift our consciousness. Often times these places are full of spiritual vibrations of the transcendental atmosphere. The spiritual world can manifest in such places, and we can perceive it if our consciousness is open to receiving the grace of God through this means.

Also, performing devotional service to the Supreme, or even sitting in meditation or quietly chanting our prayers and *mantras* in such places, allows us to feel ourselves zoom right out of this material realm and enter into the spiritual atmosphere. It is as if the spiritual world opens up to us. When one experiences such a thing, he or she never forgets it and is never quite the same. Furthermore, we can take this experience with us wherever we go and for the rest of our lives.

So this is what we are going to do. In the next section of this book we are going to go on a grand adventure and visit the major holy places of a few different religions and hear of their importance and the legends or miracles that have taken place at those temples and holy sites. Even if you cannot go personally, this tour through what I've written and the few photographs I've supplied will give you some great insights into the significance of these places and what it is like to visit them today, and the potential they supply for our spiritual advancement.

SEEING SPIRITUAL INDIA (PART 4)

The Major Historical and Holy Places of Northern India

Seeing spiritual India is like a pilgrimage into spiritual dimensions. And Northern India has some of the most important holy places in India. You can go into the mountains of the Himalayas, which are known all over the world for being an area of sages and ancient sites, many of which are described in the *Mahabharata, Bhagavata Purana,* and other classic texts. This has been where many people have ascended into lofty levels of consciousness and spiritual experience. Other places include the holy site of Kuruksetra. This is where Lord Krishna sang the sacred *Bhagavad-gita* just before the start of the Mahabharata War, along with other places relating to the Vedic legends of the universal creation. Also in Northern India is the sacred site of the Sikhs at the Golden Temple in Amritsar. Or you can visit the holy place of the Tibetan Buddhists at Dharamsala where the residence of the Dalai Lama. There is also the burial place of Issa, or Jesus, in Srinagar. These and other important places that carry spiritual significance we'll describe on our tour of Northern India. Even if you do not see all of these places, it can be fascinating to know the locations where many of these legends originated.

We will first start our travels in Haridwar and then journey on up into the Himalayan Mountains. Traveling into this part of the Himalayan region allows us to go back into history as well as experience the reason so many spiritual seekers have come here for thousands of years. This area abounds with legends. The unique beauty, peace, and high energy of the land also helps us to further our spiritual development and insights into the purpose of life. This is where various higher dimensions intermingle with the earthly plane. You will see many *sadhus,* yogis, and sages, some of whom are very powerful and who are in tune with these higher realities. So if the opportunity arises, get a little of their association.

The grand views of the tremendous mountains will inspire as well as humble

145

us before this awesome display of God's energy. This area is full of lush forests, flowering meadows, significant temples, and points of spiritual importance, as well as the tallest mountains in the world. Some of the mountains you will see include Nanda Devi (25,645 feet), Dhaulagiri (26,810 feet), Annapurna (26,504 feet), and farther south you might see Everest (29,028 feet). These alone are quite breathtaking. Simply by traveling through this area you may feel extremely fortunate and a sense of wonder and achievement. For some, this pilgrimage is but a dream, and for others it is but a once in a lifetime experience. So while you are in this region, remember to take some time in the solitude of the mountains, or in a quiet cave, or a peaceful meadow or forest, to meditate and contemplate your place in the universe and the meaning of your life.

The name "Himalayas" means the "land of the snows." But its nickname is "the playground of the *devas*." And those advanced sages can, indeed, perceive the divine dimensions in which the demigods exist.

Haridwar, population 190,000, 225 kilometers northeast of Delhi, is easily reached by bus from New Delhi. Or, if visiting Vrindavana, you can get an overnight bus straight from Vrindavana to Haridwar.

"Haridwar" means the door to Hari, the Supreme. It sits on the banks of the Ganges River. Many years ago it used to be called Kapilsthan because Kapila Muni had lived and meditated here. Haridwar is also known for being where the Ganges leaves the mountains and enters the plains. This is the reason Haridwar also has the name of Ganga-dwara. It is one of the seven major holy places of India and has plenty of spiritual significance. This is where Vidura was instructed by Maitreya. Kapiladeva also performed penances here. Daksha performed his great sacrifice nearby at Kankhal, which was attended by all the great demigods. It is about four kilometers south of the railway station. The Dakseswara (or Dakshaprajapati) Mahadeva Shiva Temple at Kankhal, the oldest temple in Haridwar, marks the place and commemorates Lord Shiva coming to help his wife, Sati. The contemporary temple was built in 1962. The central image in the temple is a Shiva-*lingam*. The little pit in the Daksha Mahadeva Mandir is saidto be where Daksha had the sacrificial fire.

Sati Kund, on Kankhal Jwalapur Road, marks the spot where Sati left her body and where she burned herself after being insulted by her father, all of which is described in the *Srimad-Bhagavatam*. Lord Nityananda also stopped here on His tour 500 years ago. However, the *kund* is in the middle of nowhere on the road and not developed in any way. It is overgrown with greenery and water lilies and can easily be overlooked.

Haridwar is known for its many temples, more of which are always being built. One popular temple is the Mansa Devi Temple, located on the hill above the city. You can walk up the hill or take a cable car which gives you a way to get a great view of the city and the mountains and plains that surround it. The Deity in the temple is small, but the temple is organized and often crowded.

Other holy temples in Haridwar include the Chandi Devi, Hanuman and a temple to Hanuman's mother, Anjani Devi, on top of the Siwalik Hills about four and a half kilometers away. Also, the Narayana-shila, Bhairava, and the Mayadevi temple, one of the oldest in Haridwar. The Mayadevi deity is a three-headed, four-armed female in the act of killing a prostrated demon. Other temples in Haridwar include the Shravannath Mahadeva, Neeleshwar, Navagraha, Bharaha Khamba, and Bolagiri temples. The Bilvakeshwar Mahadeva temple is where Parvati performed austerities to get Lord Shiva as her husband. She ate only leaves of the Bilva trees. Not far away is a temple marking the place where the Ganges originally appeared in order to supply water for Parvati to drink.

Another more modern temple in Haridwar is the Bharata Mata (Mother India) Mandir. It was consecrated in 1983 and stands eight stories tall. The first floor contains a standing image of Bharata Mata and a map of India on a raised platform. The second floor contains the Shrine of Heroes, dedicated to those who were active in India's independence movement, such as Bhagat Singh and Shivaji. The third floor is dedicated to great women of India's legends and recent history. The fourth floor is the shrine of Indian saints from various religions. The fifth floor is the assembly hall. The sixth floor contains the Shakti Shrine with various images of the goddess. The seventh floor is dedicated to Lord Vishnu with many examples of His forms. And the eighth floor is the Shiva Shrine with many images of Shiva and various gods and goddesses associated with him.

This temple is located along a road in the eastern part of Haridwar. The road has numerous temples that one can visit. There is one that is a replica of the Vaishno Devi temple, and has a route that you take in which you must cross water, crawl through caves and narrow passages before you finally reach the sanctum. Visiting it is said to equal the same merit as going to the real Vaishno Devi temple in Jammu. There are also a temple of mirrors nearby which has many deities with mirror thrones and Krishna and Arjuna on a chariot with horses, all made of colored mirrors.

One of the holiest places in Haridwar is Har-ki-Pauri, where all pilgrims come to bathe in the water of the Ganges. Some people believe that this is the spot where the celestial waters of the Ganges flow into the river. Therefore, the river is known as the Ganges from this spot onward. As the pilgrims bathe, they may hang onto chains or rails in the wall to stable them in the swift current. If they get carried away, there are also chains hanging from the bridge which they can try to grasp. Otherwise, the water can take them downstream a ways before they can reach a point of getting out of the river. The pilgrims come here first to bathe before going on the northern pilgrim tour of Char Dhama, the four major places farther north.

The Ganges at Har-ki-Pauri is actually a canal that channels the water to the side of the city. Imprints of Lord Vishnu's footprints are found on a wall under the water here. One of the priests can help you find them. There are many little shrines and temples here for Ganga devi, Haricharan and others. Every evening around six or seven PM you can see the *arati* ceremony to the Ganges as the priests offer large ghee lamps to the river while *kirtan* music goes on with banging hand cymbals and gongs. This is a major event and lots of people turn out to see it. It creates a very festive atmosphere every night. The southern end of this *ghat* is where people pour the ashes of their deceased ancestors into the Ganges so their existence becomes purified.

The most auspicious days to bathe here are the full and new moon days, plus Ekadasis, all solar and lunar eclipses, and the full moon during Kartika (Oct/Nov). The first day of Vaisaka (April/May) is also important because this is said to be the date when the Ganges first appeared here, and it also marks the beginning of the Hindu solar year.

The Kumbha Mela is a month-long festival that is very important and marks one of the most auspicious times to bathe here. It is held here every twelve years when the planet Jupiter is in Aquarius and the Sun enters Aries. This festival is, indeed, timeless and dates back thousands of years. The last one was in April/May of 1998. Over two million people attend the festival in Haridwar. After six years the Ardh Kumbha Mela is held, which is a much smaller festival. Other sacred bathing places include Neel Dhara at the main branch of the Ganges, and Gourikund, which is a small holy well.

Heading south from Har-ki-Pauri along the Ganges we'll reach Gau Ghat, where it is said that bathers can be purified of killing and eating a cow. Vishnu Ghat marks the spot where Lord Vishnu once bathed. About a half kilometer south of Har-ki-Pauri is Kushavarta Ghat, where Dattatreya did penance many years ago by standing on one leg for a thousand years.

About half a kilometer upstream from Har-ki-Pauri is Bhimagoda Kund, which is said to have been created by a blow from the knee of Bhima, one of the five Pandavas when he needed to provide water for his wife and brothers. Nearby is where we'll go to get a ricksha to Rishikesh, unless we take a bus.

About six km north of Haridwar on the banks of the Ganges is Sapta Rishi Ashram where the Ganges divided itself and created seven small islands so it would not displease the Seven Rishis who were meditating there at the time.

Haridwar is known for having many *ashramas* and places of study. But if you want to stay at an *ashrama* to study yoga or Hinduism, Rishikesh is much more pleasant. Haridwar is a nice place to visit to see the temples and holy sites, but it is also a big, noisy, and congested city.

Rishikesh, 24 kilometers away from Haridwar, is our next stop. With a population of 75,000, it is a smaller, quieter and fun place to go. It is a place in which you see the spiritual atmosphere and influence wherever you look. You will find good food, good water, clean air, a pleasant climate, plenty of temples, and many wandering *sadhus*, sages, and pilgrims. The town got its name from the time when Lord Hrishikesh, Vishnu, appeared here to grant *darshan* to Raibhya Rishi when he was performing austerities. The demons Madhu and Kaitabha were also killed here by Lord Vishnu.

One of the main temples is the Bharata Temple in the central part of town, dedicated to the Deity of Lord Narayana. This temple is only a half kilometer from

Triveni Ghat, the main bathing *ghat* in town. This *ghat* is said to be where the subterranean Yamuna and Sarasvati meet the Ganges. This is also where the *shraddha* ceremonies are made to the forefathers, and where the funeral pyres are made. North of the Bharata Temple beyond the Chandrabhaga River is the Balaji and Chandramouleswara Temple. The architecture is in the South Indian style and it is managed by the board of the famous Tirupati Temple in South India. The Shatrugna Temple, dedicated to the youngest brother of Lord Rama, is about four-and-a-half kilometers from downtown Rishikesh.

One of the nicer places to stay is in the Swargashrama area on the east bank of the Ganges across the Sivanand or Ram Jhula suspension bridge. There are some very pleasant temples here. The Divine Life Society is just north of the bridge and offers many facilities for the spiritual aspirant. Downstream a ways is the Maharishi Yogi Ashrama where the Beatles stayed for some time. However, it seems that if you don't have previous arrangements for visiting, the guard at the gate will not let you in. High on the side of a hill is the Kailashanand Shiva Temple, which has shrines on each of its several floors, and from where you can get some nice views over the town of Rishikesh. By the bridge is a small temple for Ganga Devi. You can watch the evening *arati* to the Ganges River here every evening around 6 or 7 PM. Another nice temple is the Parmath Temple. It is near the clock tower and has many diorama exhibits of the different incarnations of Krishna and Puranic legends. It has a lecture hall for Vedic discourses, spoken mostly in Hindi, and a variety of programs are held here attracting many pilgrims. It also has a nice central temple with a large Deity of Visvarupa, Lord Krishna's universal form, which is one of the few I've seen in India.

The area around the Ganges River has got some nice sandy beaches for swims in the cold river. Large boulders are scattered along the shore on which you can sit and be warmed by the sun, or sit in meditation at night. It can be a very mystical experience to sit near the flowing Ganges in these Himalayan foothills, under the stars and moon, especially as you see other sages also meditating in the twilight. There are also lots of nearby woods that you can walk through, and the days are warm and the nights are cool. The best place to eat is the open air Chotiwala Restaurant. However, it may be really crowded around noon, so nearby restaurants are also good. Wandering cows will walk by looking for a little food. You can see the children on the bridge throwing bits of food into the river feeding the schools of large fish, which you can see when the water is clear. There are rows of holy beggars along some of the lanes, and foreigners or tourists are not uncommon. In the evening you can see some of the wandering mendicants making a little cooking fire after they've taken whatever money they've received from their begging, and purchased vegetables to cook for their evening meal. Later, they will be rolled up in their cloth bedding to take rest for the night along the Ganges or on the steps near the temples or shops. You can also walk along and see old *sadhus* in their rooms near the Ganges, maybe sitting on their small bed, pictures of the deities on the wall, a few clothes hanging on a line, while they chant or read sacred books. Some of these old sages live permanently in Rishikesh, while others stay for a short while before continuing up into the mountains.

The Lakshmana Jhula area is only three kilometers upstream from Rishikesh, a pleasant walk away. This is where Lord Rama's brother, Lakshmana, performed penance, commemorated by the Lakshmana Temple. And Rishi Kund is said to be where Lord Rama and Lakshmana took bath to purify themselves from killing the demon Ravana, who was also a *brahmana*. There are some small old temples as well as large modern ones in this area. Also, you won't want to miss the seven storied temple with the diorama exhibits. Up in the hills about 12 kilometers away from the Lakshmana Jhula bridge is the Neela Kantha Mahadeva Temple. It's a four hour walk or a jeep ride up the hill.

From Rishikesh there are many important holy places we will want to visit, such as Badrinath, Gangotri (near the source of the Ganges), Kedarnath, and Yamunotri (near the source of the Yamuna River). This is called the "Char Dhama" or four shrines pilgrimage tour. There will be many other holy towns you will travel through and where you may want to stop. There are also seven holy rivers in this area, which include the Alakananda, Bhagirathi, Dhauli Ganga, Mandakini, Pinder Ganga, the Nagar, and others. These rivers form five important *sangams* or confluences where they meet. Some pilgrims bathe in all five *sangams* before having *darshan* at Badrinath.

The best way to travel to these places is to hire a taxi or car so you can go when and where you want, but this is expensive. The next best way to go is on a tour, of which there are several from which to choose. Otherwise, just take the regular buses as best you can. But be sure you make reservations the day before, usually no later than 4:15 PM, or you may be forced to deal with long lines of people the next day. The first bus of the day from Rishikesh leaves around 6:00 AM, but without a previous reservation the bus is likely to be filled by the time you arrive at the Yatra Bus Stand at 5:30 AM. So I stay at the Surichi Hotel across from the Yatra bus stand when I'm ready to travel north. That way I can purchase my bus ticket the evening before, and then simply walk to the bus the next morning.

Rishikesh and Haridwar have tourist companies which can arrange tours for your visits to the northern holy places. The GMVN complex is such a place in Rishikesh. The Nigam Tourist Office in Rishikesh can also make travel and accommodation arrangements for you, but do so several days in advance. There are several different tour packages from which to choose. Tours can also be arranged through the Garhwal Mandal Vikas Nigam Office in the Chandralok Building, 36 Janpath, Delhi. Before leaving on your tour, make sure you change all the money and travelers checks into rupees that you may need for the trip because most of the small towns that you will be visiting will have little facility for doing so.

The temples at the main places of interest, such as at Badrinath, open sometime during the last week of April to the first week of May, after consultations with astrologers and pundits. The opening is called the Akhand Jyoti Darshan. The temples stay open until the weather gets too severe, usually in the middle of November or by Diwali. Then the temples close for the season. The busiest time when most pilgrims visit this area is in May and June, and then again in September, which can create very crowded conditions when trying to find accommodations. The rainy season exists between the end of June to the beginning of September. During that period it can rain or get cold at any time, which can cause very muddy and uncomfortable conditions, and mud-slides and dangerous roads. By September, the hills are very lush and beautiful, which is why some people go at that time. At most times it is warm during the day and cool at night, but bring warm clothes and good walking shoes, especially if you plan to do any trekking to Gaumukh or other places.

Most pilgrims' priority is to at least visit Badrinath, but we will head to Yamunotri first. When we leave Rishikesh, the bus leaves at 6 AM and arrives at Hanuman Chatti at around 6 PM, a long bus ride. On the way, we will pass through such towns as Chamba (a small town on top of a hill, offering great views), Tehri (a dusty, dirty town I'd rather not have to go through, where they are building a large dam on the Ganges), Barkot, and then on to Hanuman Chatti. Then it's by foot through Kharshal and Janki-chatti before reaching Yamunotri.

Other towns that you may want to see, such as Dehra Dun or Mussoorie, you will have to take a separate bus to reach. Dehra Dun, population 367,000, is a large but pleasant city in a valley of the Siwalik mountains. The town has little to offer pilgrims compared to other places in the area, besides accommodations. It does have the Tapkeshwar Temple, dedicated to Shiva. Water from a nearby stream flows onto the *lingam* when it's not dried up. There is also the Lakshman Sidh Temple.

Dehra Dun is known mostly for the academies based there, such as the Indian Military Academy, Survey of India, and the private Doon School. There is also the Forest Research Institute, one of the best in the world. You can see the institute's six galleries of exhibits and its museum by taking a six-seater from the clock tower to the institute. The Wadia Institute of Himalayan Geology also has a museum of rocks and fossils.

Mussoorie, population 29,000, is a small but popular hill station. It's best attraction is simply its location, especially being high up in the hills where people can get away from the heat of the plains during summer. There are plenty of hotels in various price ranges for tourists. There is not that much to do here except relax and go for various walks or pony rides around the area that offer great views of the surrounding mountains and valleys.

One thing that you will have to get used to is how the buses going through the mountains get so close to the edge of the road, which often has a sheer 200 or 300 foot drop down to the bottom of the gorge. Parts of the roads are often wide enough for only one vehicle, in which case they will have to back up to the closest area that is wide enough for two vehicles to get around each other. This certainly adds to the time it takes for the journey, and to its questionable safety. One time I was on a bus that was met by three buses approaching from the opposite direction on a narrow, rebuilt section of road. So our bus had to back up. Abruptly, the people in the back of the bus started getting excited and began jumping for the door and out of the bus. Suddenly, I thought maybe I better jump off as well. The back of the bus looked like it was going over the side of the road. It would've been a long fall before the bus hit the side of the hill and rolled over until it landed in the river. Nonetheless, I stayed put, and soon everything was settled and the people started climbing back on the bus, and we were on our way again, though hearts pounding.

Going to Yamunotri, Hanuman Chatti is the end of the road. There is not much to see here in this small town. Most people simply stop to get accommodations, which are very basic, and then continue on to Yamunotri. The best place to stay is the Nigam Tourist Rest House, which is where you'll stay if you've booked a tour through their office. Otherwise it is often booked up. The rest of the places are dirty, some without water, and over-priced. If you do not care for Hanuman Chatti, then as soon as you arrive you can begin the three hour walk to Janki-chatti which is a nicer town with cleaner places to stay. But since you'll be walking, travel lite.

From Hanuman Chatti you reach Yamunotri by walking 14 kilometers, which takes a good five or six hours, so start early. It's a narrow uphill climb in most parts, which can be difficult, especially the last two or three kilometers to the top. It was too tough for me. I had to take a horse the last four kilometers up, and was very glad I did when I saw how steep the path can be. My legs were shot. The path can also be quite narrow in parts, hardly room for two horses to pass each other, with sheer drops of 200 or 300 feet straight down. However, the views are quite splendid. Even as I was walking back down the mountain, I'd pass by other people who were going up and who would ask me in a tired voice how much farther it was. I'd just try to be encouraging, however, I could tell that for some people the climb was difficult.

About halfway there, you'll pass by sulphur springs. You will also pass by Shiva Prayag, the confluence of the Nil Ganga and Yamuna rivers. Performing worship in the Shiva Temple here is said to rid one of bad astrological influences.

The legend is that Yamuna was born from the wedding of Surya, the Sun god, and Sanjana, the daughter of Vishvakarma, the architect of the demigods. There was once a time when Surya became hopelessly in love with Sanjana and after some assistance from the demigod Vayu, the ruler of the winds, and other demigods, Vishvakarma agreed to the wedding of Sanjana and Surya. From this was born Yamuna who was graceful like Sanjana and glorious like Surya. However, Yamuna wearied of Surya's intensity after some time and had Chhaya, her mythical river sister, take her place. Since then Yamuna has wandered through the mountains.

Yamunotri is considered to be where the sacred Yamuna River begins. The

Hanuman Ganga and Tons River also begin here, both of which join the Yamuna. Yamunotri is located on the western side of Bandarpoonch Mountain, which has a height of 6,315 meters, so it's always snow covered. Also, nearby is a hot spring at Kalinda Parvata. Next to the main temple is Surya Kund, the most sacred of the hot springs. You can watch the pilgrims drop small cloth bags of rice or potatoes in the boiling water and pull them up in a few minutes fully cooked. You can bathe in the Yamuna Bai Kund near the temple.

The main attraction at Yamunotri is, of course, the Yamunotri Temple, built in 1839 and dedicated to the goddess Yamuna. Inside the temple you'll find a black stone deity of Yamuna-devi and a white deity of Ganga-devi. Yamuna is the twin sister of Yamaraja, the lord of death. So if you bathe in her waters, it is said that you'll be freed from a painful death. But before worshiping in the Yamuna Temple, one is expected to visit the Dibya Shila next to it.

Although many pilgrims come to Yamunotri (3,185 meters above sea level), the actual source of the Yamuna River is at the Saptarishi Kund (4,421 meters above sea level). This is named as such because legend has it that the seven universal *rishis* performed austerities here in Satya-yuga. The *kund* is a glacial lake of dark blue water only about a half kilometer wide. However, there are six other *kunds* that are also located here. It takes a good 16 hours or more to go up to this lake and return. You have to make a 12 kilometer climb up hills and rocks, and walk through snow, ice and water, as well as deal with the high altitude. You will need a guide to help find your way and a day in Yamunotri to get used to the high altitude before going. Since it is so difficult to reach, few people visit Saptarishi Kund. But if you plan to go, do so without going on a bus tour, as the time you'll need will not be part of the tour schedule.

Once we are finished in Yamunotri, Gangotri is our next stop. You can take a 13 hour bus ride from Hanuman Chatti, which leaves at 5:30 AM. You can also take a 12 hour bus ride directly from Rishikesh. Be sure to make reservations the day before. Other buses leave later as they fill up.

One place that is out of the way as we go toward Gangotri is the place known as Dodital, considered to be where Lord Ganesha had appeared. It is a beautiful lake set in a lush forest with a temple nearby. It is said that it was here where Parvati bathed and created a boy from the dirt from her body. She then requested him not to let anyone approach while she was bathing. When Lord Shiva arrived, the boy blocked his way. Shiva, not knowing the boy was his son, cut off the boy's head. When Parvati heard what had happened, she became angry and explained the situation to Shiva. Shiva then told his associates to bring the head of the first living being they saw. So they went searching and brought back the head of an elephant. Shiva fixed it onto the boy's body, who thus became Ganesh.

Uttarkashi is another of the towns you will travel through, or even stop for the night if you take a late bus. Since it is a major stop-over place for pilgrims, there are many hotels here, but they tend to get booked up quickly, especially in the busy months of May and June. If you do stop here, the main temples to see are the

Visvanatha and Annapurna temples, similar to Varanasi, along with a temple for Parasurama. There is also a temple for Shakti, a Kali Temple, and the Ekadash Rudra Temple. Otherwise, there is not much of importance here.

Gangotri is a major place of pilgrimage and is famous for its temple to the goddess Gangadevi, the personality of the Ganges River. The present Gangotri Temple was built in the early 19th century by a Nepalese general, Amar Singh Thapa. It was severely damaged by an avalanche and was renovated a hundred years later by the Maharaja of Jaipur. About 50 feet left of the temple is the Bhagirathi Shila, the sacred stone where King Bhagiratha sat while worshiping Lord Shiva. He did this so Shiva would accept the force of the Ganges on his head from its descent from heaven to earth.

The reason why King Bhagiratha desired that the Ganges descend to earth was to purify the remains of the 60,000 sons of his great grandfather, King Sagar. What happened was that during Satya-yuga, King Sagar was going to perform an *ashvamedha-yajna* (a sacred horse ritual). This made the demigod Indra fearful that King Sagar may become more powerful than he. So Indra stole the horse and left it at the residence of Lord Kapila. King Sagar's 60,000 sons went to look for the horse and thought Kapiladeva stole it when they found it at his *ashrama*. Kapiladeva had been in deep meditation and when he was disturbed, he burned the 60,000 sons by the power of his glance. Only Asamanjas survived and went back to tell King Sagar what happened. Then the king's grandson, Asuman, returned to Kapiladeva and requested him to release the horse, which he did and explained that the king's sons could be saved if their remains could be bathed in the waters of the Ganges. But in order for this to happen, Gangadevi would have to descend from heaven to earth.

So King Bhagiratha pleased Gangadevi to descend, but she explained that the force of her water descending from the heavenly region would destroy the earth. Therefore, King Bhagiratha pleased Lord Shiva to accept the powerful force of the river on his head. Thus, the Ganges descended to earth and followed King Bhagiratha who cut a deep gorge in the earth with his chariot. This gorge went all the way to the Bay of Bengal at Ganga Sagar, the island where Lord Kapiladeva resided. There, the Ganges purified the remains of the 60,000 sons of King Sagar so they could return to the spiritual world.

It is said that the Pandavas also visited Gangotri to purify themselves of killing their relatives in the war of Kuruksetra. Now, because of King Bhagiratha, so many other pilgrims can also take advantage of the holy Ganga, and visiting Gangotri is considered a most auspicious event. Worship is performed inside the temple, and the *arati* ceremony is also performed outside the temple to the Ganges River in the evening.

Gangotri is a pleasant town and also caters to foreigners who wish to make the trek to Gaumukh, the actual source of the Ganges, which is called the Bhagirathi here. As the river runs by the town, it is extremely loud and powerful as it flows in a northerly direction. This is what gives Gangotri (Ganga going north) its name. It's a peaceful town and a nice place to stay for a few days. However, it can be crowded and most hotels, although quite basic, can be booked up early. The Kedar Ganga also flows into the Ganges here, and 100 yards below this confluence is the loud Sahasradhara Falls. From here the river squeezes into a gorge that is only about a meter wide, which shows how swift and powerful the river can be. Lord Shiva was supposed to have been sitting at this Sahasradhara Falls when the Ganges came down from heaven. That is why this is considered the beginning of the river, according to tradition. From here the water froze because of the high altitude and became the glacier that extended up into the mountains.

Although now the Ganges or Bhagirathi River starts from this glacier higher up in the mountains at Gaumukh, the glacier is said to have once extended all the way down to Gangotri many years ago. Even now the glacier is receding higher into the mountains. One lady mentioned that after visiting Gaumukh nearly 20 years ago, the glacier has receded by almost a whole kilometer already. Thus, it changes in appearance and location each year.

Gaumukh is the part of the glacier under which is the source of the Ganges. It is referred to as Gaumukh because it resembles a cow's face, and the ice cave from where the water rushes out resembles the mouth of a cow. The glacier is a wall of gray snow 328 feet tall. It spans an area of about 30 kilometers long by four kilometers wide, at an elevation of 14,000 feet. After the middle of October there is too much ice and snow for anyone to make the trek. Even without the snow it is not an easy climb.

It is 18 kilometers (though some now say 23) northeast from Gangotri to Gaumukh, the source of the Bhagirathi River. To reach Gaumukh you start by climbing the stairway up the hill by the temple that leads you to the path. Keep walking to Chirbasa, about eight kilometers out, which is nothing more than a little stop-over place with tea shops, tents, and mattresses. From here you take the path around a cliff face where the deterioration of the rock is blamed for a number of accidents. So you must be careful. After this, the path leads to a mountain desert. Once you reach Bhojbasa you may prefer to spend the night. It is very basic with no electricity. Then from here it is about five more kilometers or two hours to Gaumukh. Towering over Gaumukh is the beautiful Shivling mountain, which summits at a height of 21,470 feet.

After reaching Gaumukh, you may explore the area for a few hours and then head back to Bhojbasa for the night. The next morning you can make the day's journey back to Gangotri. However, if you want to go farther than Gaumukh, Tapovan is another five kilometers, or four hours, away near Mount Shivling. It is a dangerous climb and you should have a guide, warm clothing, food, and a tent. The famous Mount Sumeru is a few kilometers from Tapovan.

From Gangotri, Kedarnath is the next major holy sight to see. A bus from Gangotri to Gourikund, where the road ends, takes at least a day to a day-and-a-half. On our way, we will pass through the town of Uttarkashi again.

Srinagar is another one of the towns we will travel through, which is good for an overnight stop if necessary. It is a small but bustling little town with a number of hotels. It does have the Kamleshwar Mahadeva Shiva Temple.

Rudra Prayag is the next important town and is where the Mandakini River from Kedarnath flows into the Alakananda River. The Rudranatha and Jagdambi Devi Temple is the main site here, and nearby is a place where Narada Muni performed austerities for spiritual development. Another small town, Agastmuni, a good distance up the road, is where the Agastya Muni Temple is and where he performed meditation.

Guptakashi, the next town, is where Lord Shiva had fled to live incognito and even turned himself into a bull to hide from the Pandavas who later found him there. This is why this place is called Guptakashi, which means "hidden Kashi." The Pandavas pursued Lord Shiva up to Kedarnath, where he gave up the disguise. There his bull hump became the *lingam*. The main temples here are for Ardhanareeswara (Gouri-Shankar) and Viswanath. In front of the Viswanath Temple is the Manikarnika Kund which has water flowing from the head of Ganesh (water said to be from Yamunotri) and the head of a cow (water from Gangotri). Other than this, this city is another overnight stop if you are on a late bus, since they close the road here when it gets dark.

Triyugi Narayana is another town about five kilometers off the main road from Sonaprayag before you reach Gaurikund. Legend has it that the marriage of Lord Shiva and Parvati happened here during Satya-yuga at Brahma Shila. Brahma acted as the priest and Parvati was given to Lord Shiva by her brother, Lord Narayana. The marriage ritual fire is said to have been kept burning for three *yugas*. Even today pilgrims can offer pieces of wood into the fire and take ashes as *prasada*, remnants from the ceremony.

The main temple, the Akhand Dhuni Temple, was built about 1200 years ago by Shankaracharya. Inside you'll find a silver Deity of Lord Narayana standing two feet tall with Lakshmi and Sarasvati at His sides. Outside the temple is a stone that marks the spot where the marriage of Shiva and Parvati took place. Nearby are four holy *kunds* or water tanks, namely the Vishnu Kund, Rudra Kund, Brahma Kund, and the Sarasvati Kund. From here we go back to Sonaprayag and on to Gaurikund.

Gaurikund is the last stop before Kedarnath. This is where you may want to stay while visiting Kedarnath. There are a number of hotels from which to choose. This is where Parvati, Gaurimata, was born and did penance for hundreds of years in order to marry Lord Shiva. The exact spot is said to be at Gaurikund, the hot sulphur spring where you can take a bath. Nearby is the Gauri Devi Temple.

Another significant temple not far away is the Sirkata Ganesh. This temple is said to mark the place where Lord Shiva beheaded his son Ganesh and gave him the elephant head, although other places claim the same significance. As related in the *Skanda Purana*, this was when Ganesh was guarding Parvati who was bathing in Gaurikund. Ganesh, having not met his father before, forbade Shiva from coming closer. Shiva did not recognize Ganesh as his son and became angry and cut off his head. Parvati learned what happened when she returned and requested Shiva to revive Ganesh with another head. Shiva went off and returned with the head of the first creature he saw, which was that of an elephant.

The *ashrama* of Vyasadeva's father, Parashara Muni, is also located 40 km down from Gauri Kund in one of the villages. There is a big statue of him there. You may have to ask the locals to find it if you are interested.

Kedarnatha, located along the Mandakini River, is a very significant place. The route to Kedarnath from Gaurikund, which is a steep incline of 14 kilometers, is dotted with small temples, forests, lush valleys, waterfalls, and colorful flowers. If you find that you cannot walk the whole distance, which may be likely after all the walking we've done. You can hire a horse to ride up. Over 100,000 pilgrims visit each year to have *darshan* in the temple dedicated to Lord Shiva as Kedareswara, one of the 12 *jyotirlingas*, or spontaneously manifested Shiva-*lingas*. The temple is a simple stone structure located in a rich grassy area and surrounded by towering, white mountains. Inside the temple, the walls are carved with fine detailed images. There is also a large image of Nandi, Shiva's bull carrier, in the hall. Inside the sanctum, you'll find a three-faced *linga*, which is about nine feet long, three feet high, and four feet wide. Here you can perform *puja*, worship, to it and even touch the *lingam* or massage it with ghee.

Other deities in the temple include Ganesh and Parvati in front of the altar door. Then there are Lord Krishna, the five Pandavas and their wife Draupadi, and their mother Kunti outside the second door. There is also a Lakshmi-Narayana Deity believed to have been installed by Shankaracharya.

The unusual shape of the Shiva-*linga* is because it represents the hump of the bull that Shiva turned into when the Pandavas found him at Guptakashi. Legend has it that the Pandavas wanted to purify themselves after the war at Kuruksetra and went to Kashi (Varanasi, the city of Lord Shiva) to find Shiva to ask for his blessings. After a while, the Pandavas found him at Guptakashi and Bhima recognized him even though he was disguised as a bull. Bhima grabbed his tail and the bull sank into the ground, leaving only the hump above ground. Shiva appeared before the Pandavas and instructed them to worship the hump. Thereafter, the temple was constructed and worship was begun and has continued to this day. However, when it gets too cold during winter, the priest from the Kedarnath Temple continues the worship of Sri Kedarnatha at the Okhimath Temple, which is farther south of Guptakashi. Okhimath also has temples of Shiva, Parvati, Usha Mandhata, and Aniruddha.

The Kedarnath Temple is busy, so the waiting time to go in may be long, two hours in the morning and maybe only 15 minutes in the afternoon or evening. The temple is believed to have been originally constructed by the Pandavas thousands of years ago and reconstructed by Shankaracharya in the eighth century.

Kedarnath is also noted for being the place where Shankaracharya attained *samadhi* around 820 AD, when he was barely 31 years of age. This is commemorated by the marble staff behind the temple that signifies the place where Shankaracharya left his body, although some people feel he left this world in Kanchipuram. This is another of those legends which seems to be shared by more than one place in India. Behind the temple is the Mahapanth Trail, or Gate to Heaven. This path is said to go north up to heaven, Swarga-rohini. Legend has it that this was the path the five Pandavas took after engaging in a big ceremony.

Visiting the Panch (Five) Kedar Temples

Along with the hump of Lord Shiva's body when he took the form of a bull, five other parts of his body also appeared in various places in the area. The Pandavas built temples in those spots as well. These places, altogether, are known as the Panch Kedars. These include the hump at Kedarnath, the arm at Tungnath, the face at Rudranath, the hair at Kalpeswara, and the navel at Madhyamaheswara.

To reach all of these places takes 14 days or so by making a long circular trek. There is a bus that leaves Gaurikund and will drop you off at access points so you can walk to the Panch Kedar Temples. But it's for the more serious minded pilgrims.

You start, of course, at Kedarnath. After your *darshan* at Kedarnath is complete you go to Okhimath and on to the village of Mansuna. From there it is a hefty 24 kilometer trek to Madhyamaheswara, while stopping at Ransi and Gondhar on the way. It is a small stone temple.

Farther down the road you get dropped off at Chopta to go to the highest temple in India, the Tungnath Temple at an elevation of 12,065 feet. It's a seven kilometer or four hour climb to reach this temple located on a stone pavement overlooking a cliff. All around it are the beautiful mountains of Neelkanth, Kedarnath, and Nanda Devi. Inside the temple are five silver faces that represent the five Pandavas. There are also images of Vyasadeva and Kalabhairava. Tungnath represents the arm of Shiva. Also nearby is a small Parvati temple.

Next we take a bus to the village of Helang, 14 kilometers south of Joshimath, to take the nine kilometer walk to the village of Urgam, and then a one-and-a-half kilometer walk to the Kalpeswara Temple. This is a rock temple inside a cave.

Now we take a bus to Gopeswara and then to Sagar, from which we take a 24 kilometer trek to Rudranath, the last of the Panch Kedar Temples. This temple represents Lord Shiva's face. The Rudraganga River is nearby, and there are good views of the surroundings below and the Trisul, Nanda Devi, and Parbat peaks.

* * *

Badrinath will be our next place of pilgrimage. From Kedarnatha we will take a bus south back to the main road at Rudraparayag, from where we will travel northeast up to Badrinath. On our way up, there are some significant towns we

will be passing through that you may want to stop and visit if you have the time.
Or you can wait and see them on your way back to Rishikesh after your visit to
Badrinath .

One of the first noteworthy towns we will see after leaving Rudraprayag is
Karna Prayag. This is where the Alakananda joins the Pinar Ganga, and where
Karna, the Pandavas' half-brother, performed austerities to please Surya, the
Sun-god, and Shiva. Another place much farther east of Karnaprayag is Ranikhet,
from which you can take a hefty hike through the hills to the cave of Babaji, a
master who used to live there and was mentioned by Paramahamsa Yogananda in
his book, *Autobiography of a Yogi.*

The next town, 21 kilometers farther up the road, is Nanda Prayag which has
the confluence of the Nandakini and Alakananda rivers. There is also a small
Gopalji, Krishna, temple here. Ravana is said to have performed austerities here,
and Nanda Maharaja, Krishna's father, held a great ceremony here. Also, as
described in the *Puranas*, Dushyantha married Shakunthala, and Kanva Rishi had
his *ashrama* in this location.

From here we'll continue on to Joshimath. This is a town that is nice to visit
for its spiritual significance. You may have to spend the night here anyway if you
take a late bus to Badrinath. They close the roads here in the evening until the
next morning. This is also where they establish one-way traffic to Badrinatha. So
you may have to wait a while as they stop traffic to allow all buses and cars to
leave the road from Badrinatha before the long line of buses start from Joshimath.

Joshimath is significant for being the place where Shankaracharya established
one of his four original centers. He also attained enlightenment while meditating
in a cave about 1200 years ago under the Kalpavriksha (wish-fulfilling) tree. This
is where he got his realizations to write and defeat Buddhism and reestablish
Vedic authority. Thereafter, Shankaracharya wrote his *Shankara Bhasya* here. The
present Shankaracharya Math and temple is on a ridge above the town. You can
find the cave where he meditated by entering the temple and following the signs.
Plus, the Kalpavriksha tree is located up the stairs to the right of the temple
entrance. This tree is said to be over 2400 years old and is 125 feet tall with an
enormous trunk.

Another significant point about this place is the Temple of Lord
Narasimhadeva, located in the lower part of town and over 1200 years old. The
Deity self-manifested from a *shalagram-shila* stone. He sits in a lotus position and
is about ten inches tall and is very detailed. To the right are Deities of Sita-Rama,
Hanuman, and Garuda. On another altar to the right are deities of Kubera,
Uddhava, and Badri Vishal. On the left wall is a deity of goddess Kali in her form
as Chandika. And a deity of Lakshmi is found outside the temple door.

Shankaracharya is supposed to have originally installed this Narasimha
Shalagram. This means that in spite of his spreading an impersonalist philosophy
to curb Buddhism in his day, he was very much a *bhakta*, a Vaishnava devoted to
the personal form of the Supreme.

Another important point about the Lord Narasimhadeva Deity is that the wrist is very thin and continuously getting thinner. You can get a good look at the wrist when the Deity is being bathed between 7:30 and 8:30 AM. It is said that the hand will finally break off the Deity when the dark qualities of the age of Kali overcome the world. At that time, the nearby mountains of Jaya and Vijaya (appropriately named after the two guardians of the spiritual domain) near Vishnu Prayag will crumble and block the road leading to Badrinath. Then Bhavishya Badri, about 23 kilometers southeast of Joshimath, will become the new Badrinath. This is a sign of the disappearance of spiritual culture in India as we have already described in our previous volume, *The Vedic Prophecies: A New Look Into the Future*.

One other important point about this temple is that the priests of Badrinath come here to continue their worship at the Narasimha Temple when Badrinath closes during winter.

Only thirty yards away from the Narasimha Temple is the Vasudeva Temple. This has a six foot tall, black stone Deity of Lord Vasudeva, Krishna. He stands with Sri Bhu (the personality of Mother Earth), Nila, and Kama. There is also a rare image of dancing Ganesh, considered to be only one of two in all of India. This temple is extremely old, no one knows how old, and is considered to be one of the 108 (Divya Desams) most important Vishnu temples in India.

The next town 10 kilometers farther up is Vishnuprayag. This is where the confluence is for the Alakananda and Dhauli Ganga rivers.

Another 10 kilometers farther up the road is Govind Ghat. If you're interested in seeing the Valley of Flowers, especially when it is in bloom after the rainy season, or in visiting Hemkund, this is where you start the trek into that region.

Hemakund is another place of pilgrimage for Hindus and Sikhs. This place is mentioned in the holy *Granth*, the Sikh scripture, as being where Guru Govind Singh meditated on the shores of a lake surrounded by seven snow-covered peaks. The water in the lake is clear and beautiful, and it is full of lotus flowers. You can reach it from Govind Ghat and by making a 20 kilometer trek east. This is also where you will find Ghangaria and the Valley of Flowers. The last five kilometers are most difficult, so dress warm and wear good walking shoes. The Sikh Gurudwara is next to the lake.

The next town is Pandukeswara known for the site of the Yogadhyan Badri Temple. This is one of the Badri temples, which I'll explain shortly. Here is also where the priests of Badrinath bring the Deity of Badri Vishal during the winter.

Hanuman Chatti (different from the town of the same name near Yamunotri) is nine kilometers farther away. This area is significant because it was here in the Gandhamadhana Hills where Bhima of the Pandavas met Hanuman. While traveling on the road, Bhima met a very old monkey whose tail was in his way. Bhima asked if the monkey would move his tail, but the monkey replied that he did not have enough energy to do it, so Bhima could try if he liked. Bhima tried several times but could not move the monkey's tail. Then the monkey revealed himself to be Hanuman. Thus, Hanuman and Bhima realized they were brothers since they were both sons of Vayu. This area is also noted for being where Hanuman meditated and pleased Lord Badrinath.

Now, another 15 kilometers farther away (35 km from Joshimath), we come to the holy town of Badrinath, or Badarikashrama, one of the most important places of pilgrimage in India. The present temple is about 400 years old, although the site goes back thousands of years. The *Skanda Purana* even mentions that it is one of the most sacred shrines even amongst all the shrines in heaven or hell. It is considered (in *Srimad-Bhagavatam* 3.4.22) the residence of the Supreme Being in His incarnation as the sages Nara-Narayana. It is also the *ashrama* of the compiler of the Vedic literature, Srila Vyasadeva. Such great devotees as Uddhava visited this place 5,000 years ago under the direction of Lord Krishna (*Bhagavatam* 11.29.44) so that he might purify himself by bathing in the holy waters there which emanated from Krishna's holy feet.

Badrinath is also known as "Narada Kshetram" because the sage Narada Muni attained liberation here in five days. Others who have visited include the great sages Gautama Rishi, Kapiladeva, Kashyapa Muni, and Shankaracharya who installed a temple here around 1200 years ago. This temple is the Jyotir Mutt, one of the five original temples he started. It has images of Adi Shankar and a Crystal *lingam* that he worshiped. Also, great spiritual masters such as Ramanujacarya visited 955 years ago, and Madhavacharya visited a few times nearly 735 years ago. Also, Lord Nityananda visited on His tour of the holy places 500 years ago. And today up to nearly 2000 pilgrims visit Badrinath every day.

One reason for this is because it is considered to be one of the eight Svayam Vyakta Kshetras in India, or places where the spiritual realm manifests on earth. It is also one of the four holy *dhamas*, which include Ramesvaram, Jagannatha Puri, and Dwaraka, where pilgrims visit for spiritual merit and enlightenment. Badri is also the name of Maha-Lakshmi's favorite tree, the Ilandai.

The temple of Badrinatha is located across the Alakananda River. To enter the temple, you wait in the long line in front of the temple before going into the *darshan* hall. The *darshan* hall is where the ceremonies are conducted, but which can accommodate only 15 to 20 people at a time. When it is your turn to enter the *garbha griha* area, you can see the Deity of Lord Badrinath. He is a black stone Deity sitting in the lotus position, meditating, covered with silks and jewelry, barely visible. To the right is His devotee Uddhava. Farther right are Nara and Narayana. Kneeling in front on the right is Narada Muni. Kneeling on the left is Garuda, His carrier. On the left side of Badrinath is Kubera, the treasurer of the demigods, and a silver Ganesh. Hanging over the Deities is a canopy covered with a sheet of pure gold. Outside the sanctum, there is also a shrine to Lakshmi on the left of the main temple which is painted red. Outside the exit door you'll find the sitting place of Shankaracharya. Around the courtyard of the temple are other shrines that you will see. Simply by accepting the *charanamrita* or bathing water of the Deity and circumambulating the temple, it is said one will get the merit of performing an *ashvamedha* ritual.

The most auspicious time to have *darshan* of Lord Badrinath is in the early morning, so you can expect it to be crowded. The temple opens at 6:30 AM and closes between 1:00 PM and 3:00 PM, and then closes for the day at 9:00 PM. Since only a few people at a time can see the Deity, there is a long waiting line all the time, but shorter in the afternoon than in the morning when it can take an hour or two to see the Deity.

The Deity of Badrinath is also called Badarinarayana or Badri Vishal, and is said to be self-manifested from a *shalagrama-shila* stone that was two feet tall. When Buddhism was in its prime, the Deity somehow was thrown into the Narada Kund for several years. Later, Shankaracharya recovered the Deity and reinstalled Him. This small Narada Kund is found a few feet from the Alakananda River, and bathing in it is considered auspicious, especially before having *darshan* of Lord Badrinath. Another hot spring pilgrims use is the Tapta Kund near the temple steps. It has a temperature of about 45 degrees centigrade (115 degrees Fahrenheit). Nearby are the Panch (Five) Shila or rocks that represent Narada, Narasimha, Varaha, Garuda, and Markandeya.

A little upstream along the Alakananda River is Brahma Kapal Ghat. This is where many people offer *pinda* to their ancestors in a *shraddha* ceremony. Local priests are ready to assist you. The name of the *ghat* comes from the time when Lord Shiva cut off Lord Brahma's fifth head (Brahma Kapal) which fell here.

A place called Deva Darshini is where the *devas* or demigods come to have *darshan* of Badrinath. You can reach it by making a climb 600 feet up.

It is also said that Narada Muni and the demigods come here during the winter months to continue the worship of Badrinath when the other priests leave for the winter and go to Joshimath. In the middle of November the priests perform one last *puja*, leave the ghee lamps lit, and close the temple. Then in May they return, open the temple, and the ghee lamps are still burning, thanks to the demigods.

There are other noteworthy places in the area. There is also a temple to the beautiful Apsara Urvasi where she took away Indra's pride. And there is a boulder at Charanpaduka, two kilometers away, that has the footprints of Lord Vishnu. This is where He stepped when He once descended to earth. The temple to the mother of Nara and Narayana, Mata Murti, is near Keshava Prayag. Near here is also Maninag Parvat mountain, where Yudhisthira answered the *yaksha's* riddles as described in the *Mahabharata*.

You will also see many beautiful mountains surrounding the area. Across from the temple is the mountain Nara Parvata, behind the temple is Narayana Parvata, and to the left of that is Neelkantha, which rises almost 22,000 feet.

An interesting and large stone you might see or ask about is the Sesha Netra which has one eye of Ananta Sesha on it, who is said to be watching everyone.

About four kilometers past Badrinath, taking the path past Brahma Kapal, is the village called Mana. A little beyond the town is the Bridge of Bhima (Bhima Pul) which is a huge stone slab Bhima used so Draupadi and his brothers could easily cross the Sarasvati River. From there you can see the foaming milk-white water flowing out of a cave. This is the Sarasvati River, though not the original, which begins at a glacier north of Mana. The Sarasvati flows out of the cave a short distance to join the Alakananda at Keshava Prayag.

Above the town a few steep kilometers away is the place of Vyasadeva's cave, which is painted white and red in front but is dark inside. It contains a dark stone Deity of Vyasadeva. You can certainly feel the energy in this cave as you sit here and meditate on the greatness of Vyasadeva and his writings. Many say that Srila Vyasadeva still lives here.

Not far away is Ganesh's cave. This is where Vyasadeva narrated to Ganesh the *Mahabharata* and *Srimad-Bhagavatam*. There are rocks that look like piles of papers that represent Ganesh's work of writing Vyasadeva's narrations. However, there are others who say that Vyasadeva wrote the *Mahabharata*, along with the *Vedas*, *Upanishads*, and some of the *Puranas* on the banks of the Sarasvati River where it flowed through Kuruksetra. The caves of Bhima and Mucukunda are located above Vyasadeva's cave. Nearby is said to be where Lord Shiva narrated the *Skanda Purana* to the sage Skanda.

Unfortunately, Mana is near the border of China, only 48 kilometers away, so it is a restricted area to foreigners who may need permission to visit Mana. When I went, I was met by a military man who simply asked me to come to a small cabin to have an officer ask me some questions and write down my passport number. It was all very cordial and only took a few minutes and I was again on my way.

Beyond Mana is Vasudhara Falls and Satopanth Lake. Take the path and walk across the flowering meadow and about three kilometers farther out you'll arrive at Vasudhara Falls, which is 135 feet high. The path is not so easy until you reach the source of the Alakananda near the Bhagirath Kharak and Satopanth glaciers. Keep going across the Chakra-tirtha meadow. This is near where Arjuna bathed and received the Pashupati Astra weapon from Lord Shiva, which he used in defeating the Kauravas. Finally, over the steep glacier, you'll reach Satopanth Lake, 25 kilometers from Badrinath. This lake is called the Lake of Divine Trinity and at each of the three corners is where Lord Vishnu, Shiva, and Brahma meditate beside the crystal clear water. Lord Vishnu bathes in this lake on Ekadashi days. Here you are surrounded by the mountains of Neelkanth, Chaukhamba, and Swargarohini. The Swargarohan Mountain is also called the Stairway to Heaven because it is believed that the Pandavas ascended to the spiritual world while climbing this mountain, as described in the *Mahabharata*.

As with any mountain town, the weather here can be very unpredictable. I arrived at night while it was cold and rainy. The next morning it became bright and sunny, but the clouds came in and it was snowing by noon. A few hours later it was sunny and warm again. So be prepared for the way the weather changes.

The Five Badri Temples

After we have completed our tour of Badrinath we can begin to head back to Haridwar, but for some of the serious pilgrims, they may want to see the other Badri temples. Actually, there are five Badri temples scattered about in different places, which the serious pilgrim can see on his way back. The main temple is, of course, the Badri Vishal Temple at Badrinath. Then there are the additional temples known as the Adi Badri, Vriddha Badri, Bhavishya Badri, and the Yogadhyan Badri. Naturally, these temples are not as popular but some of the serious pilgrims visit them nonetheless. And some are easier to get to than others. For example, Yogadhyan Badri is in the town of Pandukeswara, 24 kilometers south of Badrinath. This is also the town where the Pandavas were born and where King Pandu did austerities for killing two mating deer who were actually two sages. King Pandu installed the bronze Yogadhyan Badri here.

The Vridha (or Bridha) Badri Temple is in the little village of Animath, about 17 kilometers south of Joshimath. Vridha Badri appeared to Narada Muni when he performed penance here.

Bhavishya Badri is situated in the little village of Subhain, a three kilometer walk east of Tapovan, which is 15 kilometers or so east of Joshimath. This will be the main Badri temple in the future.

The Adi Badri Temple is the farthest away, located 18 kilometers south of Karna Prayag. Inside a small 16 temple complex, the main temple contains Adi Badri Narayana, a black stone Deity that is three feet tall. In His hands He holds a mace, disc, and lotus. Another place in the Badrinatha region is Dhudi Prayag, where the Pundavati River flows into the Alakananda. This is another place known as the birthplace of Ganesh.

* * *

On our way back to Rishikesh, another town to take note of is Deva Prayag (or Deoprayag). This is the first major town northeast of Rishikesh by about 70 kilometers and around 32 km southwest of Srinagar. It is where the confluence of the Bhagirathi and Alakananda rivers is located. This is where the river becomes the Ganges, at least in name. This is a very important *sangam* or confluence, second only to Allahabad where the Yamuna, Ganges, and Sarasvati meet. At Deva Prayag, in Treta-yuga, Lord Rama and Lakshmana performed a *yajna*, spiritual ritual, here to purify themselves of killing the demon Ravana because he was a *brahmana*. You'll find an old Raghunatha Temple here, erected about 1250 years ago. It has a Deity of Sri Rama that is 15 feet tall. It is considered one of the Divya Desams, or one of the 108 most important temples in India. You can also see Vamana's cave, which is behind the temple and up the hill a ways. And there is also the stone throne of Lord Rama not far away.

Once we are finished with our tour of the Char Dham region, and have returned to Rishikesh, we can take a direct bus to Chandigarh. There we can decide which route we will take next. It is easy to take a direct bus from Chandigarh to Amritsar for a visit.

On our way to Amritsar, however, or while we are in the area, we may want to take a side trip to the city of Hoshiarpur. This is where the *Bhrigu Samhita* is located. This is the great astrological text, said to have been written by Bhrigu Muni, the authority on Vedic astrology. This edition is said to have been written about 5,000 years ago and is now kept by the Bhrigus there. Presently, it is a 500 year old manuscript discovered in 1923 by Des Raj, grandfather of the Bhrigu Shastris. They are known to have everyone's horoscope kept on parchment, which can be looked up if you can visit them. However, the search may take years. One such reader that you may contact in Hoshiarpur is Sneha Amritananda. Her phone number is 1882-22122. She may be able to give you a reading or additional information, but call in advance.

By taking an early morning bus, we'll arrive in Amritsar about six hours later. There are plenty of hotels near the train station, which is fine since we will be leaving Amritsar by train. I got one on the hill to the east of the station, an easy cycle-ricksha ride away. When we are ready, we can take a 15 minute cycle-ricksha ride through the town to the Sikh Golden Temple, our main point of interest. Amritsar is a good sized town, and there are many stores and pedestrians in the downtown area.

As we approach the Golden Temple complex, we first see a huge white building with a clock tower in the middle. We first go to the shoe minder's stall to leave our shoes, and then we proceed after covering our head with a hat or cloth. The head must be kept covered inside the temple complex. Outside the complex are many small shops that sell all sorts of Sikh religious paraphernalia and books. The temple also has a museum upstairs in the clock tower, and the temple also provides free vegetarian food from its large kitchen. Free accommodations to all pilgrims who need it are also available. If you want, you can get a guide at the information office by the clock tower. Then, entering under the eastern clock tower, the stairways lead down to the large courtyard.

Amritsar, population 710,000, was developed in 1577 by the fourth Sikh guru, Ram Das. The name "Amritsar," or Amrita Sarovara, means the "Pool of Nectar," which is the sacred pool in the middle of the temple courtyard. After the pool was established, it was Ram Das' son, Arjun Dev, who built a temple in the middle of the pool in the late 16th century. He also installed the Sikh scripture in it, the *Adi Granth Sahib*. The *Granth* is a collection of verses and songs by revered saints, such as Ramananda, Namdev, Kabir, Nanak, etc., that Arjun Dev had compiled. It was Gobind Singh, the 10th Sikh guru, who established the principle that there would be no more successor gurus, but the *Granth* would be the guru.

As you circle the inner courtyard, going in a clockwise direction, there is a colonnade where there are many rooms where people can stay or rest. Next to the lake, the walkways are made of marble tiles. Along the east side of the tank is the area of 68 holy places that Arjun Dev established as being equal to the 68 most holy places of the Hindus. On the south side are chains that lead into the lake so that the men can lower themselves into the water for a holy bath, which is done especially in the morning. As you continue to go around the lake, there are a few special trees and shrines, but the explanations are written in Hindi. On the northwest side of the pool is the Jubi tree, under which Baba Gujhaji, the temple High Priest, sat 450 years ago and oversaw the construction of the temple. Presently, the tree is believed to have powers to grant sons to women who hang strips of cloth from it.

While I was walking, one very nice Sikh man and his wife came up and explained that one tree we were standing near on the east side of the lake was in remembrance of the second Sikh guru. He had lived in a village and when Guru Nanak asked who he was, the boy replied, "I am the Dead One." His mother called him that because all of her sons had died young and he would probably die young as well. Then Guru Nanak blessed him and said, "Don't worry, now you will become the Old One." So later he became Guru Nanak's successor and lived to be 130 years old, long enough to see the fourth Sikh Guru.

The man went on to explain some of the tenets of Sikhism, most of which I already knew. He said that the basic principle of Sikhism is unity with God and universal brotherhood. They pray for health and prosperity, but not just for themselves or their community or other Sikhs, but for all people.

He continued to explain that there are four entrances into the Amrit Sarovara Lake and the Golden Temple itself. These represent the openness of Sikhism to all people of the four directions. There are also two temples: The central temple in the lake is for spiritual direction, while the temple on the land represents material instructions. It is by this unity of material and spiritual instructions that one can reach perfection in life and service to God and to humanity. The man went on to say that Sikhism is a world-wide community and since I was there at the Golden Temple, that meant I was also a member of their community. The man pleasantly pointed out that though we may be from different countries, because we were both at the Golden Temple, we were both brothers in spirit. And I firmly agree.

After circling the courtyard, it is time to enter the temple. The Golden Temple is called Hari Mandir, or Temple of the Lord. In 1761 the temple was destroyed by Ahmad Shah Durani. It was rebuilt in 1764 and then was roofed with copper-gilded plates by Ranjit Singh. Thereafter, it became known as the "Golden Temple." The dome of the temple is covered with 220 pounds of gold leaf. The temple is reached by a causeway called the Guru's Bridge. You can take photos most everywhere except in the temple.

Walking out to the temple, the Guru's Bridge is a beautiful walkway with brass railings. On the temple structure itself, the lower parts of the marble walls have beautiful inlaid flowers and designs, and the upper portion is plated. The temple also has beautiful embellished gold plates and doors. The first time I was there they were in the process of replacing the golden plates on the temple, which were about 250 years old. I returned a few years later when the renovations had been completed, and it is indeed a most beautiful building. Upon entering the temple, you can take a handful of halava that they give out, or take a handful when you walk back across the bridge. Inside you can see it's wonderful design and interior. It is quite exquisite. Pilgrims are always walking through and then exiting in the back or side doors and then walk back across the bridge again when they are finished. The original *Granth* scripture is kept under a jeweled pink cloth on a decorated throne. To the left are several musicians playing and singing the verses of the *Granth* with harmonium, *karatala* hand cymbals, etc. This *kirtana* singing continuously goes out over the loudspeakers and helps produce a very devotional atmosphere. On the right side of the temple interior is an area where some people sit and listen. The top floor is the Hall of Mirrors where the Sikh gurus used to sit.

At night around 10 PM the *Granth* is ceremoniously taken from the temple to the Akal Takhat building where it spends the night. It is again returned to the temple in a short procession at 4 AM (5 AM in winter). If you are there at the time, you can watch the proceedings.

South of the temple complex is the temple gardens that cover 30 acres. The eight-storied tower of Babl-Atal, dedicated to Atal Rai, the son of Hargobind, the sixth guru, is at the southern end.

In spite of all the political turbulence that has gone on here over the years, the Sikhs are generally very friendly people and more than willing to share their culture with visitors. I actually had a very nice time on both occasions that I had visited the Golden Temple and met some very friendly people who liked showing me around. It is also an example of a very open and devotional community.

The Golden Temple is a beautiful place and has a calm and meditative atmosphere. It is especially peaceful at night when you can sit underneath the stars and listen to the soothing recitations of the *Granth* over the loudspeakers next to the pool, which reflects the image of the brightly lit temple on the surface. I will never forget that experience during which I had some very strong realizations in my own meditations. Other Sikhs will be observing prayers at that time, and even if you are not sure of what is happening, you are more than always welcome.

Not far from the Golden Temple is Jallianwala Bagh, the site where the British opened fire on a crowd of men, women, and children and killed some 2,000 Indians, including Hindu, Muslims, and Sikhs. This incident was a turning point in India's struggle for independence. You can still see the bullet holes in the well into which people jumped trying to escape the bullets.

Also, not far away is the Durgiana Temple. It is also in the middle of a small lake and reached by a bridge. As you enter the gateway leading to the Durgiana Temple, there are two small altars, one on either side. One is for Ganesh and one for Durga, both of which are quite beautiful. Then you walk over the bridge out to the temple, which appears simple on the outside but is highly decorated on the inside. It has beautifully embossed silver plated doors with images of demigods and Puranic legends. There are many paintings and illustrations done in multicolored mirrors and lights and ribbons that hang throughout. It has three altars for the beautiful Deities. One is for Radha-Krishna and a Govardhan-*shila* which sits on top of a male body, the only one I've ever seen like this. The center altar is for Lakshmi-Narayana, and the third altar is for Sita-Rama, Lakshmana and Hanuman.

A short distance away from Amritsar, about 11 kilometers to the northwest, is Ram Tirtha Sarovara. This is a large sacred tank said to be dug by Hanuman. Valmiki is said to have had his *ashrama* here and was cured of leprosy by Rishi Chavan Prash by bathing in the waters. It is also said that Sita gave birth here to the sons of Lord Ramachandra, Kush and Luv.

Leaving Amritsar, I got up early to catch the 5:15 AM train to Pathankot, but this didn't leave until 6:30 AM. This meant a lot of waiting around, which is not unusual while traveling in India. It can also take a lot of energy doing this kind of traveling, but once you arrive at these holy places it can be very exhilarating and rewarding.

This train provides a slow ride, stopping every ten minutes at every village. All you can do is sit back, relax, and watch the scenery and your fellow travelers. The train got to Pathankot around 10:00 AM. We quickly get a cycle-ricksha and make it to the bus stop before the bus is filled up. Once the bus is full, we are off and rolling by 10:15 AM. Soon we can begin to see the snow-capped mountains in the distance. Towards the end of this four hour long drive, we really start climbing up into the hills, and by 2:00 PM we arrive at the bus station at the southern end of Dharamsala.

If, however, you come up to Dharamsala directly from Ambala, there are some other pilgrimage towns you may travel through which you may want to stop at to see. Or you can visit these towns later after arriving in Dharamsala if you prefer. They include the following:

Kangra, 18 kilometers south of Dharamsala, is known for its famous Bajreshwari Devi Temple. This used to be a fabulously wealthy temple. Then in 1009 the notorious Mahmud of Ghazni stole a huge fortune in gold, silver, and jewels. Then Tughlag plundered it again in 1360. In fact, it was paved in plates of silver during Jehangir's reign. But the earthquake of 1905 destroyed it, and it has been rebuilt as we see it today.

Many people still visit this temple. To reach it you will walk through narrow lanes filled with vendors selling many types of religious paraphernalia. Just follow these lanes until you reach the temple. Leave your shoes at a stall across the street and then go down the stairs and through the gates and you enter the courtyard with the temple in the center. You get in line with the rest of the pilgrims. When you finally have *darshan* you'll see the small altar of silver with multiple silver umbrellas hanging over the deity of the goddess. The deity, basically, is a small flat stone, the diameter about the size of a fist with eyes made of conchshells. A bright cloth and silver jewelry are draped around her. Behind the main deity are regular brass images of goddess Durga riding her lion carrier. Many pilgrims come through and offer sweets, flowers, and incense for the temple priests to offer to the deity. The priests in turn give some of it out as *prasada*.

Around the perimeter of the courtyard are offices, intermittent diorama exhibits, and a few other shrines. In the back and through the gate and down another stairway is a small shrine with a *lingam* in the center.

Masrur, 15 kilometers south of Kangra, has 15 carved rock-cut temples similar to the large rock carved temples in Ellora, one of which has a stalagmite that is worshiped as a natural representation of Lord Shiva. These temples are ornately detailed in the Indo-Aryan style, although partly ruined.

Another pilgrimage site is the Jawalamukhi Temple, 34 kilometers directly south of Kangra. It is famous for its eternally burning flame that is in the rock sanctum. And Baijnath, 51 kilometers southeast of Dharamsala, 16 kilometers from Palampur, is known for its old Shiva temple that dates back to 804 A.D.

Once our bus arrives at Dharamsala, take the stairway up the hill and you'll be right in the heart of town. With a population of 26,000, it is another small but nice place to visit, especially to get away from the heat of the Indian plains in summer. There are plenty of small hotels to choose from in various price ranges. I settled on one hotel that was O.K. for 130 rupees a night. It had small rooms with attached bath and a little balcony that provided a wonderful view of the mountains above and the plains below.

Some people prefer to stay at Dharamsala where it is a little warmer at night than the colder McLeod Ganj farther up the hill. The weather can be very unpredictable at times. It can be pleasant one minute and then turn cloudy and rainy at any time. I also overheard a girl monk, a Westerner, talk of finding three or four scorpions in her room at the Tushita Buddhist retreat center, which is up in the woods above McLeod Ganj. This surprised me that there would be scorpions even at this altitude and in this cool climate, and this was in the month of March.

As we wander around the town, there are lots of small shops selling all kinds of things, from clothes, household goods, great Indian sweets, touring packages, and also vegetable and fruit markets. It's also easy to get bottled water here.

On sunny days the weather is great, the air is cool and the sun is warm which provides a great atmosphere for taking long walks. And there are plenty of hills and paths to explore farther up, especially from McLeod Ganj. You can take the roads up into the hills or take the trails. On the northern end of town you can take the path that cuts through the woods for a short-cut up to McLeod Ganj. It avoids most of the winding roads and joins the street only a short distance from the Central Tibetan Administration (C.T.A.) offices. This is a complex just off the road half way between Dharamsala and McLeod Ganj that takes care of many kinds of Tibetan affairs inside India as well as outside. It was established in 1960 soon after His Holiness the Dalai Lama escaped to India in 1959. Its main focus is to work towards the Tibetan people's struggle for independence and survival. They function according to the Charter of Tibetans in Exile, which is a constitution based on modern democratic principles.

There are departments of Religion and Culture, Education, Finance, Information and International Relations, Security, Health, and so on. It also has the Library of Tibetan Works and Archives where you can find out about classes in Tibetan Buddhism and meditation that are given by noted Lamas. These are especially popular when His Holiness the Dalai Lama conducts some of the classes in March. It is also where foreign students can enroll for courses or pick up their mail. Sometimes in the backyard behind a building across from the library you can see the monks practice their debates with one another.

As we leave the C.T.A. complex, the main building near the driveway by the entrance is where you can get "A Guide to Little Lhasa in India," which is a small but very good and authoritative guide to Dharamsala and especially the McLeod Ganj area. The maps also show the many trails you can take for long walks in the hills and through the woods. This is a great adventure to see the countryside and the many little houses and retreats in the area. You could literally disappear from the world in this place.

From the C.T.A. complex we can continue up the road or we can backtrack a little to another path which cuts through the woods and takes us to a Buddhist shrine that has thousands of prayer flags flapping in the wind as they hang from high lines. This is located on the southern perimeter of the Lingkhor footpath which the Tibetans use to circumambulate the residence of the Dalai Lama. I believe this shrine is the Lhagyal-ri (Lhasol Ground) where the Tibetans perform their rituals and say their prayers to the protecting and guardian deities. It is a very quiet place and you can stay for a bit and watch as old Tibetan men and women alike walk by, chanting on their beads and turning the many prayer wheels you'll find here.

Around the path to the right of the shrine are many boulders with prayers and *mantras* painted on them. The scene is as if it was taken out of a page of history from Tibet itself. Moving on to the left you may see a little shack with an old Tibetan who carves the names of patrons on to slate rocks, for a small fee, which are then placed along the route to this shrine.

Farther along the trail, the property on our right is securely fenced off. This is the area of the Dalai Lama's residence. It was here where he came when he fled Tibet, and the Indian government set this area, as well as a number of other areas throughout India, as a place for Tibetan refugees. Farther along we come to the Namgyal Monastery and the Tsuglagkhang (Central Cathedral) which is the focus of cultural and spiritual life in Dharamsala. There are many monks who study here, and the Tantric college still performs rituals for and with the Dalai Lama. The Namgyal Monastery was originally founded by the Third Dalai Lama in the 16th century in Lhasa, and now, along with the Tsuglagkhang, has been reestablished during the exile here at McLeod Ganj.

The Tsuglagkhang Cathedral is a plain building, especially compared to the one in Lhasa, but it is nevertheless quite functional. You'll often see at least a few monks inside sitting and chanting from the texts. The Cathedral houses three important images. These are Sakyamuni Buddha, Padmasambhava, and Avalokiteshvara, the Buddha of compassion of whom the Dalai Lama is the recent incarnation. The central image is Sakyamuni Buddha which measures three meters high and is made of gilded bronze. The altar and image are very colorful.

The story of this particular image of Avalokiteshvara is quite moving. In the seventh century Songsten Gampo built and installed the jewel-encrusted image in the Lhasa Central Cathedral. It had become a major object of devotion for people throughout Central Asia. However, during the Cultural revolution, the Chinese Red Guards came and ransacked the temples in Lhasa and threw this and many other images into the streets. From what was tossed into the streets, some of the Tibetans managed to collect and then smuggle wrathful and peaceful aspects of images of Avalokiteshvara, along with other artifacts, out of Tibet. These relics passed through Nepal and then into India with the help of many people. Then another wrathful image of Avalokiteshvara and one of Amitabha, the Buddha of Boundless Light, also reached India. These were all assembled into the present image of the Buddha of Compassion in the Cathedral at McLeod Ganj. You'll now see this image encased as a precious relic and made of silver with eleven faces and a thousand arms and a thousand eyes.

The Tsuglagkhang also has full sets (100 volumes) of the Kagyur religious texts, the complete teachings of the Buddha, along with the 225 volumes of the Tengyur, the later commentaries on the Kagyur by Indian Buddhist scholars.

In the afternoon you can watch the monks in the temple courtyard practice their debates, which is fascinating and quite theatrical at times. Across the courtyard from the temple are the security checkpoints at the entrance to the residence of the Dalai Lama, which is also where you'll most likely go if you have a private or public audience with him.

Nearby is the recently opened Namgyal cafe, which is a small but nice place to eat freshly made Tibetan foods. Be sure to ask for the vegetarian preparations. A little book shop is just above it. At the cafe I met an elderly, retired Tibetan man who had taught about Tibet at Western Michigan College for two years in Kalamazoo, Michigan. He had also visited Detroit, taught two more years in Cleveland, and a few years in Oregon. It was quite interesting talking with him and unexpected to have met such a person in Dharamsala, of all places, who was familiar with Detroit, where I have been living.

Going the rest of the way into McLeod Ganj, we pass many shops and restaurants, as well as numerous vendors along the sides of the streets who sell all kinds of Tibetan items, such as jewelry, clothing, souvenirs, images, and nick-nacks. You can really feel the influence of the Tibetan culture and its people here at McLeod Ganj. The Tibetans are some of the friendliest people you could ever hope to meet. They seem to be ready to smile at any time, even with the simplest of greetings. They also seem to have a real zest for life, considering how they've all had to leave their homes, most of their possessions, and relatives in Tibet and enter India as refugees.

McLeod Ganj is a very small village composed of only two major streets that are only about two blocks long each. This forms a rectangular area around which are the major shops. At one end of the town is the Tibetan Handicraft center. You can walk in and see them in the process of making carpets, jackets, and other items on very simple equipment. These are sold to help support the Tibetan community here.

In the center of town is the Namgyalma Stupa, which is a memorial to all those Tibetans who lost their lives fighting for a free Tibet. It represents the determination of Tibetans to preserve their own distinct way of life against overwhelming odds. The main shrine is a small chamber with an image of Sakyamuni Buddha and a large "wheel of law" that people turn as they leave. Around the outside of the rectangular shrine are many paintings of Buddhas and prayer wheels that the devotees turn as they circumambulate them while chanting *mantras* on their beads. You'll see many monks walking about or eating at the restaurants in town.

At the other end of McLeod Ganj is the taxi and bus stand. The bus back to Dharamsala can fill up fast and costs five rupees. The 30 minute bus trip through the other neighboring towns is always a short but interesting adventure. Nearby is also the Nowrojees General Store which was one of the first stores to have been established in the bazaar at McLeod Ganj. From this part of town there are any number of retreat centers, paths to walk, temples or monasteries to visit, or other little towns and places to check out. You can check your guidebook for further information about this.

For example, one place you may want to visit is the Bhagsu Shiva Temple, reached by taking the mountain road north from the bus stand. The walk is pleasant and takes you through another little community of shops, restaurants, and residential houses. It's an area where many Westerners hang out or live in rented rooms in the houses offered by the locals. I happened to meet one American who lived in the area. He rented a nice room in a house owned and shared by a local Tibetan family. Although it was rustic with no modern amenities, it was only 30 rupees a night, or less than $30 a month. But he did say that it could be cold at night, rainy, and you need warm clothes at this altitude. And finding and using a toilet in the morning could be a little difficult.

A little farther is the small Bhagsu Shiva Temple which is near some bathing pools fed by the cold mountain stream which flows through them. Many people, Indian and Tibetans alike, frolic in the water in spite of the sign that says no swimming or bathing.

A little past the pools there is a hole in the wall with an arrow next to a sign that says, "Waterfall." After you walk through the wall and begin going along the path, you can soon see in the distance on the hillside a nice waterfall. You can take a lower path that is less risky or a higher path that is narrow with long, sheer drops on the side of it. Once you get there, you'll find plenty of people swimming in the cold mountain water, including hippies, tourists, and young Tibetan monks washing clothes, and others sunbathing after a swim. Off to the side is a little shack made with a tin roof setting on piles of slate stone. This is a tiny cafe that offers only eggs, fire- brewed tea and stream cooled soda pop. So I had a Pepsi and sat in its little seating area. It was a nice way to relax in the sun with the sound of the waterfall in the background and enjoy the mountain surroundings. After relaxing a bit, it was time to go back.

High in the hills above this Bhagsunath waterfall are the huts and caves of some of the Tibetan lamas and monks who seek this area for meditating in seclusion. Even though you may reach the waterfall, it is advised that you not disturb the recluses.

Coming back from the Bhagsu Shiva temple, while walking along the road, I heard the sound of drums and horns coming from a building on a hill. So I went up the drive and checked it out. I was quite fortunate to find a troupe of Tibetan dancers performing the ancient Tibetan mask dances. The place was a temple and lots of people had gathered in the courtyard to see the dancing. The members of the troupe primarily were from a Tibetan refugee camp in Mahendragada, Orissa. This type of mask dancing always depicts a story of good verses evil in the form of demons and Buddhist guardians. It was very interesting and quite colorful and full of tradition.

When I left it was starting to get cold. I stopped and had dinner at the Green Restaurant, a pleasant place that was filled mostly with Westerners, hippies, and those getting into the Tibetan Buddhist scene. Loud music from old Neil Young recordings were being played in the background.

That night I decided to walk back to Dharamsala after having taken the bus up. I hadn't taken the path back before so I was a little unfamiliar with it. I walked past the Dalai Lama's residence and when I came to the Lhagyal-ri shrine, I didn't know where to turn for the path down the hill. I hadn't dressed warmly and it was cold and dark. The moonlight was all I had, and I was getting lost. I kept walking faster along the path hoping to find some road. Then I ran into three Tibetans, one of which was an old nun. She asked me (mostly in Tibetan) where I was going, and I said Dharamsala. Then she pointed out that the way I was going was no good. She physically turned me around and boldly tapped my arm to get me going back to the Buddhist shrine. She then got someone who spoke English to show me the right path to take and how to get started. Then I was on the right track.

Thanks only for the full moon was I able to see all the rocks, bumps, and downed trees and other dangers to keep from falling or breaking a leg, and to keep from getting lost again. Finally, the path came out to the road and then I could see the lights of Dharamsala in the distance below to safely walk the rest of the way back. Later, I reached the well lit and still busy streets of Dharamsala where I picked up a few Indian sweets from a shop for a desert, and went back to my room to count my blessings. All in all, it was a great day.

There's also plenty of festivals at McLeod Ganj. One of the special ones is the Tibetan Opera and Folk Festival. This is held at T.I.P.A. (The Tibetan Institute of

Performing Arts). This place is about a 15 minute walk out of McLeod Ganj. Simply take the road toward the Bhagsu Temple and there soon will be a dirt road that breaks off to the left and goes up into the hills. After some walking you will come to the T.I.P.A. center. This is the home of Ihamo, a unique and very colorful Tibetan folk opera. The center preserves and trains its students in a number of musical dance and theatrical traditions of Tibet. It also makes its own costumes, masks and musical instruments.

The Tibetan Folk Opera Festival is an annual event in April which lasts five days or so. It costs a nominal fee to attend, but is very interesting. Lots of families gather in the courtyard for picnics and celebration and to see the exhibits, dancing, plays, singing, and opera. The costumes are extremely colorful in the sunlight. The opera is, naturally, all in Tibetan, but it is also full of humor that almost anyone can understand. Even though the Tibetans are all refugees, having escaped from Communist Chinese occupied Tibet, they have a great joy in life and are quick to laugh and smile at the humor in the opera.

Late in the afternoon, after standing for hours where I could look over most everyone's head to view the opera, an old Tibetan lady in the crowd pointed to me and then pointed out a seat where I could sit. I didn't feel much like moving, suspecting that the opera would be over soon, but I thought fate was calling me and I should go. So I moved through the crowd and found the seat. Shortly after that the opera did end, and then the Dalai Lama, who attended, came out of his room a few storeys up in the building behind the crowd, and spoke to everyone. Where I happened to be was one of the best places to be situated to see and take a few photos of him, which I couldn't have gotten if I had remained where I was. Then after he spoke for about 10 minutes, he came down the stairway and walked through the crowd greeting people as he went, not far from where I was standing. The special relationship and respect between him and the Tibetan people is obvious.

One of the things you might want to do while you are in Dharamsala is ask for a public audience with the Dalai Lama. To get a private audience can take up to four months of waiting. But as long as he is in town, you can check to see when he plans to give the next public audience. To do this you must go to McLeod Ganj and take the road toward the Bhagsu Temple from the bus stop. Go to the Branch Security Office in the same building (upstairs) as the Tibetan Welfare Office across from the Kokonor Hotel. This is where they'll let you know when the Dalai Lama is having his next public audience and how to sign up for it. If you're accepted, they'll give you a permit and tell you not to bring any bags or cameras for security reasons. They will also tell you where and what time to go. You'll usually go to his residence and wait in the temple courtyard until everyone starts getting called, which will be around noon. They will call people in groups of ten according to your ticket number. Once inside the security gates, you get frisked twice and any cameras or bags people have are left in a room.

Beyond the security gates are the huts and quarters for servants and security personnel. Then there is a driveway that leads up the hill to a hall or reception building, and you wait outside along the driveway. Farther over is a house which is the actual residence of the Dalai Lama. Around 1:00 PM everyone is directed to get in a single line. I managed to be one of the first 25 in this group of around 300 people. Then the Dalai Lama and some of his assistants showed up and we circled around the driveway, as directed, to meet him. Each person approached and was able to shake his hand. When it was my turn, I took his hand in both of mine, bowed my head and looked up into his smiling face and said, "It is a pleasure to meet you." His hand was very soft but his handshake was firm. His face was so full of expression, with a big smile, that I thought he was about to say something. The exchange and moment was good enough. I then turned, accepted a piece of red string with a knot in it that the priest was handing out, and then I was on my way back out through the gates. The string is like a blessing and you tie the ends around your neck, which most of us were doing as a sign of having met the Dalai Lama. This indeed was a joyous occasion to have met the current incarnation of the compassionate Buddha. This made my visit to Dharamsala, Little Lhasa, as complete as it was going to be. And I certainly loved my visit here.

Now we can decide if we are going back south toward Ambala or Chandigarh or head farther north. To go south, we can easily take buses back to Chandigarh. For me it was better and more comfortable to head to Hoshiarpur and then take a train south.

If we are going to continue our way north to Jammu, then from Dharamsala we can take a 10 hour bus ride to visit the town of Chamba if we like, which is a small town north of Dharamsala. Chamba, population 17,000, 56 kilometers from Dalhousie, has some temples that some people may want to visit. (This town also can be reached from Pathankot or Nurpur.) This town used to be the headquarters for the district. The old palace is now a hotel. The town is still a trading center, which is especially the focus during the Minjar festival in August which draws crowds from many of the surrounding towns. There is a colorful parade during the festival lead by the Deity of Raghuvira, with other deities on palanquins following behind.

The Lakshmi-Narayana Temple complex is near the palace and contains three Shiva temples and three Vishnu temples, the oldest of which dates to the 10th century while the most recent temple was built in 1828. There is also a Hariraya Vishnu Temple with a Sikhara form of architecture. A steep climb up the hill is the Chamudra Temple, which also offers grand views of Chamba, as well as the Ravi River below and the surroundings. From this side trip we go to Pathankot from where we catch the next bus or train to Jammu, if we wish to go.

Jammu is a large city, population 225,100, known for problems with militant Muslims in the area and political unrest between India and Pakistan. For us it is little more than a stopover place, if we decide to brave the travel restrictions. However, while we are here, there are a few very large and impressive temples we can see. The Raghunath Temple is near the center of town and it's visited by many thousands of pilgrims, especially during the annual pilgrimage to the Vaishno Devi shrine. The temple was built in 1835 by Maharaja Ranbir Singh. It includes several other shrines to see. The interior of the temple is plated with gold and there are as many as 125,000 Shalagrama-*shilas* (stone representations of Lord Vishnu, Krishna). The Deity of Lord Ramacandra is in the main sanctum.

About half a kilometer away is a large Rambireswara Shiva Temple in town built in 1883. It is unique in having one large, five foot tall *lingam* and ten smaller ones outside, and 125,000 Shiva-*lingams* which come from the Narmada river in South India. It also has eleven rock crystals that have been formed in to Shiva-*lingams*. With its tower reaching up to 225 feet, it's one of the largest temples in North India. Across from this temple is the Dogra Art Gallery, which has a good collection of sculptures, manuscripts, and Pahari miniature paintings, terracottas, and other items. The Amar Mahal Museum also has some paintings showing scenes from the *Mahabharata* along with portraits and items of royalty.

From Jammu we take a two hour bus ride (48 kilometers) to Katra. This is where the road ends for the trek to the popular Vaishno Devi cave temple. Katra is the home of the Kalka Mata Mandir, a very old Shiva and Kali temple which has self-manifested deities. It is a very popular temple and visited by many of the traveling pilgrims. The care of the temple has now been given over to Iskcon, the Hare Krishna Movement, which is building a temple and guest house.

Twenty kilometers from Katra is the town of Raisi, which has a Sikh Gurudwara and another important cave temple. From Katra we continue to Vaishno Devi.

The reason why Vaishno Devi became so significant is that it is the place where Durga, as a girl, killed the demon Bhairon. The story is that around 700 years ago Bhairon and his guru, Goraknath, attended a festive feast for Kanya Puja that was arranged by Baba Shridar who lived in Hansali, a village about two kilometers from Katra. A divine girl appeared to him and told him to have a feast for the *puja*, and then she disappeared. Shortly thereafter he met Gorakhnath and his 360 disciples and invited them to attend.

During the feast the divine girl again appeared and served all the guests whatever food they wanted from her Kamandal pot. However, Gorakhnath and Bhairon wanted to make trouble for her and asked for meat and wine. She said she could not serve such things in the home of a *brahmana*. The goddess turned into her subtle form and went toward Trikuta Hill while being chased by the angry demon Bhairon. She then entered the Garbha Joon cave and meditated for nine months. Bhairon finally reached the cave and the goddess used her trident to break through the other side. Bhairon chased her to a cave at the peak of the mountain where the goddess Durga killed him.

Vaishno Devi is reached from Katra by a steep and tough 13 kilometer climb. It takes about four hours to reach it, or longer if you're not in shape, and three hours to get back. So plan on starting early to get there and return in one day. Before you start, pick up a Yatra Slip at the tourist center by the Katra bus stand in order to go past the Ban Ganga Temple, which you must reach within six hours of getting the slip. This is a checkpoint that monitors the people coming through, after which you get another slip at the Darbar Yatri Check Post.

The first important place we'll visit is the Bhumika Temple, about one kilometer out from Katra. This is where the goddess disappeared. This place is also called Darshani Darwaza because you can see the three peaks of the Trikuta Parvat that is the dwelling of the goddess Vaishno Devi.

The next place we arrive at is the Ban Ganga Temple. This is where the goddess shot an arrow into the ground which produced the sacred river, Ban Ganga, to satisfy the thirst of Langoor Vir. The goddess is supposed to have washed her hair at this place, which gives it the name Ban Ganga. Pilgrims usually take bath here. You must also show your checkpoint slip here in order to proceed.

Another one-and-a-half kilometers farther, and at an altitude of 3,380 feet, is the Charan Paduka Temple. Her holy footprints, *charanpaduka*, are visible on a stone at this place where she rested for a time while being chased by Bhairon. Four-and-a-half kilometers more is Ardh Kuwari where there is the Garbha Joon cave where the goddess hid for nine months. When the demon, Bhairon, found the cave in his search for the goddess, she escaped by using her trident to make a new opening. The cave is 15 feet long and very narrow.

From here the path to Vaishno Devi gets quite steep for the next two-and-a-half kilometers. The mountain resembles the forehead of an elephant, therefore, this climb is called the Hathi Matha. You'll find both a footpath and a stairway to make this climb, but the path is easier. After you climb to Sanjhi Chatt, there are four more kilometers to the Vaishno Devi cave, which has an altitude of 5,100 feet.

The Vaishno Devi cave is the only temple in India where all three goddesses of Lakshmi (the goddess of fortune and wife of Lord Vishnu), Sarasvati (the goddess of learning), and Kali are worshiped together. This is also where the goddess Durga killed the demon Bhairon, so it is an important place. It is also believed that Sati's arm fell here after her immolation at Daksha's fire ceremony in Haridwar.

The best time to visit this temple is between March and July, as it can get cold the remainder of the year. The busiest time is during March-April and September-October. There can be up to 15 to 20 thousand pilgrims a day visiting this temple, and the line of people waiting to get in can be up to four kilometers long on holidays, such as the Kartika (Oct-Nov) full Moon.

Once we reach the cave, before entering most pilgrims bathe in the water that comes out of the cave. Only 12 to 15 people are permitted in the cave at a time, so it can be a long wait to get in. You first get a number from the counter for the group with which you'll go in the cave. You'll wait at gate number two until your group is called. You then go through a low entrance for a couple yards and then walk in water that is from ankle to knee deep for 100 feet. This is called Charan

Ganga. The cave ceiling is only about five feet high, so you cannot stand straight. Finally, you reach the end of the cave and walk up four steps to see the *pindies*, which are consecrated rocks that represent the three deities of Maha-Sarasvati on the left, Maha-Lakshmi in the middle, and Maha-Kali on the right. Also inside is a lamp that never goes out.

Before leaving Vaishno Devi, we can also visit the nearby Sri Ram Temple and see the Shiva-*lingam* in a cave 125 steps down. The Bhairon or Bhairav Temple is about two-and-a-half kilometers and another 1600 feet up. It is traditional for pilgrims to visit this temple after visiting the Vaishno Devi cave. It is here where Bhairon's head landed when he was killed by the goddess, and the huge stone outside the cave represents his body. Legend has it that the demon prayed to the goddess after he was killed, and he was thus absolved of all sins by Durga. Also, tradition has it that Durga gave the benediction that all desires would be fulfilled for her devotees who visit this place.

Once our *darshan* is complete, we then make our way back and prepare for our return journey to Katra. If, however, we need to spend the night at Vaishno Devi, a town of 20,000, you may be able to find a place here or at Ardh Kuwari, which has basic rooms.

Kashmir

Unfortunately, if you have not already visited Kashmir before around 1994 or earlier, things have now got so unsettled there that presently the U. S. Embassy has posted travel restrictions for U. S. citizens. If you go, they take no responsibility for you. And it is difficult to say when this will change. The last time I was in India, you could still visit Srinagar with few worries, although there were plenty of police checkpoints. But now it is advised that you travel at your own risk. So I am still keeping my descriptions of the things to see in Srinagar, and the journey from there to Leh, in the hopes that things may change one day. However, if you still cannot go to Kashmir, then from Jammu we can head back to Ambala or Chandigarh and head north from there.

Unfortunately, there are also plenty of scams and methods of cheating tourists in Kashmir that have developed. Some of these start with the Kashmiri tourist agents in Delhi. They are the only ones who will try to convince you that Kashmir is absolutely safe. Other Indians will never say that. Most Indians do not tour Kashmir, but will tell you that Kashmir may be settled and safe one day, and then unsettled with outbreaks of violence the next. An example is the last time I was in India, I was thinking that things had been quiet in Srinagar, so maybe it would be safe to go. Three days later the war in Kargil broke out, which had strong connections with the militants in Srinagar. So you never know.

Furthermore, I have heard the stories of how Kashmiri tour agents will convince naive tourists to travel to Srinagar and stay on a houseboat. They especially try to get you to go as soon as you reach India, before you've gone anywhere else, and while you still have all of your travel money. Once you get there, on a houseboat, they scheme to get your money. They will send vendors to sell you things, or beggars to beg for your money, or the family who is taking care of you will ask for money for their children, and they will take cash, traveler's checks, or credit cards. If you don't buy or give anything, sometimes they will threaten your life, or kidnap you for your money, or even kill you and turn you into food for the fish.

One story I heard was of a Swedish girl who had been to India before but not to Kashmir. She was convinced by a Kashmiri travel agent to go to Srinagar and stay on a boat. Two weeks later she was back in Delhi crying with no money and no way to get back to Sweden because of the schemes described above. An Indian friend loaned her some money and with the help of her Embassy, she was able to get back home. She has since returned to India, but not to Kashmir. However, I have heard of people still going to Srinagar without any previous arrangements and staying on a houseboat for a few days with no problems. So that may be the best way to do it. Nonetheless, I did meet a man in Haridwar who had to flee Kashmir, leaving his property, business, and money six years earlier. He said he loved Kashmir, it was the best place but he would never return because of the way the Muslims acted toward others in the region.

Furthermore, because of the recent (summer, 1999) fighting by the Pakistani intruders in Kashmir, commercial jets from Delhi to Srinagar have been accompanied by Indian Mig fighter jets for protection because two passenger jets had been shot down. So there is definitely some risk at present in going to Kashmir.

In any case, if we can go to Srinagar from Katra and Jammu, we continue north and can make another side trip to the famous Amarnath cave, 145 kilometers east of Srinagar. Check at Jammu for a bus to Pahalgam.

As we travel this route, we will pass through the town of Udhampur. Ten kilometers from here is a town with temples that have fine carvings and sculptures. And Ramnagar, a town southeast of Udhampur and reached by bus, has the Palace of Colors, known for the beautiful Pahari-style wall paintings.

As we continue, we'll pass through the towns of Kud, Patnitop, and Batote. Kud, at 1738 meters, and Patnitop, 2024 meters, are both popular hill stations that offer simple places to stay and pleasant walks. An eight kilometer walk from Kud or Patnitop will take you to Sudh Mahadev, a popular Shiva temple. Many pilgrims visit for the three-day festival of singing, music, and dancing during the Asad Purnima festival in July-August.

Once we reach Banihal, we are 17 kilometers from the Jawarhar Tunnel. It is 2500 meters long and once we exit the tunnel we are in the lush Valley of Kashmir. This is about 93 kilometers from Srinagar. In spite of the political violence of the region, this is one of the most beautiful areas of India. As we head north, we'll pass through Avantipur, which has two ruined temples built from 855 to 883 AD. The larger Avantiswami Temple is dedicated to Vishnu, and the other is a Shiva temple. There are still some interesting and detailed relief sculptures.

On the way to Srinagar, we'll stop at Anantnag and take a bus to Pahalgam. We'll pass through the town of Achabal, which has one of the many noteworthy Moghul gardens in Kashmir. This is said to have been built in 1620 by Jahanara, Shah Jahan's daughter. Farther on is Kokarnag, famous for its rose gardens. At Mattan is a spring-fed pool filled with fish, and the large but ruined temple of Martland on the plateau above Mattan.

Pahalgam, at 2130 meters, is a good place to stay during a pilgrimage trek to Amarnath Cave. There's some hotels here but not much to see, although it is surrounded by tree green mountains with snow caps in the background, and the lovely Lidder River flows through the town. Pahalgam does offer many walks through the hills to such places as the small, 12th century Mamaleswara Shiva Temple about one kilometer away. Or you can go to Baisaran and Aru, 11 kilometers upstream for a day's walk. There are many shepherds taking flocks of sheep here and there throughout the area. But save your walking energy if you are going to Amarnath.

Over the years, this area has been a political hotbed with terrorists and militants that occasionally cause trouble for the pilgrims going to Amarnath. India has sent many police and army personnel to keep the peace. It is an especially sensitive area for foreign tourists who have been, at times, completely forbidden to make the pilgrimage. So check in advance if you want to go. Furthermore, the weather can be a serious factor in the pilgrimage to Amarnath. In 1996, 250 pilgrims died in the unexpected snow storms that occurred. Now the state governments will be using modern weather forecasting equipment and will restrict the pilgrimage period to 30 days only. Further regulations will be that pilgrims must be between the ages of 15 to 65 years old and no more than a maximum of 100,000 pilgrims can make the trek with a limit of 8,000 per day.

Reaching Amarnath requires a three to five day uphill trek. It is located in a glacial valley at an elevation of 13,700 feet. The pilgrimage traditionally starts on the eleventh day after the new Moon (Ekadashi). The cave is only open between July and August, which is the rainy season. So the ground can be damp and slippery, and you can get plenty wet. But the area is snow-covered the rest of the time. Many thousands of people journey to this cave each year. Many attend the annual Sravana (July-August) festival when it's said that Shiva first appeared.

As we reach the cave, pilgrims bathe in the Amaravati before going in the cave for *darshan*. The cave is large, about 90 feet long and 150 feet high. Once we get inside, the main attraction is a large ice formation that looks like and is accepted as a Shiva-*lingam*. Although it changes size according to the seasons, it can be nearly six feet tall. It is largest usually on the full Moon day of July-August. Unfortunately, there have been times when it's been disappointingly small.

Nearby are several other ice formations that represent other demigods. The left side of the Shiva-*lingam* is a formation representing Ganesh, and on the right is one of Parvati and Bhairava. Once we are finished with our trek and *darshan* at Amarnath, we'll continue on our way to Srinagar.

On our way, the town of Parshaspur, just outside of Srinagar, has the massive ruins of an ancient temple, with huge blocks of stone scattered about a wide area.

Srinagar, population 650,000, is the capital of Kashmir and the stopover place for going to Ladakh. This has been and still is a great tourist place, although the political unrest in the area has certainly put a damper on things. So first check the level of political unrest before going to determine whether you should visit or just make a short stay, or forget about it altogether. For the serious spiritual pilgrim, however, Srinagar does not have much to offer.

We'll find Srinagar to be a crowded but colorful city that exudes a distinct Asian atmosphere. It is indeed different from the rest of India in language (Kashmiri and Dogri), climate, and in the way people look. The old city is the place to avoid and where most of the fighting takes place. It looks war-torn and there are plenty of soldiers, roadblocks, and bunkers on the street corners. So if we visit Srinagar, stay near the lakes as much as possible for the safest places.

Dal Lake, one of the top tourist attractions in Srinagar, is actually three lakes, which are separated by dikes or "floating gardens." The main area for the houseboats is at the southern end near the tourist district, not far from the main part of town. You'll find many shops, handicrafts, restaurants, hotels, and travel agents in this area. The Tourist Reception Centre is also where we can get buses to and from Jammu and Leh. Srinagar is where you can stock up on the supplies you may need, or change money, or send parcels home before we head into Ladakh, if you are going there, or if you can go there. More about this later.

While in Srinagar, we can walk around the lake and take some boat rides or even rent a houseboat for a few days. Houseboats on Dal Lake can be a great way to relax. Of course, floating on the water and getting away from everything is a great experience in itself. And now that tourism has declined in the region, you can get some great values for accommodations. To check out the boats, you don't need to go to the Tourist Reception Centre or the Houseboat Owner's Association. You can go right to the lake and see what's there. The touts will try to sell you a boat as soon as you arrive, or even as you walk through town, or anywhere they can. Don't agree to anything without seeing the boat itself or you may regret it.

Most houseboats have a verandah where you can sit and watch the view of the lake, mountains, and other boats go by. Behind this is a living room, furnished, along with a dining room, two or three bedrooms, each with a bathroom. There are different categories for the level of facility, and prices that also include meals. You can rent a room with others or rent the entire boat. Make sure that the *shikara* boat trips to shore are free, and that they supply a bucket of warm water for bathing each morning. Also, don't be bothered by the many vendors who float by trying to sell you all kinds of things.

The water of the lake is very clear, in spite of all the sewage from the city and houseboats. To take a leisurely cruise around the lake on a rented *shikara* boat can take all day to see most everything. In the lake, Silver Island and Gold Island are popular picnic spots.

You can also walk or bicycle around the lake and see the Moghul gardens, or the Kotar Khana, the (House of Pigeons) once royal summer house. From the Kotar Khana we go on to the Chasma Shahi gardens, which are about nine kilometers out of Srinagar town. These are the smallest of the Moghul gardens, established in 1632, located up a hillside. Farther on is Pari Mahal. Another kilometer away is a Sufi College with a nicely maintained garden on the arched terraces. It is a pleasant area with lovely views over the lake. Also in the area, nearer the lake, is Nishat Bagh, the gardens that were established in 1633 by Asaf Khan. These offer great views over the lake with the Pir Panjal mountains in the background. The garden design follows a traditional Moghul plan with a central channel flowing down the terraces. If you are not interested in going all the way around the lake, you can head toward the long central causeway that cuts right through and then head back to town.

On the northern side of the lake, at the end of a small canal, is Shalimar Bagh. These gardens were built by Jehangir in 1616 for his wife, Nur Jahan, "light of the world." The top terrace used to be reserved strictly for the emperor and the court ladies during the Moghul period. Farther around the northern end of the lake we will arrive at Nasim Bagh. These are the oldest of the Moghul gardens in Kashmir, established by Akbar in 1586. These are no longer maintained and are used by an engineering college. A little farther on is the Hazratbal Mosque, said to house a hair of the prophet. This is a new mosque on the shores of Nagin Lake and has the snow-capped mountains in the background. Nagin Lake is considered the cleaner and quieter lake, and farther away from everything, which can be good in one way, and also riskier in another as you get farther away from town.

Now we start reaching the older area of Srinagar where we have to be more careful of the Islamic militant activity. There are a few other noteworthy sites, although visiting them may not be all that worth while. One site that I'll mention, although you can't visit it since the Army has moved in, is the Hari Parbat Fort on top of Sharika Hill on the west side of Nagin Lake. The early part of it was built between 1592 and 1598 during the reign of Akbar, while the newer parts date to the 18th century. A shrine to the sixth Sikh Guru is located at the southern gate.

Farther south is the local Jami Masjid Mosque. This was originally built in 1385 by Sultan Sikander. Then it burnt down in 1479, was rebuilt in 1503, and burnt down again. The present structure, built in 1674, is wooden with over 300 pillars which support the roof, each made of single deodar tree.

Nearby is the Bulbul Shah Mosque, and also the tomb of Zain-ul-Abiden, the son of Sultan Sikander. It has a dome and glazed tiles in its traditional Persian architecture.

Farther down the river is the Shah Hamdan Mosque with a pyramidal roof. If you are a non-Muslim, you will have to stay outside. Across the river is the Pather Masjid Mosque, which is an unused and run-down stone structure, built by

Nur Jahan in 1623. Farther south is a Raghunath Temple dedicated to Lord Rama. Another noteworthy temple in Srinagar is the Pandrethan Shiva Temple on Jammu road heading out of town. It is in the military cantonment and dates back to 900 A.D.

We also can stroll along the Jhelum River where it flows through Srinagar. There are nine old bridges and a few newer ones that cross it, and, along with the buildings and mosques nearby, walking through this area provides for a very picturesque way of absorbing the cultural atmosphere. You can also visit the Shri Pratap Singh Museum just south of the Jhelum River, which has more Kashmir artifacts and exhibits.

Kashmir is well-known for the handicrafts you can buy here at the many emporiums in town or in the area. But if you buy anything of considerable size, ship it home before going on to Leh. There are also workshops you can visit to watch the workers in action. Things you can buy here include the famous Kashmir carpets, embroidery, shawls, sweaters, coats, along with paper mache items, wood carvings, saffron spice, and much more. And, of course, there are plenty of people who will expect you to buy something.

Behind the Boulevard near Dal Lake is Shankaracharya Hill. There is a Hindu temple here, but an earlier temple was built here around 200 B.C. by Ashoka's son. The top of the hill provides a great view over the lake. The hill used to be called Takht-i-Sulaiman, the Throne of Solomon, which definitely represents some of the history of this region.

Let me explain how there is an accepted connection with this hill and Solomon. The small temple on top of the hill is called Takht-i-Sulaiman, or the Throne of Solomon. An inscription on the remnants of the old building states that the new temple was restored in 78 A.D. by King Gopadatta (or Gopananda). According to tradition, Solomon had visited the land of Kashmir. In fact, the local Moslems know Kashmir as "Bagh Suleiman," the Garden of Solomon. This would go in accord with the theory that some scholars believe that Kashmir was the "Promised Land," or the "Land of the Fathers" that the "ten lost tribes of Israel" wandered to in northern India where they found peace and tranquillity. This was after they had moved eastwards when they had been driven out of Israel by the Assyrians, never to be heard from again. Therefore, it may have indeed been Solomon, as tradition declares, who divided the Barehmooleh Mountain and created an outlet for the water that later formed Dal Lake. He also may have constructed the original building of the Takht-i- Suleiman on top of what is now Shankaracharya Hill.

The Grave of Jesus

Another interesting monument, in the center of Srinagar's old part of town, is the Rozabal, which means "tomb of the prophet." This is the burial place of Yuz

Asaf. The name Yuz Asaf relates to Jesus. Jesus' Hebrew name was Yazu, similar to Yuz. In Arabic and the Koran his name was Hazrat Isa or Isa, and Issa in Tibetan. Both of which are similar to the name Isha in Sanskrit. This tradition has been carried down through the *Farhang-Asafia*, Volume One, which explains how Jesus healed some leper who then became *asaf*, meaning purified or healed. The word *yuz* means leader. Thus, Yuz Asaf became a common reference to Jesus as "leader of the healed."

There are other accounts of how Yuz Asaf preached throughout Persia, present-day Iran, converting many people. Some of these details can be found in Agha Mustafai's *Ahivali Ahaliau-i-Paras* which confirms that Jesus and Yuz Asaf are the same person. Even the well-known and liberal Emperor Akbar had a court poet who referred to Jesus as *Ai Ki Nam-i to: Yuz o Kristo*, which means, "Thou whose name is Yuz or Christ."

Other records and place names that relate to Jesus point to his presence in Afghanistan and Pakistan. The Acts of Thomas describe the journey of Jesus and Thomas in Pakistan (then Taxila) at the court of King Gundafor in the 26th year of his rule, which would be about 47 A.D.

Also, when Jesus came to Kashmir he came with a group of followers which included his mother, Mary, who must have been over 70 years old, and was no doubt weakened by the journey. Seventy kilometers east of Taxila, and 170 kilometers west of Srinagar on the border of Kashmir, is a small town called Mari, or Murree in English, near Rawalpindi. In that town is a very old grave called *Mai Mari da Asthan*, meaning "the final resting place of Mother Mary." Here is where she must have died before Jesus reached Kashmir, which was considered Paradise, or Heaven on earth. Even to this day this grave is maintained by Muslims as the resting place of Jesus' mother because he (Isa) is considered one of the main prophets of Islam.

Also near the villages of Naugam and Nilmag, about 40 kilometers south of Srinagar is a large plain called the Yuz-Marg, the meadow of Jesus. It is here that some of the tribes of Israel settled after 722 B.C. to live as shepherds, which is still a major occupation in the area today.

Even at Akbar's city, Fatehpur Sikri, near Agra, as you enter the main gate toward the mosque, there is an inscription which states: "Jesus (Peace be with him) has said: 'The world is a bridge. Pass over it, but do not settle down on it!'"

More evidence of Jesus in Kashmir is found in an inscription that was carved on the sides of the steps at the threshold on the Throne of Solomon in Srinagar. The meaning of this is described in detail by Mullah Nadiri, a historian during the rule of Sultan Zainul Aabidin, in 1413 in his book on the history of Kashmir, *Tarikh-i-Kashmir*. He relates that Gopananda, or Gopadatta, ruled Kashmir and had the Temple of Solomon refurbished by a Persian architect. During the renovation four sayings in ancient Persian were set in stone that said, in essence, that Bihishti Zagar is the constructor of these columns in the year of 54. Khwaja Rukun, son of Murjan, had these columns built. In the year 54, Yuz Asaf proclaimed his prophetic calling. He is Jesus, prophet of the sons of Israel.

Mullah Nadiri goes on to relate that during the rule of Gopadatta, Yuz Asaf came from the Holy Land to the Kashmir valley and proclaimed to be a prophet and preached to the people. Gopadatta ruled sixty years and two months before he died. It is calculated that Jesus came to Kashmir nearly 16 years after the crucifixion and lived to be around 80 years old. Even the *Koran* (23.52) explains that Jesus did not die on the cross but survived the crucifixion and ascended to live in a peaceful hill-side watered by a fresh spring.

All this means that not only did Jesus come to India to learn from the *brahmanas* and Buddhists as records show, but after returning to his land of Israel to preach and was later crucified, he did not die on the cross but suffered and recovered. After that he ascended to Heaven, known as Kashmir, where, after some years, he died and was buried in Srinagar.

According to various records, during his missing years Jesus was supposed to have studied for four years at the temple of Jagannatha Puri. Then he traveled and studied with the Buddhists at Kapilavastu (present-day Lumbini), the birthplace of Buddha in Nepal. Then he went to Lhasa in Tibet for five years. After that he went homeward and then to Greece for sometime before going on to Egypt. Then at the age of 25 he went to Heliopolis and studied for five more years before returning to his homeland.

The story of Jesus' crucifixion is also interesting because, generally, most people die on the cross by starvation or suffocation when the ribs press down on the lungs so that the person can no longer breathe. This often takes several days. According to tradition, Jesus was nailed on the cross in the early afternoon of a Friday and taken down as dusk was approaching, after being nailed on the cross only four or five hours. So it is most unusual that a young and healthy person like Jesus died after only four hours on the cross. Thus, it is more likely that as a yogi he was able to enter an altered state and appear as if dead, only to be revived later. This is not uncommon with some yogis in India. Furthermore, there are modern commemorations of Jesus' crucifixion wherein people are crucified every year in the Phillippines and Mexico and survive quite easily. A person does not die of crucifixion after only four hours. Thus, it is quite likely that he survived the crucifixion and died elsewhere.

To visit the grave of Jesus, you'll find it in Anzimar next to a Muslim cemetery in the Khanjar (Khanyar) quarter of Srinagar's old town. You find Rauzibal Khanyar down a narrow, winding alley in an old, wooden mausoleum in much disrepair. The grave itself is in a building called Roza bal, an abbreviation of *Rauza*, which means "tomb of a prophet." You enter the rectangular building through a small doorway. On your way in you'll see an inscription that explains that Yuz Asaf came to Kashmir many centuries ago and dedicated himself to the search for truth. The inner chamber has two graves on the floor, each covered with heavy cloth and with wooden railings around them. The first and smaller grave is for the Islamic saint Syed Nasir-ud-Din, buried here in the 15th century. The larger grave behind it is for Yuz Asaf. Near the gravestone of Yuz Asaf are footprints carved in the stone showing the scars Jesus would have suffered during his crucifixion. It is the custom for pilgrims to place candles around the gravestones, and when years of wax was removed by Professor Hassnain, not only did he discover the footprints, but he also found a cross and rosary. As typical with Muslim mausoleums, these graves are a covering and the actual graves are in a crypt under the floor. A look into the real burial chamber is provided by a small opening. The grave which contains the remains of Yuz Asaf points east to west, according to Jewish tradition.

This all points to the fact that this could indeed be the burial place of Jesus. The grave has been maintained by attendants since its construction, which is established by ancient records to be as far back as 112 A.D.

Moses in Kashmir

While in Kashmir, another point of interest is that not only was Solomon and Jesus in Kashmir, but there is significant history that Moses was also here. In fact, Kashmir is considered to have the burial site of Moses. There is a grave-site that has been maintained for over 2700 years near the plains of Mowu, once called Moab, above Pishnag, once known as Pisga. This is on Mount Nebo and about 15 kilometers across from Bandipur, which was once known as Behat-poor and Beth-peor. This is considered to be the burial place of Moses.

The logic behind this is that the book of Deuteronomy (34.4-6) explains that Moses died in the land of Moab and was buried near Beth-peor. It is also explained elsewhere in the chapter that Mount Nebo in the Abarim Mountains, and Mount Pisga and Heshbon are in the vicinity. The biblical land of Moab is now called the plains of Mowu. Biblical Pisga is now called Pishnag. Beth-peor was later called Behat-pur near the Jhelum River, which is called the "Behat" River in Persian. Now Behat-pur is called Bandipur, and the village with the biblical name of Heshbon (*Deuteronomy* 4.46) is now called Hasba or Hasbal. This area is about 80 kilometers north of Srinagar.

If we travel to this area today, Bandipur (Beth-peor, meaning "the place that opens") is near where the Jhelum (Behat) River opens into the plains of Lake Wular. Another 18 kilometers north we find the village of Hasbal, both towns mentioned in the Bible. Mount Nebo, in the Abarim Mountain range, is across from Bandipur, and above the village of Pishga. Mount Nebo offers a great view of the heavenly land of Kashmir.

Twelve kilometers north of Bandipur we come to the town of Aham-Sharif. From here we go by foot to reach the village of Booth at the base of Mount Nebo. We head west for an hour, taking a vague path up a steady slope. Several fields away is the tiny town of Booth with Mount Nebo rising behind it. Here we'll need to get the attendant of the grave, called the "Wali Rishi" who will guide us the rest of the way. He willingly leads us up to an open garden where there's a small mausoleum. This is the burial site of Sang Bibi, an Islamic female saint and two of her followers. Nearby is a stone column in the grass that stands about a meter tall which designates the grave of Moses.

Other places in Kashmir are also related to Moses. Near Shadipur north of Srinagar, the cliffs near the confluence of the Jhelum and Sindh rivers are called Kohna-i-Musa, "the cornerstone of Moses," where Moses is said to have rested. Three kilometers north of Bandipur is another of Moses' resting spots at Ayat-i-Maula.

About 46 kilometers south of Srinagar is a place called Bijbihara. This is a spot on the river bank referred to as Moses' Bath. The stone lion there is said to be about 5000 years old. The "Stone of Moses" or Ka-Ka-Bal is said to have been the subject of Moses' magic. It is also explained that, though it weighs 70 kilograms, the stone will rise a meter high of its own power if eleven people each touch it with a single finger and all properly recite the magic formula "ka-ka, ka-ka."

At Bijbihara's cemetery there is an inscription in Hebrew on an old grave. A few kilometers away you can see the Temple of Martand that resembles the steps, vestibule, pillared hall, and interior of a traditional Jewish temple, in spite of the Hindu demigods carved on the outside.

* * *

When our visit to Srinagar is complete, make sure you've gotten a bus ticket to Leh because they are usually fully pre-booked. If you don't want to take a bus, flights to Leh are on Tuesdays and Thursdays, which offers quite spectacular views while flying over the mountains.

Other ways to get to Leh is to fly in from Delhi, Chandigarh, or Jammu, depending on availability, which can change quickly since flights are often over booked and if the weather permits it. You can also take a 485 kilometer, two-day bus ride from Manali. It is a very rough road which is open only from mid-June or later to mid-September, so plan accordingly.

If we were to go to Leh from Srinagar, it's a long 434 kilometers on a mostly paved road which travels along the Indus much of the way. The journey takes two days, and, although there are overnight accommodations in many towns, the buses stop for an overnight stay at Kargil. However, the military roadblocks and checkpoints don't help to speed things up.

The road to Ladakh heads through the Sindh Valley, a beautiful area. The Dachigan Wildlife Reserve is also along this route, which is to the northeast of Srinagar. After traveling for some distance we'll arrive at Sonamarg, which is at a height of 2740 meters. This is the last major town before the Zoji La pass. It has pine trees and meadows everywhere with the beautiful snow-covered mountains in the distance. It is like a wild west town with wooden shacks and a truck stop.

There are a few places to stay here and is a good base for trekking. The next stop is at the tiny town of Baltal, at the base of Zoji La. Here is another town from where you can make the trek to the Amarnath Cave to see the natural Shiva-*lingam* in the form of ice.

Zoji La, at 3529 meters, is the first mountain pass on our journey and is the first to be snowed over when it starts getting cold. It's only open from around mid-June to mid-September. So plan your trip accordingly. The road is unpaved here and offers breathtaking views. However, where the road has long, sheer drops along the edge will also take your breath away as you pray to get through it. But if you've already traveled to Badrinath, you should be a little used to this by now.

Ladakh

Zoji La is like the entrance into Ladakh, which is called Little Tibet. It is just like a portion of Tibet in northern India. It is Tibetan in culture, religion, and its people. It has been open to outside visitors only since the mid-70s, so it can be and is called at times the "last Shangri-la." It is situated in a high plateau north of the Himalayas, which form a barrier to the rain. This is why Ladakh is so barren and dry, except where the rivers flow from the distant glaciers. There can be drastic temperature changes, turning from warm to cold in minutes. The nights are usually very cold. So bring warm clothes and a sleeping bag.

Ladakh is like a different world, and worth the endeavor to see. It offers strange scenery, spectacular sights, ancient hillside palaces, a colorful culture, and friendly people. However, during the tourist season, make sure you have small change in currency because most people won't.

Drass is the first town we come to after the Zoji La pass. This can be a bitterly cold town in winter with lots of snowfall. We will have to stop here to register our names and passport numbers as we enter Ladakh from Srinagar. Kargil is the next town and is good for an overnight stop. It has various places to stay, mostly for basic accommodation. The buses arrive daily late at night and leave at dawn.

By the time we reach the small village of Shergol we will have entered the area of Buddhist influence and left the Muslim area. This will be noticed by the little *gompa* monastery on the eastern side of the mountain.

Mulbekh is the next town we come to. It has two *gompas* on the hillside, which may or may not be open. So check in town before climbing if you wish to visit since someone may know who has the keys. One thing to watch for a little ways beyond Mulbekh is a huge image of the future Buddha, Chamba, carved into the face of the rock near the road.

From here we encounter the Namika La pass, at 3718 meters, then the Bodh Kharbu military camp, and then the Tatu La pass, the highest on our journey at 4094 meters. Then we'll come to the village of Lamayuru with its *gompas* on the hilltop, which is attended by 20 to 30 monks.

The next towns worth noting are Rizong, which has the Julichen nunnery and a monastery, and Alchi, which has a low *gompa* with huge Buddha images and detailed wood carvings. Inside are Kashmiri wall paintings. Throughout the village are numerous Buddhist *chorten* shrines. Thereafter is the Lekir *gompa* and monastery. Then Basgo has a *gompa* with interesting images of Buddha as well as a fort, although it's quite damaged. Finally, we arrive at Leh.

Leh, population 22,000, is not a large city and is small enough to easily find your way around. During the season it is crowded with western tourists. It is mostly a military base, but it is still a very interesting town with fascinating sites and plenty of hotels from which to choose. It's also a good town for arranging treks into the surrounding hills. It especially allows you to have a good look at the ancient Tibetan lifestyle without going to Tibet. Of course, we've already had a good taste of this when we visited Dharamsala, which is easier to get to and very interesting.

In the central part of town is the 16th century Leh Palace, which looks similar to Potala in Lhasa. From the roof you can get great views over the city and of the Zanskar mountains across the Indus. If you can, find a monk who has keys to the now unused interior. The prayer room is especially interesting but dark, and the huge masks can make the place a little frightening.

Above the palace are the Leh and Tsemo Gompas, which house paintings and old manuscripts, and a large three-storey tall seated Buddha. Above is another *gompa*, ruined but worth the views over Leh.

From the palace, it's a couple kilometers north of town to the Sankar Gompa which has a great image of Avalokitesvara with 1000 arms and heads. This *gompa* is only open from 7 to 10 AM and 5 to 7 PM, but it does have electricity. So you can visit it in early evening.

Walking through the small lanes of Leh is interesting, and if you want you can check out the Mahabodhi Society for meditation sessions and courses. You can also visit the Centre for Ecological Development which promotes the development of Ladakh through solar energy, organic farming, health education, etc. If you want to stay in Ladakh for an extended visit with a Ladakhi family, the Student's Educational and Cultural Movement of Ladakh can provide some assistance. You can also check out The Cultural and Traditional Society for their cultural shows each evening. It's across from the Hotel Yak Tail. And if you are in the buying spirit, the handicrafts you can get here are rather expensive compared to similar items in Dharamsala or Kashmir. So you may consider saving your money.

There are other significant *gompas* in the area that we will want to visit while in Leh, which is actually one of the main reasons for coming here. Ten kilometers south of Leh, near the airport, there is the 1000 year old Spitok Gompa on a hill where you can get great views above the Indus River. Across the Indus is the Pharka Gompa.

Farther south of Leh is Choglamsar where there is a Tibetan refugee camp. This has become known as an important center for the study of Tibetan literature, history, and Buddhist culture. There is the temporary residence of the Dalai Lama near the river.

Farther along the road toward Manali is the village of Shey, above which is the 560 year old summer palace of the kings of Ladakh. The palace is in ruins, but you can see the 12-meter-high seated Buddha in the palace *gompa*. However, it's only open from 7 to 9 AM and 5 to 6 PM. Otherwise, you'll have to locate a monk named Tashi in the village to find the key.

Farther south, 17 kilometers from Leh, is the Tikse Gompa, which you can see from Shey. This is probably one of the nicer *gompas* to visit and is nicely situated on the hilltop above the village and Indus river. It is known for its library of Tibetan books and artwork, and you can observe the religious ceremonies in the early morning (around 6:30 AM) or at noon. You'll know when they start by the long sounds of the horns from the roof. If you wish, you can spend the night at the hotel.

Forty-five kilometers south from Leh, a half-day, bumpy bus ride past the Shey Gompa and the Tickse Palace, located six kilometers off the main road and on the western side of the Indus River, is the Hemis Gompa. You can get off at Karu, and walk the several miles up to the Hemis Gompa, which cannot be seen from the road. You walk up the hill and to a narrow valley with a prayer wall and many Buddhist *stupas*. It is one of the largest and most well-known of the Ladakh *gompas*, and also has nice copper images of sitting Buddhas, about 20 feet tall, plus wall paintings, and a respectable library. There is also a statue of an evil demon named Mirza, commemorating the invasions of the Muslim chieftan, Mirza, in the 16th century. It is especially famous for its large Hemis Festival. This is a two-day event in late June or early July with mask dances and lots of spectators. The Cham or Setchu festival is when they have the mystery plays which honors the Buddhist saint and prophet, Padmasambhava.

The Hemis Gompa, as it stands today, is over 400 years old. However, the previous monastery, the Go San Gompa, existed here for well over 1000 years earlier. Many inner rooms are filled with ancient writing, much of which are uncataloged.

The Hemis Monastery is where, in 1886, Nicolas Notovitch discovered the ancient manuscript that describes the life and travels of Saint Issa, Jesus. This, as Notovitch explained, was a compilation of scrolls from the library in Lhasa that were brought from India, Nepal, and Magadha about 200 years after the time of Christ. It was originally written in the Pali language, and translated into Tibetan. The manuscript describes how Jesus traveled to India and to the north to Nepal and the Himalayan region. Swami Abhedananda also confirmed the existence of these texts at Hemis in 1922, and published his account of it in his book, *Kashmiri O Tibetti*. Nicholas Roerich also visited in 1925 and published his own account of the manuscripts in his book, *The Heart of Asia*.

The next noteworthy *gompa* in the area is north of Hemis on the west-bank road along the Indus at the valley of Matho. They hold a significant festival here where the monks go into trance and become possessed by spirits.

Heading north of Matho back toward Leh, a road turns off the west-bank road, near the Choglamsar bridge, and goes to the Stok Palace. This is where you can visit the museum of this 200 year old palace, where the Rani of Stok, widow of the last king of Ladakh, still lives. Her eldest son is likely to become the next king when he is of age.

The best way to get to some of these *gompas* is to simply take a few day trips out from Leh, or hire a taxi or car, or rent a jeep.

When our visit to Leh is complete, it will be time to head south toward Manali. If we take a bus, we have to be sure we get our ticket at 9 AM the day before we want to leave since there may be a long queue in the high tourist season. The bus leaves at 6 AM for the 2-day journey, but we must be ready to stay in Leh another night in case the bus doesn't show up, which occasionally happens.

The 485 kilometer road is open from mid-June or later to mid-September. The road also reaches heights of 5328 meters at Taglang La pass, so if you haven't gotten used to the altitude in Leh, you may get headaches or nausea along the way. Only about half of the road is paved, so it is a rough ride.

As we head south, the Taglang La offers some great views. If the bus stops for tea, you can visit the little temple here. After a while you'll go through Pang Camp, which is where most buses stop for lunch at the few restaurant shops in tents by the river. Prices are good for the food. Farther along is the Lachlung La pass, the second highest pass at 5065 meters.

Once we arrive at Sarchu, we are back in the state of Himachal Pradesh. Most buses stop here for the night. Prices are too high for the accommodations in tents, but this is all that is available if you stop here. The next pass is Baralacha La at 4883 meters, where the road soon starts to accompany the Chenab River.

After some time we arrive at Tandi where the road meets the Chenab and Chandrabagha Rivers. Then Keylong, or Kvelang, is the first major town on our route, and then on to Kosar, or Khoksar, for a lunch stop. A lovely waterfall is located in this town. Also along the route is Gondhla which has an eight-storey tall castle of the Thakur of Gondhla. There is also a *gompa* that has some historic importance. Finally, after we cross the Rohtang La Pass at 3978 meters, we'll make our descent into Manali.

Manali is a small resort town, population 2600, and is a good place to relax after our journey through Ladakh. It gets really crowded in the months of May-June and through September. It has plenty of places to stay, but the prices may be high and places get quickly booked up in the tourist season. It also offers many nice walks, treks, and biking trips you can take through the nearby country and villages which are quaint but beautiful if you are into that. People come for the cool atmosphere, but there are some spiritual points of interest here, too.

For example, the Manu Temple, located three kilometers from downtown, marks where Manu first stepped onto dry land after saving the *Vedas* and the animals in his boat after the great flood. In fact, the name Manali is in reference to this. The name "Manali" is short for the name "Manu-Alaya," which means the "home of Manu." It is one of the only temples to Manu in all of India.

There is also the Hidimba Temple in the Dhoongri area of town, dedicated to the wife of Bhima. It was here that Bhima married Hidimba after he killed Hidimb, her man-eating brother. They had a son, Ghatotkatch, who was a great warrior who died in the Kuruksetra war. A temple for him is also nearby.

There are a number of places around Manali which you can visit, if you have the time and energy. Some of these places are not easy to find or reach. But I mention them since they are in the area.

Vashisth is a small town three kilometers from Manali across the river. There are some small but interesting temples here. Tat Baba, located a short walk away from the Vashistha Temple, is where the ashram of Vashistha, the spiritual master of Lord Rama, is said to have been. This is where he performed austerities. Legend has it that Vashistha once tied himself with ropes and jumped into the river when the *rakshasha* Kalmashped killed his 100 sons. But the river loosened the ropes and released him, which gave the river the name of Vipasha, or that which liberates one from bondage. There are also a number of sulphur hot springs around Vishisth, including some within the Vasistha Temple grounds.

About five kilometers south of Manali, not far from Jagatsukh, near the Prime Cafe, is the Arjuna Gupha, or cave of Arjuna. This is where Arjuna underwent austerities to acquire the Pashupata Astra weapon from Lord Shiva. He fought and pleased Shiva, who was disguised as a Kirata, thus earning the weapon. To reach this place is a tough two hour climb with little to see upon reaching it. Furthermore, this may not be the exact place of the event since two other places in India claim the same history.

Six kilometers south of Manali is the small village of Jagatsukh, off the main road, where you'll find an old temple to Lord Shiva with a Sikhara-style structure. There is also another temple to Sandhya Gayatri and Brahma. The Pandavas are also said to have visited these temples.

Bhrigu Kund is a beautiful place where Bhrigu Muni is supposed to have performed austerities, but it takes a rugged, six hour walk to reach it. There is also the Beas Kund, source of the Beas River where Vyasadeva performed austerities.

Thirteen kilometers south of Manali is the town of Katrain. High above it is Naggar. This has the Naggar Castle hotel where you can get excellent views of the area. The castle used to be headquarters for the local Raja. The small old fort is built around a courtyard that has the Jagtri Patt Temple. There is a story that a five by eight foot stone slab in the temple was cut from a stone at Deotiba and carried through the air by a swarm of honey bees. These bees had been transformed from a group of demigods. The stone was carried to Naggar Castle after it had been decided to be the seat of all the gods.

There are also a few old temples here, such as the Gauri Shankar Shiva Temple that has deities of Shiva and Parvati. It is located at the small bazaar below the castle, and dates to the 11th or 12th century. Across from the front of the castle, off the main road, is the small Chatar Bhuj Vishnu Temple, which has a beautiful Vishnu Deity that stands four feet high. Higher up is the Tripura Sundri Devi Temple, dedicated to Durga, with its pagoda-like structure. On the ridge higher up is the Murlidhar Krishna Temple, reached after a tough 20-minute climb.

From here we travel south to Kulu, population 14,500. Kulu is a more mellow town and less crowded by tourists than Manali. Kulu is particularly known for the Raghunathji Temple, dedicated to Lord Rama. The temple is on a hill behind the Kulu Raja's Rupi Palace that overlooks the city. It is reached by traversing a path from near the Kailash Cinema by the bus stand. The Deity is considered to preside over the Kulu valley region and was brought here by Raja Jagat Singh in 1651 from Ayodhya.

Kulu is also well known for its Dussehra Festival in October. They have a huge festival here that celebrates the victory of Lord Rama over the demon Ravana. The Deity of Raghunatha is brought into the valley on a chariot in a grand procession where He stays for a week. Then the other 200 or so deities in the area are brought to Him to offer worship. The town becomes very crowded with pilgrims at this time, so accommodations become very limited.

Three kilometers out from Kulu is Bhekhli village where the Jagannatha Devi Temple is located up a steep climb. And four kilometers out of Kulu toward Manali is a Vaishno Devi Temple, with a representation of the goddess Vaishno in a small cave.

Eight kilometers southeast of Kulu is the Bijli Mahadeva Shiva Temple. This is reached by a difficult climb up a six kilometer incline. It has a 65-foot tall flagstaff that attracts lightning. When it's struck by lightning, the Shiva-*linga* is broken, after which it is put back together with a paste made from roasted gram and wheat powder.

Fifteen kilometers south of Kulu in Bajaura is the temple of Basheshar Mahadeva (Shiva) with ornate stone carvings.

When we leave Kulu, we can get a bus directly to Shimla, or we can take a leisurely tour through several more little towns in the area that have some interesting things to see. From Kulu we can go south to Aut and then west to Mandi. Mandi, population 23,000, is considered the gateway to the Kulu Valley. It has a popular Bhutnath Shiva Temple and the festival of Shivaratri is especially famous. It lasts a week and deities are brought here from all over the area.

Returning to Aut, we can now go southeast through Rampur, which is the site of a significant trade fair in November, and on to Sarahan farther east, the home of the Bhimkali Temple which has a combination of Buddhist and Hindu architecture. From here we can backtrack and go on to Narkanda. This town, population 700, is a popular place for seeing the Himalayas, especially from Hattu peak at 3300 meters. This whole area is popular for ski resorts. From here we go south to Shimla, if we haven't taken the direct bus from Kulu or Manali.

Shimla is a much larger town, population 110,000, and crowded with lots of buildings, streets and alleys packed onto the hillside. It is popular as a cool hill station during the summer with an altitude of 21,000 meters. However, when I was there in June, it was still 30 degrees Centigrade, and I was sweating in the sun. So I didn't think it was so cool. Nonetheless, it was especially used by the British when they would move here for the summer. There's not much of spiritual interest here, but you can certainly have a little fun exploring the town and walking to nearby points of interest, such as to Summer Hill, Prospect Hill, the Hanuman Temple at Sankat Mochan, Chadwick Falls, or the Tara Devi Temple seven kilometers out of town. Of course, that's if you still have the energy after everything else we've done.

If you want, you can go farther west to Bilaspur, which has the Vyas Gufa cave, and the Lakshmi-Narayana and Radha Shyama temples.

Once our visit is over, from Shimla we head south to the town of Chail, which has the hilltop Chail Palace and an ancient Sikh temple. Then we go on to Solan where we find the Soloni Devi Temple located on the southern side of town. After this we go on to Pinjore if you'd like to see more Moghul gardens and the Shish Mahal Palace, and the Rang and Jai Mahals. Otherwise, or afterwards, we go on to Chandigarh. Chandigarh really has little to offer the pilgrim, unless you want to stop and see the museum or art gallery. Otherwise, we simply keep going south to Kuruksetra, a very significant town in relation to Krishna. If you do not want to see these small towns, you can take a small train from Shimla to Kalka where we switch to the Himalayan Queen on the broad faster gauge line. This train goes directly to New Delhi but also stops at Kuruksetra.

Kuruksetra is a spiritually important and peaceful town which no pilgrim should miss. It's 118 kilometers north of Delhi, or about a four hour train ride away. It is most noted for being the place where Lord Krishna sang the *Bhagavad-gita*, which means the "song of God," to his friend Arjuna. The *Bhagavad-gita* is a classic text of India and Vedic thought. Every December there is the festival of Gita Jayanti, which is the celebration of Krishna relating the *Bhagavad-gita*.

Although there are plenty of *dharmshalas* in town where we can stay, there is one hotel located about a 30 minute cycle-ricksha ride away from the train station: The Nilkantha Tourist Complex. It is a simple affair with two floors of rooms surrounding a courtyard. It is not far from the Brahma Sarovara, Sannihit Sarovara, and other temples. Rooms here are fairly nice: A double with a balcony was 150 rupees a night. From my room I could hear the holy recitations coming from the loudspeaker from a temple across the field which I could see from my balcony. In the evening there are also plenty of fireflies that look like stars in the grass.

The hotel also has a restaurant with a limited selection. I ate there in the evening, but the electricity was out and the door was left open, which allowed for many mosquitoes to come in. So eating in the growing darkness while dealing with the mosquitoes was not the best of arrangements. There are a few places nearby that also sell cold drinks, and you can get Cokes at one of the vendors across the street if you wish. I never saw any bottled water for purchase except at the train station.

The Iskcon temple is in the older part of town. If you can get there in the morning you can have *darshan* of the beautiful Radha-Krishna Deities, which stand about two feet tall, and the smaller Gaura-Nitai Deities. You can also attend the *arati* and have a nice *prasadam* breakfast. The temple is quite nice and expanding. In fact, they only had acquired the property and erected the building in the six months prior to my first visit here, which included guest quarters on the top floor where visitors can stay. The number of devotees is small, but they are very friendly and helpful. In fact, they helped arrange my motor ricksha transportation to see the holy places in town.

Not only was the *Bhagavad-gita* sung by Lord Krishna in Kuruksetra, but other spiritually important events also took place here. Krishna met his friends and residents of Vrindavana here during an eclipse while He was living in Dwaraka. He also took bath in Brahma Sarovara and the Sannihit Sarovara water tanks. It is said that the Brahma Sarovara tank is one of the most important in all of India, and that all the holy waters of India are found in the Brahma Sarovara during an eclipse, which is why millions of pilgrims come here to bathe during such an event. It is also said that those who bathe here, live here, visit, or die in Kuruksetra go to heaven after death. In the *Kuruksetra Mahatmya* of the *Mahabharata* the sage Pulastya says that even the dust of Kuruksetra will cause one to reach the highest goal. This is the benefit for all who died in the battle of Kuruksetra 5,000 years ago, and one reason why the battle took place here. It is another reason why every pilgrim should visit this holy place.

Furthermore, it is said that Manu wrote the *Manu-samhita* here. Some people also believe that Vyasadeva wrote the *Mahabharata* at his *ashrama* along the banks of the Sarasvati River when the Sarasvati used to flow through Kuruksetra. The *Rig* and *Sama Vedas* may have been written here as well. Even Lord Buddha is said to have visited Kuruksetra.

While we are here, there are several places we want to visit. First of all, Jyotisar is the place where Krishna related the *Bhagavad-gita* to His devotee Arjuna. This is about 10 kilometers out of town. It is a pleasant ricksha ride away and provides a time to meditate on the occasion when the huge armies gathered on these plains thousands of years ago. Jyotisar is now a small park with a central banyan tree over a small marble chariot that marks where Krishna sang the *Bhagavad-gita* and showed Arjuna His universal form. The banyan tree is said to be the same tree as when Krishna and Arjuna were present and, thus, the only living witness to the event. There is a large pond of water here that provides for a refreshing atmosphere. There are also a few other small shrines, like an old Shiva temple. It is most pleasant to sit and meditate on the significance of the area and read some of the *Bhagavad-gita* while visiting.

The history of the Battle of Kuruksetra and the speaking of the *Bhagavad-gita* can be told briefly. The five Pandava brothers, born of King Pandu, were the legitimate heirs to the kingdom of India. However, when the Pandavas were still young, Pandu died untimely and Dhritarashtra, the head of the Kuru family, assumed control until the Pandavas were grown. However, due to his love for his own sons, Dhritarashtra engaged in many plots and intrigues to eliminate the Pandavas so his sons, the Kauravas, could inherit the kingdom. After many years of tribulations, close escapes from death, and fourteen years of exile, the Pandavas returned to reclaim their rights to the throne. The Kurus were not inclined to honor the Pandavas in any way. Even after asking for only five villages, one for each of the Pandavas to rule, Duryodhana, the chief of the Kauravas, said he would not give them enough land with which to stick a pin.

After all peaceful negotiations were exhausted, the Pandavas agreed that there was no other choice than to fight. Even Lord Krishna asked the Kauravas to settle the matter, but this was not what was destined to be. Each side then amassed huge armies from all over India and beyond. In fact, the Kurus had a much larger army and far greater warriors than the Pandavas. However, the greatest ally of the Pandavas was their great moral and spiritual character, and their friend Sri Krishna, the most powerful personality.

When it was time for the huge armies to face each other on the plains of Kuruksetra, there were many millions of warriors, horses, chariots, and elephants ready to fight. Before the battle, Krishna, who was serving as Arjuna's chariot driver and advisor, drove Arjuna's chariot between the two great armies. Seeing the number of friends and relatives on each side ready to fight each other, Arjuna hesitated and felt much grief over the situation. He felt it was useless to fight. It was then that Krishna took the opportunity to sing the *Bhagavad-gita* to Arjuna.

The *Bhagavad-gita* is the essence of all Vedic philosophy and is composed of 720 verses and explains such topics as the nature of the soul, God, the material universe, activities and *karma*, reincarnation, and the purpose of life. After explaining all this to Arjuna, he took courage with proper understanding and fought. Thereafter, the war of Kuruksetra lasted for 18 days in which several million warriors died in the fierce fighting. Then the Pandavas were rightfully established in their kingdom, and Sri Krishna had provided His eternal instructions in the form of the *Bhagavad-gita*. This is all explained in the *Mahabharata* which is composed of 100,000 verses, making it the longest poem in literary history.

When we leave Jyotisar, our next stop is at Bana Ganga. This is where Grandfather Bhisma left this world on the 11th day of the Battle of Kuruksetra. The battle was so fierce that Bhisma's back was covered with arrows. Finally, he fell on his back and laid on what appeared as a bed of arrows. Then Krishna and the Pandavas, hearing the news, gathered around him as he prepared to leave this world. Bhisma was one of the greatest and most respected of the warriors on the battlefield. As he lay there, he became thirsty and Arjuna shot an arrow into the ground from which sprang Ganges water to quench Bhisma's thirst. This later formed into what is now a small *kund* or water tank called Bana Ganga, or Bhisma Kund. Bathing in it is said to give the benefits of bathing at all the holy *tirthas*.

Next to the *kund* is a small temple that has images of Bhisma on the bed of arrows surrounded by Krishna and the Pandavas in the act of listening to Bhisma as he instructs Yudhisthira on the path of *dharma*, or spiritual merit. There is also a Deity of Krishna in His universal form. At one end of the *kund* is a huge 26 foot tall deity of Hanuman. There is also a little temple here of Sita-Rama, Lakshmana, Hanuman, and Durga. When we are finished here, next we'll go to the large Brahma Sarovara tank.

Brahma Sarovara is one of the holiest tanks in India and is where millions of pilgrims gather to bathe during an eclipse. One who bathes here is said to receive the merit of performing an *ashvamedha* ritual, and one is freed from all sins by bathing here during an eclipse. This is where Lord Brahma performed a large sacrificial ceremony and also from where he manifested the earth planet in the process of creation. Legend has it that Brahma Sarovara was excavated first by King Kuru long before the epic battle of Kuruksetra. It is a huge tank (half a kilometer wide and one kilometer long) with an island in the middle connected by a road that cuts through it. On the island is a well called the Chandra Kupa Well, one of the oldest sacred wells. Tradition has it that in ancient times the water in the well would change to milk during the solar eclipse. Next to the well is a small Radha-Krishna temple where Yudhisthira is said to have built a victory pillar after the successful culmination of the war. This lake is also where Krishna, His brother Balarama, and His sister Subhadra came from Dwaraka to bathe during an eclipse. Along the side of the tank is a smaller island with the Sarveshvar Mahadeva (Shiva) Temple on it.

The streets nearby have a number of other temples that we can visit, such as the Birla Gita Mandir. This has a Deity of Krishna in the act of explaining the *Bhagavad-gita* to Arjuna. Outside is a chariot with images of Krishna and Arjuna on it. Down the road along Brahma Sarovara are other temples and *ashramas*, many of which are quite nice.

Nearby is Sannihit Sarovara, another water tank that is very significant. It is not as large as Brahma Sarovara, but it is fairly big (1500 by 450 feet). Sannihit means the assembly of the entire range of holy *tirthas*, which is said to happen every Amavas, or eclipse, especially the Somavati Amavas (lunar eclipse). It is also said that all of the sacred holy places gather here on the new Moon day, and that this is where the seven sacred Sarasvatis meet. Performing the *shraddha* ceremony to the ancestors and bathing during the eclipse is said to purify you of all your sins and give you the merit of having performed 1,000 *ashvamedha* ceremonies. Lord Krishna also bathed here and met the *gopis* and residents of Vrindavana when He was present.

On the eastern end of the tank are several small temples to Vishnu, Dhruva, Hanuman, Durga, Lakshmi-Narayana, etc. Across the road is a large, beautiful temple to Lakshmi-Narayana. There are also numerous *sadhus* found here, and those who merely *look* like *sadhus*. In fact, as I walked around the lake, I came upon a group of *sadhus* who, instead of engaging in meditation or reading scriptures, etc., were sitting and playing a game of cards. When I asked them if I could take a photo, a few instantly said no. Playing like a naive tourist, I asked why not, and one answered, "What do you think?" They thought I was going to give it to the newspapers. Of course, I knew why they didn't want their photo taken: They didn't want to be seen that way because they would lose their credibility. This made me realize how few real *sadhus* actually exist.

Not far from here is a very impressive, government operated Krishna Museum. This museum is all related to the pastimes of Krishna and the various ways to express devotion to Him. The museum has a wide assortment of brass, metal, and wood Deities of Krishna, Jagannatha Deities, paintings, drawings, sculptures, and artwork from all over India. There was also a life-size image of Mother Yasoda with Krishna and Balarama. It also has an assortment of costumes and dress from different eras of Indian history. This museum is very nicely done and well worth the visit, but don't take any photos or, as I was told, that may take away your camera.

Our next stop is Kamal Nabha or Nabhi, which is said to mark the place where Brahma was born out of the lotus flower that arose from the *nabhi* or navel of Lord Vishnu. Though it is small, it is very significant. This is located in the old town of Thanesar. The water tank here is not that large and is green with algae. There is only a small shrine with Lakshmi-Narayana Deities and a picture on the wall of Vishnu with Brahma on the lotus coming from Vishnu's navel. In the entranceway are a few other small Deities.

The Sthaneswara Temple and Tank are also very interesting and is where the Pandavas prayed to Lord Shiva for blessings to be victorious in the war of Kuruksetra. The water from the tank is considered sacred and to have healing powers. A few drops of the water from the tank is said to have cured King Ban or Vena of leprosy. The temples around the tank have very beautiful Deities of Krishna, Radha-Govinda, Sita-Rama and Lakshmana, Shiva, Durga, etc., and an ancient Shiva-*lingam*.

Down the road is the Bhadra Kali Temple which marks the place where Sati's ankle fell when Lord Vishnu cut her dead body as it was being held by Lord Shiva. This was after she left her body when she had been insulted by her father, Daksha, in Haridwar for having Shiva as her husband.

There is an assortment of other noteworthy places around Kuruksetra, some of which you may want to visit if you have time. The mound called Amin, eight miles outside of town, is where Arjuna's son, Abhimanyu, was caught in the Chakra Vyuha during the battle of Kuruksetra, as described in the *Mahabharata*. And the Karna Vadha trench is where Karna, the Pandavas half-brother who fought against them, was killed when his chariot got stuck there. And Jind and Safidon are towns where you'll find such *tirthas* as Ram Hridaya where Parashurama performed a spiritual ceremony. At Birhi Kalan near Jind is Varaha

Tirtha where Lord Varaha appeared in order to save the earth. Sarp Damam, in Safidon, is where Janamejaya performed a fire sacrifice in order to destroy all the snakes, as described in the *Srimad-Bhagavatam*. If you have the time to do some research, the library at Kuruksetra has a good collection of Vedic literature in Sanskrit as well as English.

After our visit to Kuruksetra, we can travel down to New Delhi where we can decide what is next on our agenda: More traveling or a return home. Even in New Delhi we can see some of the important temples, such as the new and beautiful Hare Krishna "Glory of India Temple" in the south part of the city. This and other temples can continue to uplift our consciousness even within the environs of the city, and before we move on with the adventure of our lives.

So now we have completed our pilgrimage to all of the major holy places and more in Northern India. These have included the holy sites of several major religions in many locations, along with places that are related to the Vedic legends and the creation of the world, as explained in this book. We have now also been to places that have provided inspiration and deep realizations for many sages and holy men, not to mention ourselves. And by visiting these places and witnessing and feeling the atmosphere of the various cultures, we also have been able to expand our consciousness and realizations about life in this world and beyond. Many of these places are like jumping-off points that can help propel us into the higher dimensions and realities of life. This can certainly play a very important part of our spiritual development, which can help catapult us back to the spiritual dimension. This, after all, is the main purpose of life, as we have explained in the previous chapters of this book. And if we have traveled with a seeker's humility and quest for higher experiences, then some of us who have gone on this journey, or even parts of it, have certainly attained glimpses into the same visions of the sages that have gone on before us, and viewed similar levels of higher reality. The effects and memories of such encounters will stay with us forever and, thus, change our lives. This is priceless experience.

PHOTOGRAPHS

PAGE 204: Top, Pilgrims happily bathing in the Ganges at Har ki Pauri.

Bottom, After a holy bath, many pilgrims visit the nearby shrines to offer respect to the many Deities, which include Radha and Krishna, Shiva and Parvati, Ganga Devi (the personality of the Ganges River), Yamuna Devi, and others.

PAGE 205: The Dakshesvara Temple. One of the most important of the historic temples of Haridwar, where Daksha, one of the mind-born sons of Brahma, performed a great sacrifice, and where his daughter, Sati, wife of Lord Shiva, immolated herself after being insulted by Daksha.

PAGE 206: Top Left, the pit that marks the original location where Daksha had his fire ceremony many thousands of years ago. The Deity of Durga (Parvati) is in the background behind the glass.

Top Right, A shop keeper behind his brass pots.

Bottom, The Ganges flowing out across the plains from Haridwar.

PAGE 207: Top & Bottom, Many people gather at Har-ki-Pauri to watch the Ganga *puja*, evening worship of the Ganges, a highlight of the day.

PAGE 208: Top, Priests holding large ghee lamps for worship of the Ganges.

Bottom, Many people gathering along the Ganges River with shops brightly lit at night create a festive atmosphere.

PAGE 209: Top, People listening to a spiritual discourse near the Ganges.

Bottom, An evening look at Rishikesh, surrounded by the Himalayan foothills in the background with the calm Ganges flowing by.

PAGE 210: Top, The Lakshmana Jula suspension bridge overlooking the Ganges with both new and old temples nearby.

Bottom, Many wandering sages and sadhus come through Rishikesh on their way to and from the holy places in the mountains. In this photo, people give sadhus packets of curd (yogurt) as a gesture of goodwill.

PAGE 211: Top Left, A Vaishnava devotee of Lord Ramachandra.

Top Right, A wandering mendicant.

Bottom Left, A Shaivite *sannyasa* (renunciant).

Bottom Right, Another wandering *sadhu*.

PAGE 212: Top, On the bus going up through the Himalayan mountains to Yamunotri. You can see one bus on the right on the road high on the hillside.

Bottom, Pilgrims high up in the hills on their way to Yamunotri.

PAGE 213: On the path from the small village of Hanuman Chatti walking to Yamunotri. If you look closely, you can see the path in these big hills going up into the mountains.

PAGE 214: The Yamunotri Temple with the snow capped peaks high above. This temple marks the symbolic beginning of the holy Yamuna River.

PAGE 215: Top, Another view of the Yamunotri Temple.

Bottom, A *sadhu* boiling rice in the hot springs at Yamunotri.

PAGE 216: The Ganges flowing through the hills on our way to Gangotri.

PAGE 217: Top, On the streets of Gangotri.

Bottom, The sitting place of King Bhagirathi when he called the Ganges to come down to Earth from the heavens. The river is known as the Bhagirathi until it reaches Deoprayag.

PAGE 218: The loud and forceful Sahasradhara Falls. This is where Lord Shiva was supposed to have been sitting when he caught the Ganges on his head when it came down to earth from the heavens. From here the water froze in the cold season and became a large glacier. Over many years it has since melted until now the mouth of the Ganges is nearly 21 kilometers farther up in the mountains, and continues to change and recede farther away.

PAGE 219: From the waterfall in the background, the Ganges forces its way into this narrow gorge that is only one meter in width.

PAGE 220: The main temple at Gangotri dedicated to Ganga Devi.

PAGE 221: The mouth of the Ganges River. Its appearance keeps changing because it keeps receding farther up into the mountains.

PAGE 222: Top, One of the beautiful mountains behind the holy town of Badrinatha.

Bottom, The major portion of the town of Badrinatha with the Badrinatha Temple in the center and the Alakananda River below. This is one of the major holy places in India.

PAGE 223: Top left, Crowds going into the Badrinatha Temple.

Top Right, Four kilometers farther from Badrinatha in the town of Mana is Vyasadeva's cave. This is said to be the place where he dictated the great *Mahabharata* and the *Srimad-Bhagavatam*, his conclusion to all Vedic literature, 5000 years ago.

Bottom, The Deity of Srila Vyasadeva in his cave.

PAGE 224: Top Left, The foamy white Sarasvati River flowing under Bhima's Pol, the stone bridge Bhima made to allow his family members, the Pandavas, to travel up into the mountains on the path that became known as the stairway to heaven. High up on this mountain route they left this world, as described in the *Mahabharata*.

Top Right, Even in the cold weather of Badrinatha some *sadhus* like this one are not affected by it and wear little else than a thin cloth.

Bottom, The village of Deoprayag, one of the most important river confluences of India, where the Bhagirathi River on the left meets the Alakananda River and becomes the Ganges.

PAGE 225: Top, The beautiful Sikh Golden Temple at Amritsar.

PAGE 225: Bottom, A view of the Golden Temple at night. It is breathtaking.

PAGE 226: Top, The beautiful Deities of Sri Sri Radha-Krishna and Govardhana Shila at the Durgiana Temple at Amritsar.

Bottom, The town of Dharamsala and the magnificent mountains above, viewed from the balcony of the hotel where I had stayed.

PAGE 227: The image of Avalokiteshvara Buddha at the Namgyal Monastery at McLeod Ganj, above Dharamsala.

PAGE 228: Top, Buddhist monks practice the often theatrical art of debate. One challenges with philosophical points, and the other responds.

Bottom, McLeod Ganj and the neighboring towns are the home of many exiled Tibetan people, including these monks.

PAGE 229: Top Left, A typical Tibetan Buddhist monk spinning his prayer wheel.

Top Right, This retired professor, Narkyid Ngawangthondup, taught about Tibet at Columbus, Ohio, Kalamazoo, Michigan, and in Seattle. He had also visited Detroit where I have been living, and I met him here at the tiny Namgyal Cafe near the monastery.

Bottom Left, A happy monk enjoying a refreshment in town.

Bottom Right, A Tibetan girl at the Shoton Festival.

PAGE 230: Top Left, Even this old woman escaped the Chinese in Tibet.

Top Right, Carpet making in a crafts shop shows some of the ways Tibetans support themselves.

Bottom, A Tibetan lady making handicrafts.

PAGE 231: Top, Tibetans selling jewelry along the streets of McLeod Ganj.

Bottom, Tibetan Buddhists of all ages share in turning the prayer wheels at the central shrine at McLeod Ganj.

PAGE 232: Top Left, An old monk turning a large prayer wheel at the central shrine, McLeod Ganj.

Top Right, A Tibetan mask dancer.

Bottom, Thousands of prayer flags fly in the wind at the shrine behind the residence of the Dalai Lama.

PAGE 233: Top & Bottom, Tibetan dancers at the Gyalsa Balsa Opera at the Shoton Festival.

PAGE 234: Top, Even though the Tibetans in India are all refugees, having given up family and property, they can still laugh and enjoy life while watching the humor of the Tibetan Opera at the Shoton Festival.

Bottom, The Dalai Lama addressing the people at the Shoton Festival and then walking through and greeting his devoted people.

PAGE 235: Top, The northern end of the lovely Kulu Valley at Manali.

Bottom, The Manu Temple at Manali which represents the place where Manu first touched ground after the global flood thousands of years ago.

PAGE 236: Top, When we are ready to return to Delhi, we can take this small train south from Shimla through the hills to Kalka and points south.

PAGE 236: Bottom, The park at Jyotisar in Kuruksetra, where Lord Krishna spoke the *Bhagavad-gita*.

PAGE 237: The exact spot where Lord Krishna spoke the *Bhagavad-gita* to His devotee Arjuna 5,000 years ago. This banyan tree is said to be a surviving witness to the event.

PAGE 238: Top, Nabhi Kamal at Kuruksetra, the water *kund* which represents where Lord Brahma was born when the cosmic lotus was growing from Lord Vishnu's navel during the process of universal creation.

Bottom, Back in Delhi there are still plenty of places to visit that can enhance our spiritual life, such as the new Glory of India Temple in the southern part of New Delhi.

PAGE 239: The beautiful Sri Sri Radha-Krishna Deities at the Glory of India Temple. Krishna's name here is Paratha Sarthi, which relates to His pastime of being Arjuna's chariot driver when He spoke the *Bhagavad-gita* at Kuruksetra.

Our journey to the holy places of Northern India starts in Haridwar, which means the doorway to God. Here we see the holy place of Har ki Pauri in the morning with lots of people starting their day with a holy bath in the Ganges.

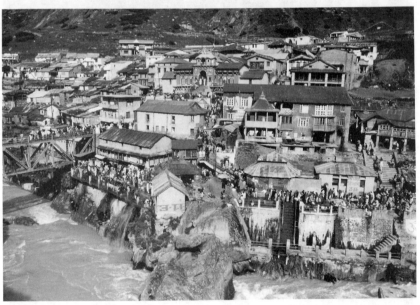

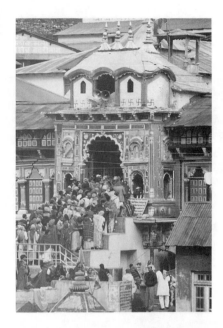

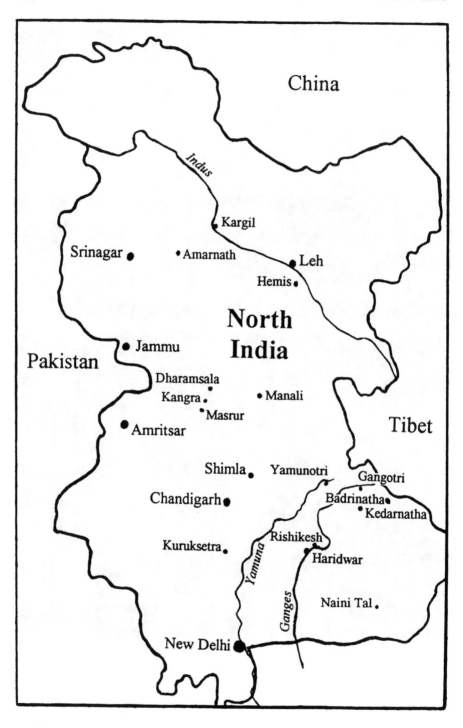

APPENDIX ONE

Summary of the Creative Process

Since we have gone through the finer details of how everything is created, we should not let that overwhelm us with information. So here is a short description of the process.

In the beginning there was the void of the *pradhana*, the unmanifest material ingredients. By the glance of the Supreme Being, the innumerable conditioned souls and the time element are carried into the material energy. This glance is Shambhu, who also carries the material element of ego. With the element of time, the *pradhana* produces the *mahat-tattva*. From this comes the false-ego, which begins to mix with the modes of nature. When the false-ego is transformed by the mode of ignorance, the sky or ether is manifested. From the ether comes the air. From air, fire is manifested. From fire, water is produced. From water comes earth. Thus, the five main elements, called *pancha-maha-bhuta*, are manifested. When time agitates the mode of ignorance, impersonal knowledge (*jnana*) and fruitive activities (*karma*) are produced from the *mahat-tattva*. From this *karma*, the modes of goodness and passion are manifested, which produces knowledge and action (*kriya*). This produces the subtle element of intelligence, which paves the way for the manifestation of sound, carried by the ether. After sound is produced comes the ability of touch. Sound and touch are enabled by air. From them comes the life-force (*prana*), energy (*ojah*) and strength (*bala*). Through fire, the potential for form, touch and sound exists. By fire's transformation caused by time, water is manifested. In water is the characteristics for taste, form, touch, and sound. A further transformation brings earth, in which are fragrance, taste, form, touch, and sound. It is under the guidance and assistance of the Supreme Controller that these changes are manifested.

When false-ego mixes with the modes of nature, further creation takes place. False-ego in the mode of goodness brings forth material objects. From false-ego in the mode of passion, the ten material senses are produced. These include the

241

knowledge acquiring senses (eyes, ears, nose, tongue, and skin) and the working senses (voice, hands, feet, genitals, and rectum). Even when all of these elements, both gross and subtle, and assembled together, nothing can happen until the individual spirit soul enters into the combination. Only after the Supreme Being, by His glance, places the *jiva* soul into the body, only then does it begin to move. Thus, the senses, manifested by the modes of goodness and passion, come into contact with the sense objects that are manifested from the *pradhana* through the mode of ignorance.

In this way, *maya*, the illusory energy, is manifested and divided into twenty-four categories, namely the five elements, five knowledge acquiring senses, five working senses, and five characteristics of fragrance, taste, form, touch, and sound. In addition, there are the mind, heart, intelligence and false-ego. The individual spirit soul is the twenty-fifth category, and the Supreme Being is the twenty-sixth that can be found within the material creation, although these two are actually beyond the limited material distinctions.

Thereafter, once the universes are ready to manifest they appear like innumerable golden eggs in the Karana Ocean. Lord Vishnu then expands Himself to enter each and every universe as Garbhodakashayi Vishnu. From His navel rises the lotus flower composed of the fourteen planetary systems, on top of which Lord Brahma is manifested. After Lord Brahma realizes his spiritual position and prays to Lord Vishnu, he is granted the powers to create. Then the secondary stage of creation begins from Lord Brahma.

First created from Brahma are the planets. Once the facility for life throughout the universe is manifested, then the variety of living beings are created. Immovable living beings are created first. Then the animal species of life are brought into being. Humankind is created next, followed by the various demigods and beings of the subtle realm. These include some of the demigods or co-managers of the universe, the angel-like beings, the Yakshas and Rakshasas, and other beings with demoniac mentality. These also include the ghosts, as well as the higher perfected beings, such as the Siddhas, superhumans, and celestial persons.

Next there is the creation of the Kumaras, Rudra, and the great sages, which are Brahma's mind-born sons. Then there is the manifestation of the *Vedas*, the four social orders, and then Svayambhuva Manu and his wife Shatarupa, the man and woman whose descendants populate the universe. How these descendants spread throughout the world is described further in Appendix Two.

APPENDIX TWO

Further Levels of the Process of Creation

This is an overview of further levels of creation, continued from Appendix One. This takes place after the universe has already been manifested as described in the *Puranas*. This explains how more of the population within the material creation came into being by special arrangement, as well as how additional species of life manifested through the progenitors who had been empowered by Brahma. So this is a continuation from the chapter on the creation from Lord Brahma.

As previously explained, Svayambhuva Manu and Shatarupa begot two sons, Priyavrata and Uttanapada, and three daughters, Akuti, Devahuti, and Prasuti. The two great sons of Manu, Priyavrata and Uttanapada, ruled the world, which consisted of seven great islands or continents.[1] They became very powerful kings, and their sons and grandsons spread all over the three worlds during that period.[2] Manu handed over his daughters to three of the great sages. Akuti went to the sage Ruci, Devahuti to Kardama, and Prasuti to Daksha. From them many generations filled the world.[3] Daksha was one of the mind-born sons of Brahma, and the descendants of Daksha spread throughout the universe.[4]

From Ruci, one of the progenitors or Prajapatis, and his wife Akuti was born one son, Yajna, who was an incarnation of the Supreme, and one daughter, Dakshina. She was a partial incarnation of Lakshmi who is the Lord's internal potency, the goddess of fortune, and Lord Vishnu's eternal consort. Later, they married and twelve sons were born to them who were demigods called the Tushitas or Yama-devas. From Daksha and Prasuti came 16 [some *Puranas* say 24] daughters. Thirteen were given in marriage to Dharma and one was given to Agni. They all gave birth to one son each, but Murti gave birth to Sri Nara-Narayana, an expansion of the Supreme Lord. One other daughter was given to Pitriloka, and the remaining daughter was given to Lord Shiva. From these daughters and their husbands came many more great personalities, the names of whom are given in the *Puranas*.[5]

From Devahuti and Kardama were born two daughters, Samrat and Kukshi. Uttama was born as the son of Uttanapada through Saruchi, and Dhruva was born as the son of Uttanapada through Suniti. Dhruva did penance to gain fame and pleased the Supreme Lord in the process.[6] Kardama Muni and Devahuti also produced nine daughters and one son, Kapila Muni, an incarnation of the Lord. Kardama handed his daughters over to the great sages at the request of Lord Brahma. Kala went to Marici, Anasuya to Atri, Shraddha to the sage Angira, Havirbhu to Pulastya, Gati to Pulaha, Kriya to Kratu, Khyati to Bhrigu, Arundhati to Vashistha, and Shanti to Atharva.[7]

It is from these descendants of Manu, known as the Prajapatis or progenitors, consisting of the greatly powerful sages and their qualified wives, that filled the world with many more varieties of population.

Kardama Muni's daughter Kala, who was married to Marici, gave birth to two children, Kashyapa and Purnima. Their descendants spread throughout the world. Purnima begot three children, Viraja, Vishvaga and Devakulya. Devakulya was the form of the presiding Deity of the Ganges River.[8]

From Atri Muni and his wife, Anasuya, came three sons, Soma, Dattatreya and Durvasa Muni. They were incarnations and partial manifestations of Brahma, Vishnu and Shiva.[9]

Angira's wife, Shraddha, gave birth to four daughters, Sinivali, Kuhu, Raka and Anumati, along with two sons, Utathya and the learned scholar Brihaspati. Pulastya and his wife, Havirbhu, begot Agastya and Vishrava. Vishrava had two wives, the first of which was Idavida, from whom was born Kubera, master of the Yakshas. The second wife was Keshini from whom were born the three brothers, the great demon Ravana, Kumbhakarna and Vibhishana.[10]

Pulaha and his wife Gati gave birth to three great sages, Karmashrestha, Variyan and Sahishnu. Kratu and his wife, Kriya, gave birth to 60,000 great sages called the Valakhilyas, all advanced in spiritual knowledge.[11]

The grea sage Vasistha and his wife Urja (Arundhati) begot seven great sages, named Citraketu, Suroci, Viraja, Mitra, Ulbana, Vasubhridyana and Dyuman. Atharva and his wife Citti gave birth to a great sage Ashvashira. The great Bhrigu and his wife, Khyati, begot two sons, Dhata and Vidhata, and a daughter, Sri, who was a great devotee of the Supreme Lord. The sage Meru had two sons, Mrikanda and Prana. Markhandya Muni was born to Mrikanda, and the sage Vedashira from Prana, whose son was Ushana, also called Shukracarya or Kavi. Thus, the population of the universe was increased by the descendants of these sages and the daughters of Kardama Muni.[12]

From the demigod Agni and his wife Svaha came three children named Pavaka, Pavamana and Shuci. From these three sons came another 45 descendants who are also fire gods. They exist by means of the oblations offered in the Vedic sacrificial fires by the impersonalist *brahmanas*. The daughter of Daksha given to

Shiva was Sati. She produced no offspring because Daksha always criticized Lord Shiva, after which Sati gave up her body.[13]

Later, Daksha and his wife Panchajani begot 10,000 sons for creating population in the universe, but these sons were delivered by Narada Muni from this activity by his teaching of spiritual knowledge. So these sons gave up the idea of engaging in householder life. Then Daksha produced another one thousand sons and the same thing happened. So Daksha and his wife Asikni produced 60 daughters. He gave ten daughters to Yamaraja, thirteen to Kashyapa Muni, 27 to the moon-god, Chandra, and two each to Angira, Krishashva and Bhuta. The remaining four were also given to Kashyapa Muni. From these daughters, produced by Daksha for the purpose of creating progeny to populate the worlds, came many types of living entities and personalities that filled the universe.[14]

This is also explained and further elaborated in the *Vishnu Purana*.[15] Therein it is repeated that Daksha, obeying Brahma to create progeny for the furtherance of creation, made movable and immovable things, bipeds and quadrupeds. Subsequently by his will, he produced daughters, ten of whom he gave to Dharma, thirteen to Kashyapa, and 27 to the Nakshatras, demigods who regulate the course of time on the moon. Of these, the gods, the titans, the snake gods, cattle, birds, the singers and dancers of the courts of heaven, the spirits of evil, and other things were born. From that period onwards living creatures were engendered by sexual intercourse. Before the time of Daksha sex was not necessary for conception and they were variously propagated by the will, by sight, by touch, or by the influence of religious austerities practiced by devout sages and holy saints. [This sheds some light on how so many offspring, and different species, could be conceived from one woman, or even mystically without a woman. It is similar to the way Brahma could create various entities and species by his special power. Nonetheless, this certainly may be a little difficult to understand for those who are less spiritually conversant or experienced.]

The *Bhagavatam* continues to explain that from Yamaraja and his ten wives came such sons as Vidyota from the womb of Lamba, who generated clouds. From the womb of Bhanu came Deva-rishabha, who produced a son named Indrasena. From Kakud came a son named Sankata, whose son was Kikata, from whom came demigods named Durga. From Yami came the son Svarga, whose son was Nandi. The sons of Vishva were the Vishvadevas. From Sadhya came the Sadhyas. From Marutvati came Marutvan and Jayanta. Jayanta, also known as Upendra, was an expansion of Lord Vasudeva, Krishna.[16]

From Muhurta came the demigods named Mauhurtikas who deliver the results of actions to the living beings. The son of Sankalpa produced lust. The eight Vasus were born of the womb of Vasu. These included Drona, Prana, Dhruva, Arka, Agni, Dosha, Vastu and Vibhavasu.[17]

From the wife of Vasu named Vastu came the great architect Vishvakarma. He became the husband of Akriti from whom the Manu named Chakshusha was born. The sons of Manu were known as the Vishvadevas and Sadhyas.[18]

From Svarupa, the wife of Bhuta [Shiva as lord of the Bhutas] came ten million Rudras, of whom eleven are topmost, namely Raivata, Aja, Bhava, Bhima, Vama, Ugra, Vrishakapi, Ajaikapat, Ahirbradhna, Bahurupa and Mahan. Their associates, the ghosts and goblins, were born of the other wife of Bhuta.[19]

Angira had two wives, named Svadha and Sati. Svadha accepted all the Pitas as her sons, and Sati accepted the Atharvangirasa Veda as her son. Kashyapa Muni, also called Tarkshya, had four wives--Vinata, Kadru, Patangi and Yamini. Patangi gave birth to many kinds of birds, and Yamini gave birth to locusts. Vinata (Suparna) gave birth to Garuda, the carrier of Lord Vishnu [from whom many other birds were created], and to Anuru or Aruna, the chariot driver of the sun-god. Kadru gave birth to different varieties of serpents.[20]

From the other wives of Kashyapa came many more types of living beings, all of which populated the entire universe. From the womb of Timi came the aquatics, and from Sarama came the ferocious animals like tigers and lions. From Surabhi came the buffalo, cow and other animals with cloven hooves. From Tamra came the eagles, vultures and other large birds of prey. From Muni came the angels. From Krodhava came the serpents known as dandashuka, along with other serpents and mosquitoes. The various creepers and trees came from Ila. From Surasa came the Rakshasas and bad spirits. Gandharvas came from Arishta, and animals with hooves not split, such as horses, came from Kashtha. Danu gave birth to 61 sons, of which 18 were very important. Of these sons, Svarbhanu's daughter, Suprabha, was married to Namuchi. The daughter of Vrishaparva, Sarmishtha, was given to the powerful king Yayati, the son of Nahusha.[21]

Vaisvanara, the son of Danu, had four beautiful daughters, named Upadanavi, Hayashira, Puloma and Kalaka. Hiranyaksha married Upadanavi, and Kratu married Hayashira. Thereafter, at the request of Lord Brahma, Prajapati Kashyapa married Puloma and Kalaka, the other two daughters of Vaisvanara. From the wombs of these two wives of Kashyapa came sixty thousand sons, headed by Nivatakavaca, who are known as the Paulomas and the Kalakeyas. They were physically very strong and expert in fighting, and their aim was to disturb the sacrifices performed by the great sages. When Arjuna went to the heavenly planets, he killed all these demons, and King Indra became extremely affectionate toward him.

Then Vipracitti begot one hundred and one sons through his wife Simhika. The eldest was Rahu, and the others are known as the Ketus. All of them attained positions in the influential planets.

In the dynasty of Aditi [another wife of Kashyapa Muni] the Supreme Lord descended in His plenary expansion as Lord Narayana. The other sons of Aditi were Vivasvan, Aryama, Pusha, Tvashta, Savita, Bhaga, Dhata, Vidhata, Varuna, Mitra, Shatru and Urukrama. Samjna, the wife of Vivasvan, the sun-god, gave birth to the Manu named Shraddhadeva, and the same fortunate wife also gave birth to the twins Yamaraja and the River Yamuna. Then Yami, while wandering on the earth in the form of a mare, gave birth to the Ashvini-kumaras. Chaya, another wife of the sun-god, begot two sons named Shanaishcara and Savarni Muni, and one daughter, Tapati, who married Samvarana. From Matrika, the wife of Aryama, were born many learned scholars. Among them Lord Brahma created the humans which are endowed with an aptitude for self-examination.[22]

Through these men and women, and others not mentioned in this summary, whose power was to create many kinds of living entities, the whole universe gradually became populated.

The above information about the genealogy of Kashyapa, with particular additions, is also found in Chapter 19 of the *Agni Purana*, Chapter 30 in the *Umasamhita* of the *Shiva Purana*, and in the *Padma Purana* from 1.6.2 onwards. Chapters 65 through 69 of the *Vayu Purana* give long descriptions and explanations of this information.

Later, in another *manvantara*, the austere Pracetas accepted a particular girl, Marisha, as their wife, as recommended by Lord Brahma. From this girl, Daksha took his second birth, after having been killed for his offenses to Lord Shiva many years earlier during the time of Svayambhuva Manu. Now he took a birth during the Cakshusha *manvantara*. After being born, Daksha again was engaged by Lord Brahma to help generate living beings, with assistance from other Prajapatis [progenitors].[23]

It is from these progenitors described above, and the genealogy of these great sages, that come the original beings that scatter across the universe and populate it with varieties of species. These species accommodate the many levels of consciousness for the conditioned souls who long for some kind of activity, according to their mental and intellectual development.

APPENDIX THREE

Seeing Beyond the Illusion: The Ultimate Purpose of this Book

So what is the purpose of reading this book? To assist ourselves in seeing through the illusory nature of this material world. When you understand how this world is manifested and how it works, you have an easier means of recognizing the temporary nature of it and why we are here. The first thing to understand is that it is better not to try to see what is beyond the illusion, but to know how to recognize the illusory nature itself. Then the Truth beyond the veil will reveal itself.

Now, using the information we have learned in this volume, let us begin to see beyond the illusory nature and recognize the reality that exists behind it all. One of the first steps is to recognize that everything is but a display of the Lord's energies. So as you begin to see everything in this way, then you will also recognize how everything is but an expansion of God. Then you will reach that state of being wherein you will understand, as the sages ask, "What is not God?" You will see that God is everywhere. Then you will also see that you are never alone. God is here, there, everywhere, omniscient through His energy. Prahlada Maharaja was such a devotee who saw God everywhere, even in a stone pillar. And that is from where Lord Narasimha manifested when He appeared to protect Prahlada. God is already everywhere. Only our ignorance keeps us from seeing this.

Furthermore, you must recognize that everyone is a part of God. This is an impetus for our love and compassion toward all. After all, how can you say you love God if you do not love all His parts and parcels? Thus, as you rise above dualities, above seeing people and things in the designations of good and bad, pleasant and unpleasant, favorable or unfavorable, you will see spiritually that they are all the same. Only materially and superficially they may temporarily display what seems to be good or bad qualities, while the core of each person, the soul within the body, is completely spiritual, beyond all temporary designations.

So, as you look around this material existence, you can see how everyone is entrapped in various material bodies, through which they act out their many desires and goals. All these forms are but different packages filled with the same substances of material energy. If you strip away the packaging, or skin, you see the network of nerves, bones, blood, muscle, mucus, urine, etc. This is the mechanics of the bodily vehicle. Deeper within the gross physical body is also the subtle body of mind, intelligence, and false ego. In this way, these multidimensional bodies are most wondrous machines and tools for acting within and experiencing the material realm. What is entrapped in these bodies is the soul, the spark and cause of consciousness, which is the same in each body. It is this consciousness when mixed with the body, along with the many material circumstances in which it becomes involved, that produce the innumerable thoughts and feelings one has. Thus, your own thoughts are but temporary material emotions flowing through the mind like the wind. As long as these thoughts are focused on the innumerable varieties of material nature, they are but forms of *maya*. Getting free of these material thoughts is an essential part of any spiritual system, which, thus, allows you to get closer to perceiving what lies beyond the illusion.

While in these bodies, and while conditioned by materialistic consciousness, the living entities are pushed and pulled, or attracted and repulsed, by the various forms of *maya*. They are attracted to objects, sensations, as well as each other, in hopes of finding pleasure and happiness. In this attempt to acquire such happiness, they often merely go through the motions of social activities that they may not completely understand, but do so because of being entrapped in the hopes that they will find meaning and fulfillment. Therefore, this search is almost never ending because within the material energy, which is temporary in substance, they hanker for what they want and then lament for what they have lost. In this way, they often remain disappointed when all is said and done, and still searching for or something more to make them feel fulfilled.

Actually, this feeling of being unfulfilled is natural because until the living being is living and acting on the spiritual platform, which is his normal state of being, he is living in an incompatible and foreign environment to his eternal spiritual condition. It is like a fish being out of water. Until the fish is back in the water, no matter what else he finds, he will not be happy. This situation can also be compared to a person in a desert with only a few drops of water to quench his thirst. A few drops of water in a desert is just not enough to satisfy anyone. So, being disappointed or even frustrated in one's attempt to find true happiness in the material world is not unusual. It is not that such happiness does not exist, it is simply that the material domain is the wrong place to look for it. So in order to be happy here, you often have to accept less than what you hoped for, or move on and work toward understanding your real spiritual identity and reach the spiritual platform. Then you can rise above the influence of what you thought you wanted.

Another aspect of rising above what you thought you wanted is that the closer you get to realizing your spiritual nature, the less inclined you are for that which is connected with the temporary body. Going further than this, the more you regain your relationship with the Supreme, which is always on the basis of eternal, transcendental love, the more you are automatically fulfilled. The more you will feel a completeness that is not available through any material facility. This is the point of really progressive material existence: To attain a state of realizing that willingly or unwillingly we are all servants of God related through spiritual love. We can realize this through knowledge and enlightenment, or by being humbled through suffering or the approach of death until we understand that ultimately God is in control and we are but servants. So we can serve Him directly and willingly, or serve Him indirectly through His energies, such as we find in *maya*. It is up to us. It is similar to being a servant of the state. We can be good and have our freedom by obeying the laws, or we can be bad or rebellious and be an unwilling servant confined in jail where we will be forcibly restrained from breaking the laws. While there, we may even be coerced to engage in various forms of service, such as making license plates or other labors for the state. Jail or freedom is our choice. In either case, we are but servants. In the same way, we can live in the spiritual world and serve the Lord directly, or be placed in the material worlds where we are servants of His energies or parts and parcels in the forms of wife, children, landlord, boss at work, etc. The easiest and most blissful way is to be a willing servant of God and follow His instructions. Everyone is a servant. This cannot be changed. This is our natural position. So we are either serving God directly, or we are serving Him indirectly through His various material energies. It is our choice.

As we continue to look at everyone wandering in the material world, we can also recognize that they are all, ultimately, looking for love: To love and be loved, this is the goal. In all the innumerable forms in which this need may appear, this is ultimately all people want. It is what makes the world go around. However, the only place where that loving propensity can be fulfilled completely is on the spiritual level, not the material. The material level offers only the chance to find the *reflection* of what we want, not the real thing that offers complete depth and continuity. And when the saintly, those who have perceived the Truth of this existence, see how people everywhere are searching in this way, they feel compassion and want to show the way to find this real love in the spiritual strata that can offer the ultimate fulfillment for which everyone is searching.

Once you can begin seeing through the facade of *maya*, or the candy coating attraction of these bodies and material existence in general, you will also understand that true love and concern for others actually takes the form of compassion. It is not simply a matter of working together in cooperation, or appreciating each other's talents, culture, etc. It is seeing that we are all bound by the influence of *maya* and need to be freed. And you cannot free others if you are also tied up. The best thing you can do to help free others from the illusion of *maya* is to make sure you are not one of those who are bound by it. You have to be free to free others. We also have to remember that compassion is the basis of the material universe. The cosmic manifestation is manifested by the compassion of God for the innumerable, materially conditioned living beings. All saintly people will feel this compassion in their view of those who are still enveloped in the drama of *maya*, stumbling in the darkness of ignorance, looking for love in any way they can find it, and not knowing the purpose of life or how to be free of their suffering.

In this way, compassion for the predicament of those lost in the illusory energy is the true expression of concern and goodwill. As explained earlier, the compassion of God is the basis of the material creation for the conditioned souls. Therefore, any spiritual leader must reflect this compassion of the Supreme, otherwise he or she cannot be a real representative of God. Such compassion is not merely a matter of helping people in their struggle with the forces of *maya*, such as with their finances, catastrophic storms, floods, or hunger, shelter, etc. Of course, such assistance should be given if you have been blessed by God to have no such problems and have the facility to help others. But such problems will always continue as long as we are bound in this material energy. This shows the importance of helping others to become disentangled from material conditioning and to be free spiritually. So you have to go beyond basic humanitarian assistance if you want to truly solve the problems of the living beings in a permanent way.

Of course, there will be those who feel they are fine, or are not interested in working toward freedom from material existence. But any spiritual assistance that can be given can make a difference and provide an eternal benefit to the individual. After all, the more you work to help others, the more you also help yourself. The benefit works both ways and affects all involved. That is the nature of spiritual work. And the highest spiritual work is to offer knowledge of one's spiritual identity and relationship with God, and the process for regaining that forgotten relationship. As Krishna explains in the *Bhagavad-gita*, He is most pleased by those who spread this knowledge. There is no higher service than that.

As you continue to develop your consciousness in this direction and consider everything you have learned about the process of creation from God, you will realize that the spiritual atmosphere pervades the material cosmos. The material creation is limited, like a cloud in the spiritual sky. However, the spiritual sky has no limitations and its energy spreads throughout the cosmic creation and manifests in various ways. It is unlimited, but our ability to perceive it is all that is limited. Actually, we have never left it, although we may think we have. We do not regain something that was never lost, like our relationship with God. We only have to remember it. That is the key to any spiritual process; how effective it is in helping us remember our spiritual identity and relationship with the Supreme. That is the meaning of being awakened. We have to awaken from this dream of forgetfulness.

So knowing that the spiritual dimension pervades the material realm, which universe are you in? The material or spiritual? It is only a matter of perception. If you think you are in the material worlds, and that your material body is what you are, then when did you begin thinking this way? In which lifetime? This shows how long our conditioning has been going on. It is this conditioning from which we must free ourselves.

If you think you are the material body, then you also will think that the life you lead, the temporary drama that you are in, is your reality. That is your world. And it is only a world of appearances. However, with a snap you can change your consciousness and your perception when you recognize that the spiritual dimension is everywhere, and that actually you are a spiritual being and a part of that spiritual dimension. It is this spiritual strata to which you belong. So although you may be functioning to a certain degree in this material dimension, you are actually a part of the eternal spiritual domain, which is everywhere. In this case, you are already home. Then you will see that in spite of the material energies around you, they are a development from the Supreme Being's spiritual energy, and you are actually in the spiritual universe which pervades the material worlds. Then you will also understand that the material aspect is only a temporary appearance, a charade. It is as if we are dressed in costumes and playing parts in a drama that is not based on who we really are. It is based on these temporary bodies, and not the reality of the soul. However, this can be changed when we realize that we are eternal spiritual beings simply having a temporary human experience at this time.

Once you rise above the bodily perception, your awareness is no longer limited to only what your senses and mind can pick up. You become aware of what is your true identity and potential, and that the spiritual dimension is all-pervading. So, once again I raise the question, what universe are you in, the spiritual or material?

As you begin to see the spiritual reality all around you, you become more attached to God and less concerned with material necessities. When you experience the bliss of God consciousness, you automatically become more detached from your surroundings, regardless of whether they are pleasant or unpleasant, such as nice house, nice clothes, etc. You become completely fulfilled through your attachment and longing for God. Attachment to guru and God is the culmination of spiritual life, no matter where you are. The more attached you are to God, the more detached and forgetful you become to things of the world. Seeing God everywhere is also a form of meditation of the highest caliber. Such a meditation will remove the veil of illusion and bring you to the spiritual dimension after, or even before, you leave your body.

Now let us perform an experiment. Go to your local mall or shopping center (which is where I am writing this), or wherever there is a lot of people. Have a seat. Now look around. Do not be judgmental about the forms and bodies you see, or the construction of the buildings and the content of the stores. See them as different manifestations of the Lord's energy. See the people. Are you attracted to some or repulsed by others? You must see beyond that.

The bodies are merely containers. They are sparked into action and alive only because of the spirit soul within, and motivated by the modes of nature. The people become motivated as the pure inclinations of the soul become filtered through the polluted desires of the materially conditioned mind and senses. Thus, instead of acting for the pleasure of God and the soul, they engage in the shallow attempt to satisfy their mind and senses.

However, the more spiritual you become, the more you can perceive that which is beyond the bodily limitations. The more you will see how the spiritual dimension is all around us and is the essential network that keeps everything together. This spiritual aspect, which is our real eternal identity, is what motivates us to search for love and happiness. The reason for this is that the soul is *sat-chit-ananda*, eternal, full of bliss and knowledge. That bliss is essentially based on loving relationships. So that is what we always want and need. Everything is but a reflection of that need.

As you continue to develop spiritually, you will see as the sages do. As a sage sees the natural spiritual reality, you can also perceive the living being within the body. You can see beyond the imperfect form and ego to see the spirit soul within. You see beyond the drama of actions and reactions of the living beings in this material world. You know you may be in the drama but are not of it. In such a case, it is as if you are watching a movie or play. You look and may be amused by what you see, may even enjoy the experience, but never become involved. In this way, you stand apart from it, even if it is all around you. You know it is separate from the reality of the real you. Thus, you can always remain detached from the activities that go on in this play on the stage of *maya*, the illusory world. You can be compared to a tourist, someone who is but a transient, traveling through this world, observing but detached, and never enticed by the attractions or aversions that others take so seriously. In this way, you can be the master of your mind, not the slave of it. Thus, you can go about giving words of wisdom to those who are sincerely seeking the knowledge that you can deliver. Otherwise, you may feel that there is little else in this world that is more worthwhile to accomplish.

So, when we begin to see beyond the illusion, we first recognize:

1. That everything is but a manifestation of the Lord's energy. The Supreme Absolute is the point and center of all creation, both spiritual and material. The energies of matter and spirit vibrate at different frequencies and manifest on different levels. Yet they both originate from the same source, which is the pure consciousness of the Supreme Being. Thus, the material strata is subservient to, and pervaded by, the unlimited spiritual energy. It is the spiritual energy which is the foundation of the material realm and interacts with it in all phases, however unbeknownst to those who are spiritually unaware.

2. Then we see the spiritual sparks in all bodies, and that each soul as a tiny part of God, practically dormant, waiting to regain its spiritual identity and activities, in spite of all the material affairs in which the body is engaged. It is the bodily concept of life that cages the real person within and tends to keep him from

remembering his true identity. It is only the light of spiritual knowledge that can open this cage to reveal the reality of our true identity.

3. Also, we should recognize the presence of the Supersoul inside everyone. It is by the power of the Supreme that the *jiva* soul has the ability of movement, intellect, speech, etc., while in the container of the material body.

4. In the midst of all this, the sage sees that spiritual love is the only relationship for which anyone really hankers and searches. It is this loving relationship which is the ultimate motivator and reason for living. However, we often only find its reflection in the material realm. Nonetheless, it is the loving relationship with God that gives the highest bliss that, in our forgetfulness in material existence, impels our need to find it in whatever form or reflection that we can. Once we have a taste of the happiness attained on the spiritual level, and in the bliss of love of God, nothing in the material realm ever looks the same. It simply loses its appeal and its thrill.

5. Meanwhile, the sage sees the people are but wearing different dresses (bodies) as participants in the temporary drama on this stage called planet Earth. And this planet is merely but one amongst innumerable others that orbit in this universe, while this universe is among countless others that manifest from the immeasurable form of Maha-Vishnu, who is lying in the Karana Ocean. This Karana Ocean, which holds all of the material energies, is but like a cloud in a corner of the infinite spiritual sky, and this spiritual sky is filled with innumerable and gigantic spiritual planets where the true reality of life exists eternally without limitations.

When you can begin to see like this, which is only a portion of what the spiritually developed sage can observe, you are starting to see beyond the illusory energy.

APPENDIX FOUR

The Material Creation is Proof of the Existence of God

As the Vedic literature progressively explains, the fullest understanding of God is that the Absolute Truth culminates in the Supreme Person. All of creation comes from this Person. And the material creation is proof of the existence of this Supreme Personality.

After all, one of the questions that we can ask is, if God was merely an impersonal void or great energy only, how can the impersonal create the personal? How can a divine energy or force, or a non-entity, give birth to, or create, entities? How can that without a personality create the innumerable beings that have personalities and characteristics and idiosyncracies?

So, if God was merely a nonentity, or without activities, there would be no need for Him to create His separated parts and parcels with whom He could have relationships or loving exchanges. Actually, there would be no need of beings of any kind, in which case there would be no need for a cosmic creation to allow the materially inclined living beings to engage in material relationships and activities.

We need to remember that one of the purposes of this creation is to allow the materially conditioned souls the freedom to express their individuality. If this individuality was not an intrinsic aspect of our nature, why would we have the propensity for self-expression or the need to chase after so many desires? And without it, once again, there would also be no need for a material manifestation. In other words, if the Ultimate Reality was but a void or great white light only, in which there is no activity, what need would there be for a cosmic creation in which the living beings are allowed to express so many desires or activities?

To explain further, it is said that variety is the spice of life, and that particular spice or enjoyment is found only in activities. Furthermore, activity is generally based on relationships of various kinds with others. If we were all one, or all merged into a void, there could be no relationships nor desires for such. Without individuality, there is no need for relationships, or activity, loving exchanges, nor any variety or fun. In such a case, the Lord would be inactive in a spiritual world that offered no variegatedness. There would also be no need for a material creation where so many relationships take place, or where the conditioned souls can chase after their own particular material desires. Actually, there would be no need for anything at all. However, we can plainly see all around us that such is not the case. There are innumerable living beings of many varieties of species, all determinedly engaged for self-preservation and expression, and the fulfillment of so many desires.

Therefore, the material creation is proof of the existence of God. It is proof of the personal form of the Supreme Being and the nature of His parts and parcels to long for and engage in a variety of activities and loving relationships, the highest of which is to engage in spiritual loving relations with the Supreme Lord. This is our natural constitutional position for which we have been brought into existence. This is the eternal nature of the soul, our real identity. That is why nothing will ever change our natural inclination toward varieties of activities, individual self-expression, and the need to love and be loved.

APPENDIX FIVE

More About the Retreating Glaciers of the Himalayas

As reported in an article by Charles Arthur in the June 8, 1999 edition of *The Independent* in England, new information has been gathered by scientists at the Jawaharlal Nehru University in Delhi, India, regarding how the glaciers in the Himalayas are retreating. As we had explained, the glacier above Gangotri, from which the Ganges River starts, has retreated about one kilometer in the past 20 years or so. In fact, it has been determined that these glaciers are retreating faster than anywhere else on the planet. Professor Syed Hasnain, the main author of the report, relates that all of the glaciers in the middle Himalayas are retreating. He warns that many of the glaciers in this region could disappear by 2035. New fears are that the meltwater could produce catastrophic floods as mountain lakes overflow.

As I explained in a previous book, *The Vedic Prophecies: A New Look into the Future*, the Vedic texts reveal that such holy rivers as the Ganges will dry up and become only a series of small lakes, at best. In this way, they may practically disappear, as did the Sarasvati. This latest report surely seems to show the possibility of this happening sooner than expected. This also shows the reason that the mouth of the Ganges, at Gaumukh above Gangotri, is retreating farther away as the years go by. So those travelers who wish to journey to the mouth of the holy Ganga will have to travel farther up into the hills as time goes by. This also indicates why the mouth of the Ganges is always changing in its appearance.

Getting back to the way the glaciers are retreating, at the University of Colorado in Boulder, a research team has found that the mountain glaciers are diminishing in the West as well. The Alps have lost nearly 50% of their ice in the last 100 years. The Major glacier at Mt. Kenya has lost 8% of its size, and 14 of the 27 glaciers in Spain are gone.

The disappearing of the mountain glaciers is also reported in an article by Lily Whiteman in the January/February issue of *National Parks*. It stated that there were more than 150 glaciers in Glacier National Park in Montana back in 1850.

Now there are only 50, and it is expected that these will also disappear within the next four decades. This is primarily blamed on the increase in global temperatures by only one degree since the 1800's. Glaciers, because of being too solid and stable to show short-term variations in climate, are particularly good barometers of global warming.

In regard to the Vedic tradition, it explains that the Ganges fell from heaven to earth and was caught on the head of Lord Shiva. This was to prevent the intense damage that the force of it would cause to the earth if it fell directly on to the planet. This took place at Gangotri, where the water backed up into the mountains where much of it froze. The course of the Ganges is said to still flow through the universe and come down to the earth planet. However, much of the river water comes from underneath the glacier. If the glacier at Gaumukh does continue to recede or melt away, and if the Ganges would ever cease its flow or begin to dry up, it would certainly mean the end of an era and a drastic affect on the spiritual culture as we have known it in India. Indeed, it would never be the same.

Notes

CHAPTER TWO

1. As quoted from, *The Pentateuch and Book of Joshua Critically Examined,* by the Right Rev., John William Colenso, Bishop of Natal, London. Longmans, Green & Co., 1863
2. *Brahmanda Purana,* 3.4.4.55

CHAPTER THREE

1. *Chaitanya-caritamrita, Madhya.lila,* 6.143
2. *Vishnu Purana,* 1.12.57
3. *Chaitanya-caritamrita, Madhya-lila,* 24.72
4. *Srimad-Bhagavatam,* 7.9.31
5. *Chaitanya-caritamrita, Madhya-lila,* 20.150
6. Ibid., *Madhya-lila,* 6.153
7. Ibid., *Adi-lila,* 7.120 purport, quote from the *Vishnu Purana*

CHAPTER SIX

1. *Srimad-Bhagavatam,* 3.21.20
2. Ibid., 3.26.5
3. Ibid., 10.87.31
4. Ibid., 1.3.1

CHAPTER SEVEN

1. *Chaitanya-caritamrita, Madhya-lila,* 20.255-6
2. Ibid., *Adi-lila,* 5.4-6, 8-11
3. Ibid., *Adi-lila,* 5.41 & purport
4. Ibid., *Adi-lila,* 2.56, purport
5. Ibid., *Madhya-lila,* 20.268-271
6. *Brahma-samhita,* 5.11-12
7. *Chaitanya-caritamrita, Adi-lila,* 5.54
8. *Brahma-samhita,* 5.47
9. *Chaitanya-caritamrita, Madhya-lila,* 5.120-124
10. *Srimad-Bhagavatam,* 10.87.12-13
11. *Chaitanya-caritamrita, Madhya-lila,* 20.272
12. *Srimad-Bhagavatam,* 3.26.19
13. *Chaitanya-caritamrita, Madhya-lila,* 20.275-282
14. *Brahma-samhita,* 5.48

15. *Chaitanya-caritamrita, Madhya-lila,* 20.324
16. Ibid., *Madhya-lila,* 20.284-6
17. Ibid., *Madhya-lila,* 20.292, 294-5

CHAPTER EIGHT
1. *Chaitanya-caritamrta, Adi-lila,* 5.51
2. *Srimad-Bhagavatam,* 2.5.22
3. Ibid., 3.5.27.purport
4. Ibid., 2.5.23
5. Ibid., 3.5.28
6. Ibid., 3.5.30
7. Ibid., 12.7.11
8. Ibid., 2.5.24
9. Ibid., 3.26.20
10. Ibid., 3.26.21-22, & *Chaitanya-caritamrita, Madhya-lila,* 20.276
11. Ibid., 3.26.19
12. Ibid., 3.5.26
13. Ibid., 3.5.27
14. Ibid., 2.5.21
15. *Chaitanya-caritamrita, Adi-lila,* 5.59 & *Madhya-lila,* 20.259-62
16. *Srimad-Bhagavatam* 3.26.27
17. Ibid., 2.5.30
18. Ibid., 3.5.31
19. Ibid., 3.26.30-32
20. Ibid., 3.26.32-34 & 2.5.25
21. Ibid., 3.26.35-37 & 3.5.33 & 2.5.26
22. Ibid., 3.5.34-35 & 2.5.27
23. Ibid., 3.26.38-44 & 3.5.36 & 2.5.27-29
24. Ibid., 3.26.49, purport
25. Ibid., 2.5.31-33
26. Ibid., 2.5.34-5

CHAPTER NINE
1. *Chaitanya-caritamrita, Adi-lila,* 5.58 & *Madhya-lila,* 20.271
2. Ibid., *Adi-lila,* 5.64-66
3. Ibid., *Madhya-lila,* 15.176
4. Ibid., *Madhya-lila,* 6.154-156
5. *Srimad-Bhagavatam,* 10.22.4, purport
6. *Chatanya-caritamrita, Madhya-lila,* 21.53
7. Ibid., *Madhya-lila,* 20.307-8
8. *Srimad-Bhagavatam,* 3.2.21.purport

CHAPTER TEN

1. *Srimad-Bhagavatam*, 2.10.46-47
2. Ibid. 3.5.6.purport
3. Ibid., 11.22.12
4. Ibid., 11.22.13
5. Ibid., 11.22.30
6. Ibid., 11.22.33
7. Ibid., 1.7.5
8. *Chaitanya-caritamrita, Madhya-lila*, 20.276
9. *Srimad-Bhagavatam*, 10.85.11
10. Ibid., 3.24.4.purport
11. Ibid., 11.22.29
12. Ibid., 11.22.26
13. Ibid., 11.22.8, 14-17
14. Ibid., 3.6.2
15. Ibid., 11.22.18
16. *Chaitanya-caritamrita, Madhya*, 20.277-83
17. *Srimad-Bhagavatam*, 3.11.41 & *Vishnu Purana*, Book Two, Chapter Six, and *Garuda Purana*,3.10.3-17
18. *Srimad-Bhagavatam*, 3.20.15
19. *Brahma-samhita*, 5.13 & 51
20. *Chaitanya-caritamrita, Madhya*, 20.284-86

CHAPTER ELEVEN

1. *Srimad-Bhagavatam*, 3.26.51-2
2. Ibid., 3.26.53
3. Ibid., 3.6.5-6
4. Ibid., 3.6.6.purport
5. Ibid., 3.6.7
6. Ibid., 3.6.8-9
7. Ibid., 3.6.10-11
8. Ibid., 3.26.54 & 3.6.12
9. Ibid., 3.6.13
10. Ibid., 3.6.14
11. Ibid., 3.6.15
12. Ibid., 3.26.54-55 & 3.6.17
13. Ibid., 3.6.16
14. Ibid., 3.6.18
15. Ibid., 3.26.56-57
16. Ibid., 3.6.19
17. Ibid., 3.26.58 &3.6.20
18. Ibid., 3.6.21
19. Ibid., 3.6.22 & 3.26.58

20. Ibid., 3.26.59
21. Ibid., 3.26.60
22. Ibid., 3.6.23
23. Ibid., 3.6.24
24. Ibid., 3.6.25
25. Ibid., 3.6.26
26. Ibid., 3.6.27-29
27. Ibid., 3.6.30-34
28. Ibid., 3.26.62-72
29. Ibid., 2.5.36-42

CHAPTER TWELVE
1. *Srimad-Bhagavatam* 3.10.14-16
2. Ibid., 3.10.17
3. *Kurma Purana* 1.7.2
4. *Srimad-Bhagavatam* 3.10.18-29. Also described in *Vishnu Purana* (Book
    One, Chapter Five), *Padma Purana* 1.3.76-84, *Agni Purana* (Chapter
    17 & 20), *Narada Purana.* 1.3.25-35, *Kurma Purana* 1.7.1-19, *Garuda
    Purana* 1.4.14-22, and others
5. *Chaitanya-caritamrita, Madhya-lila*, 20.292-3
6. *Srimad-Bhagavatam* 3.6.6.purport
7. *Chaitanya-caritamrita, Adi-lila*, 5.95-101
8. Ibid., *Adi-lila*, 5.102-3
9. *Brahma-samhita* 5.18 & *Srimad-Bhagavatam* 11.24.10
10. *Srimad-Bhagavatam* 3.8.14-15
11. *Brahma-samhita* 5.22 & *Chaitanya-caritamrita, Madhya-lila*, 20.287-288
12. *Chaitanya-caritamrita, Madhya-lila*, 20.305
13. Ibid., *Madhya-lila*, 20.288-291
14. Ibid., *Madhya-lila*, 20.314-316 & *Brahma-samhita* 5.46
15. *Brahma-samhita,* 5.45
16. *Chaitanya-caritamrita, Madhya-lila*, 20.309-311, 317 & *Srimad-
    Bhagavatam* 10.88.3
17. *Brahma-samhita* 5.48 & *Srimad-Bhagavatam* 3.11.38
18. *Srimad-Bhagavatam* 3.8.16-21
19. Ibid., 2.9.6-7
20. Ibid., 3.8.22
21. *Brahma-samhita* 5.27
22. Ibid., 5.28
23. *Srimad-Bhagavatam* 2.9.4
24. Ibid., 3.8.23-33
25. Ibid., 3.9.1-44
26. Ibid., 3.10.1-9
27. Ibid., 11.24.11-14

28. *Chaitanya-caritamrita, Madhya* 21, 58 purport
29. *Srimad-Bhagavatam* 2.5.40-1
30. *Srimad-Bhagavatam* 2.5.38-9 & *Narada Purana* 1.3.37-9 & 40-46. Other descriptions of the universe are found throughout the Fifth Canto of the *Srimad-Bhagavatam*. Additional descriptions of the nether worlds and the 14 planetary systems of the universe are found in Chapter 50 of the *Vayu Purana*.
31. *Srimad-Bhagavatam* 5.26.5
32. Ibid., 4.20.35-6
33. Ibid., 4.9.25.purport & 4.12.27
34. Ibid., 4.12.39
35. Ibid., 8.11.5 & 8.15.22
36. Ibid., 5.26.37
37. Ibid., 5.19.28
38. *Narada Purana* 1.3.49-55
39. *Srimad-Bhagavatam* 3.11.1-13
40. Ibid., 3.10.11-12
41. Ibid., 3.11.17-23
42. *Brahmanda Purana* 1.1.5.29-31
43. *Srimad-Bhagavatam* 3.12.2
44. *Brahma-samhita*, 20-21
45. *Bhagavad-gita* 10.4-5
46. *Kurma Purana* 1.7.64-66 & *Brahmanda Purana* 1.2.8.59-60 & *Padma Purana* 1.3.118-119
47. *Brahmanda Purana* 3.4.4.13
48. Ibid., 1.2.7.43-56
49. Ibid., 3.4.4.30-31
50. *Srimad-Bhagavatam* 4.29.4
51. *Bhavagad-gita* 13.22
52. *Vishnu Purana*, Book One, Chapter Five, p49 & 58
53. *Srimad-Bhagavatam* 3.10.19-20
54. *Vishnu Purana*, Book One, Chapter Five, p49 & *Narada Purana* 1.3.34, & *Kurma Purana* 1.7.5-6, 54-55
55. *Srimad-Bhagavatam* 3.10.21-25 & *Padma Purana* 1.3.105-110
56. *Vishnu Purana*, Book One, Chapter Five, p58
57. *Garuda Purana* 1.4.31-34
58. *Srimad-Bhagavatam* 3.10.26
59. *Kurma Purana* 1.7.9-10 & 50
60. *Vishnu Purana*, Book One, Chapter Five, p51
61. *Padma Purana* 93-97 & *Kurma Purana* 1.7.50-51
62. *Srimad-Bhagavatam* 6.18.30
63. *Srimad-Bhagavatam* 3.20.18-19, & *Garuda Purana* 1.4.20-25

64. *Kurma Purana* 1.7.41-43 & *Padma Purana* 1.3.84-90 & *Vishnu Purana,* Book One, Chapter Five, p.55-56

65. *Srimad-Bhagavatam* 3.20.22

66. *Padma Purana* 1.3.90-92 & *Garuda Purana* 1.4.24-25 & *Kurma Purana* 1.7.45 & *Vishnu Purana,* Book One, Chapter Five, p56

67. *Vishnu Purana,* Book One, Chapter Five, p.56

68. *Kurma Purana* 1.7.46-49 & *Padma Purana* 1.3.92-93 & *Brahmanda Purana* 1.2.8.13-17

69. *Padma Purana* 1.3.93-97

70. *Srimad-Bhagavatam* 3.20.23-29

71. *Garuda Purana* 1.4.28-29

72. *Vishnu Purana,* Book One, Chapter five, p58 & *Brahmanda Purana* 1.2.8.30-36, & *Kurma Purana* 1.7.51-53

73. *Brahmanda Purana* 1.2.8.36-38 & *Vishnu Purana,* Book One, Chapter Five, p.58, & *Garuda Purana* 1.4.29

74. *Srimad-Bhagavatam* 3.20.38-39

75. *Brahmanda Purana* 1.2.8.40 & *Vishnu Purana,* Book One, Chapter Five, p.58, & *Garuda Purana* 1.4.30

76. *Padma Purana* 1.3.104

77. *Srimad-Bhagavatam* 3.20.40-41

78. *Brahmanda Purana* 1.2.8.39-40 & *Garuda Purana* 1.4.29

79. *Srimad-Bhagavatam* 3.20.42-43

80. Ibid., 3.20.44

81. Ibid., 3.20.45-46

82. Ibid., 3.20.47-48

83. *Vishnu Purana,* Book One, Chapter Five, p.62 & *Padma Purana* 1.3.115-124

84. *Srimad-Bhagavatam* 3.12.2-4. Other references to the creation of the *Kumaras,* but with less detail, are found in the *Brahmanada Purana* 1.1.5.58, *Agni Purana* 17.14, *Kurma Purana* 1.7.18-21, *Padma Purana* 1.3.166-9, as well as the *Vishnu Purana* 1.7.1-8.

85. *Srimad-Bhagavatam* 3.12.2-4 & *Padma Purana* 1.3.197-204

86. *Srimad-Bhagavatam* 3.12.2-14

87. Ibid., 3.20.52-53

88. Ibid., 3.12.21-24 & *Vishnu Purana,* Book One, Chapter Seven, p.71 & *Padma Purana* 1.3.166-169

89. *Kurma Purana* 1.7.35-39

90. *Srimad-Bhagavatam* 3.12.25-27

91. Ibid., 3.12.34

92. Ibid., 3.12.37-39 & *Brahmanda Purana* 1.2.8.50-55 & *Vishnu Purana,* Book One, Chapter Five, p.60. Other references for the creation of the *Vedas* is found in the *Kurma Purana* 1.7.57-60, *Garuda Purana* 1.4.34, *Agni Purana* 17.13, & *Padma Purana* 1.3.110-114.

93. *Srimad-Bhagavatam* 3.12.35, 41
94. *Vishnu Purana*, Book One, Chapter Six, & *Padma Purana* 1.3.129, &
     Garuda Purana 1.4.35
95. *Srimad-Bhagavatam* 3.12.42-47
96. *Vishnu Purana* 1.6.6-12, p.63-4
97. Ibid., Book One, Chapter Six, p.69
98. *Padma Purana* 1.3.155-164 & *Garuda Purana* 1.4.36-38
99. *Srimad-Bhagavatam* 3.12.50-57
100. Ibid., 4.1.47-8, & *Padma Purana* 1.3.176-194 & *Kurma Purana* 1.8.6-30
     & *Vishnu Purana*, Book One, Chapter Seven
101. *Srimad-Bhagavatam* 3.21.1
102. Ibid., 3.24.22-24

CHAPTER THIRTEEN

1. *Srimad-Bhagavatam* 11.22.29
2. Ibid., 3.11.22-30
3. Ibid., 12.7.12
4. *Bhagavad-gita* 9.7-8
5. *Vishnu Purana*, Book One, Chapter Seven, p.81-82
6. *Srimad-Bhagavatam* 11.24.20
7. Ibid., 10.85.5
8. *Bhagavad-gita* 9.6
9. Ibid., 15.13
10. *Chaitanya-caritamrita, Adi* 4, 8-11, 13
11. *Srimad-Bhagavatam* 8.14.7-9

CHAPTER FOURTEEN

1. *Srimad-Bhagavatam* 1.2.34
2. Ibid., 1.3.5
3. *Chaitanya-caritamrita, Madhya-lila* 20.263-4
4. Ibid., *Madhya-lila* 20.245-246
5. Ibid., *Adi-lila* 3.6
6. Ibid., *Adi-lila* 2.112
7. Ibid., *Adi-lila* 2.133-115
8. *Srimad-Bhagavatam* 1.3.5.purport
9. *Bhagavad-gita* 4.7-8
10. *Srimad-Bhagavatam* 10.86.45
11. *Chaitanya-caritamrita, Madhya-lila* 20.352
12. *Srimad-Bhagavatam* 2.7.2.purport
13. *Chaitanya-caritamrita, Adi-lila* 14, 18.purport
14. Ibid., *Madhya-lila* 20.354
15. Ibid., *Adi-lila* 3, 93-94
16. *Srimad-Bhagavatam* 10.14.37

17. Ibid., 10.14.55
18. Ibid., 10.40.16
19. Ibid., 3.2.7
20. *Chaitanya-caritamrita, Madhya-lila* 20.382
21. *Srimad-Bhagavatam* 1.3.6
22. Ibid., 2.7.5
23. Ibid., 1.3.7 & 2.7.1
24. Ibid., 1.3.8
25. Ibid., 2.7.19
26. Ibid., 1.3.9
27. Ibid., 2.7.6
28. Ibid., 1.3.10
29. Ibid., 2.7.3
30. Ibid., 1.3.11 & 2.7.4
31. Ibid., 1.3.12
32. Ibid., 1.3.13 & 2.7.10
33. Ibid., 2.7.11
34. Ibid., 1.3.14
35. Ibid., 2.7.9
36. Ibid., 1.3.15 & 2.7.12
37. Ibid., 1.3.16
38. Ibid., 2.7.13
39. Ibid., 2.7.21
40. Ibid., 1.3.17
41. Ibid., 1.3.18 & 2.7.14
42. Ibid., 1.3.19 & 2.7.17-18
43. Ibid., 1.3.20 & 2.7.22
44. Ibid., 1.3.21& 2.7.36
45. Ibid., 1.3.40-43
46. Ibid., 1.3.22
47. Ibid., 2.7.23-5
48. Ibid., 1.3.23 & 2.7.26
49. Ibid., 1.3.24 & 2.7.37
50. Ibid., 1.3.25 & 2.7.38
51. Ibid., 1.3.35, 37
52. Ibid., 1.3.38
53. Ibid., 1.3.5.purport & *Chaitanya-caritamrita, Madhya-lila* 20, 319-328
54. *Bhagavad-gita* 8.17 & *Srimad-Bhagavatam*.3.11.20 & *Vishnu Purana*,
    Book One, Chapter Three, p.35
55. *Chaitanya-caritamrita, Adi-lila* 3, 7-10 & *Srimad-Bhagavatam* 4.30.49
    purport
56. *Srimad-Bhagavatam* 1.3.5.purport & *Chaitanya-caritamrita, Madhya-lila*
    20, 329-333

57. *Chaitanya-caritamrita, Madhya-lila* 20, 334-347 & *Srimad-Bhagavatam*
        11.5.32, 36 & 12.3.51-2
58. *Chaitanya-caritamrita, Madhya-lila* 20.369-73

CHAPTER FIFTEEN
1. *Srimad-Bhagavatam* 11.22.19-25
2. Ibid., 10.14.56-7
3. Ibid., 11.2.48
4. Ibid., 11.2.38

CHAPTER SIXTEEN
1. *Srimad-Bhagavatam* 1.3.28, purport
2. *Jaiva Dharma*, Volume Three, Chapter 15, page 69
3. *Jaiva Dharma*, Chapter 15, page 76
4. *Bhagavad-gita*, 13.20, purport
5. *Jaiva Dharma*, Chapter 15, page 74
6. *Chaitanya-caritamrita, Adi-lila*, 5.45
7. Ibid., *Adi-lila*, 2.36 purport
8. Ibid., *Adi-lila*, 5.41
9. *Jaiva Dharma*, Chapter 15, page 90
10. Ibid., Volume Three, Chapter 15, page 72
11. Ibid., Volume 3, Chapter 16, p. 94
12. Ibid., Volume Three, Chapter 15, page 73
13. *Srimad-Bhagavatam* 7.10.3, purport
14. *Jaiva Dharma*, Volume 3, Chapter 16, p. 90
15. Ibid., Volume 3, Chapter 15, p.69
16. *Srimad-Bhagavatam* 5.5.19, purport
17. Ibid., 4.28.53, purport
18. *Bhagavad-gita* 15.7, purport
19. *Srimad-Bhagavatam* 11.14.25
20. *Bhagavad-gita* 13.20
21. *Jaiva Dharma*, Volume 3, Chapter 16, p.95
22. *Sri Caitanya Siksamritam*, p. 160
23. *Srimad-Bhagavatam* 3.9.9, purport
24. *Jaiva Dharma*, Volume 3, Chapter 16, p.99
25. Ibid., Volume 3, Chapter 15, p.74-5
26. *Chaitanya-caritamrita, Adi-lila*, 7.116, purport
27. *Teachings of Lord Chaitanya*, p. 217-8
28. *Srimad-Bhagavatam* 9.4.64, purport
29. *Jaiva Dharma*, Volume 3, Chapter 16, p. 88
30. *Srimad-Bhagavatam* 9.9.47

CHAPTER SEVENTEEN
1. *Srimad-Bhagavatam* 11.22.39-40
2. Ibid., 11.22.41, 48
3. Ibid., 3.7.11
4. Ibid., 6.15.24
5. Ibid., 6.15.25
6. Ibid., 9.9.47
7. *Chaitanya-caritamrita, Madhya-lila* 20, 118
8. *Srimad-Bhagavatam* 11.2.29
9. Ibid., 11.20.17
10. Ibid., 11.22.54-56
11. *Bhagavad-gita* 18.54

CHAPTER EIGHTEEN
1. *Srimad-Bhagavatam* 3.20.12
2. Ibid., 9.24.58
3. Ibid., 11.3.3
4. Ibid., 1.2.16.purport
5. Ibid., 1.2.19.purport
6. *Chaitanya-caritamrita, Madhya-lila* 6, 173
7. *Srimad-Bhagavatam* 3.15.23
8. *Chaitanya-caritamrita, Madhya-lila* 6.162
9. Ibid., *Madhya-lila* 20, 141

CHAPTER NINETEEN
1. *Chaitanya-caritamrita,.Madhya-lila* 6, 174
2. *Srimad-Bhagavatam* 12.6.43
3. Ibid., 12.6.44-6
4. Ibid., 12.7.5-6 / 9-10 / 22-24
5. Ibid., 12.13.10
6. Ibid., 2.7.51
7. Ibid., 3.13.8.purport
8. Ibid., 1.1.3
9. Ibid., 12.13.11-12, 14, 16
10. Ibid., 1.3.43

CHAPTER TWENTY
1. *Srimad-Bhagavatam* 10.48.23
2. Ibid., 11.20.4
3. *Chaitanya-caritamrita, Madhya-lila* 20, 122-4
4. Ibid., *Adi-lila* 7, 146

CHAPTER TWENTY-ONE
1. *Srimad-Bhagavatam* 1.2.6
2. *Narada Purana* 1.11.4
3. *Srimad-Bhagavatam* 6.16.41-2
4. *Chaitanya-caritamrita, Madhya-lila* 19.174
5. Ibid., *Adi-lila* 7.141-2
6. *Srimad-Bhagavatam* 5.1.35
7. Ibid., *Adi-lila* 17.22
8. *Srimad-Bhagavatam* 5.12.12
9. Ibid., 3.2.6.purport

APPENDIX TWO
1. *Srimad-Bhagavatam* 3.21.1
2. Ibid., 4.1.9
3. Ibid., 3.12.50-57
4. Ibid., 4.1.11
5. *Srimad-Bhagavatam* 4.1.47-8, *Padma Purana* 1.3.176-194, *Kurma Purana* 1.8.6-30 & *Vishnu Purana*, Book One, Chapter Seven.
6. *Agni Purana*, 18.1-4
7. *Srimad-Bhagavatam* 3.24.22-24
8. Ibid., 4.1.13-14
9. Ibid., 4.1.15
10. Ibid., 4.1.36-38
11. Ibid., 4.1.39
12. Ibid., 4.1.40-46
13. Ibid., 4.1.60-2
14. Ibid., 6.6.1-3
15. *Vishnu Purana*, Book One, Chapter 15, pp 172-3
16. *Srimad-Bhagavatam* 6.6.4-8
17. Ibid., 6.6.9-11
18. Ibid., 6.6.15
19. Ibid., 6.6.17-8
20. Ibid., 6.6.19-24
21. Ibid., 6.6.26-32
22. Ibid., 6.6.33-36, 37, 38-39, 40, 41, 42
23. Ibid., 4.30.48-51

REFERENCES

The following is a list of all the authentic Vedic and religious texts that were referred to or directly quoted to explain or verify all the knowledge and information presented in this book.

Agni Purana, translated by N. Gangadharan, Motilal Banarsidass, Delhi, 1984

Atharva-veda, translated by Devi Chand, Munshiram Manoharlal, Delhi, 1980

Bhagavad-gita As It Is, translated by A. C. Bhaktivedanta Swami, Bhaktivedanta Book Trust, New York/Los Angeles, 1972

Bhagavad-gita, translated by Swami Chidbhavananda, Sri Ramakrishna Tapovanam, Tiruchirappalli, India, 1991

The Song of God: Bhagavad-gita, translated by Swami Prabhavananda and Christopher Isherwood, New American Library, New York, 1972

Bhagavad-gita, translated by Winthrop Sargeant, State University of New York Press, Albany, NY, 1984

Bhakti-sandarbha sankhya

Bhavisya Purana

Bhavartha-dipika

Bible, New York International Bible Society, 1981

Brahma Purana, edited by J.L.Shastri, Motilal Banarsidass, Delhi 1985

Brahmanda Purana, edited by J.L.Shastri, Motilal Banarsidass, 1983

Brahma-samhita, translated by Bhaktisiddhanta Sarasvati Gosvami Thakur, Bhaktivedanta Book Trust, New York/Los Angeles,

Brahma-Sutras, translated by Swami Vireswarananda and Adidevananda, Advaita Ashram, Calcutta, 1978

Brahma-vaivarta Purana

Brihad-vishnu Purana

Brihan-naradiya Purana

Brihadaranyaka Upanishad

Caitanya-caritamrta, translated by A. C. Bhaktivedanta Swami, Bhaktivedanta Book Trust, Los Angeles, 1974

Caitanya Upanisad, translated by Kusakratha dasa, Bala Books, New York, 1970

Chandogya Upanishad

Garbha Upanishad

Garuda Purana, edited by J. L. Shastri, Motilal Barnasidass, Delhi, 1985

Gautamiya Tantra

Gheranda Samhita, translated by Rai Bahadur Srisa Chandra Vasu, Munshiram Manoharlal, New Delhi, 1980

How to Know God, The Yoga Aphorisms of Patanjali, translated by Swami Prabhavananda and C. Isherwood, New American Library, 1969

Jiva Gosvami's Tattvasandarbha, Stuart Mark Elkman, Motilal Banarsidass, Delhi, 1986

Kali-santarana Upanishad

Katha Upanishad

Kaushitaki Upanishad

Kurma Purana, edited by J. L. Shastri, Motilal Banarsidass, Delhi, 1981

Linga Purana, edited by J. L. Shastri, Motilal Banarsidass, Delhi, 1973

Mahabharata, translated by C. Rajagopalachari, Bharatiya Vidya Bhavan, New Delhi, 1972

Mahabharata, Kamala Subramaniam, Bharatiya Vidya Bhavan, Bombay, 1982

Matsya Purana

The Law of Manu, [*Manu-samhita*], translated by Georg Buhlerg, Motilal Banarsidass, Delhi, 1970

Minor Upanishads, translated by Swami Madhavananda, Advaita Ashram, Calcutta, 1980; contains Paramahamsopanishad, Atmopanishad, Amritabindupanishad, Tejabindupanishad, Sarvopanishad, Brahmopanisad, Aruneyi Upanishad, Kaivalyopanishad.

Mukunda-mala-stotra

Mundaka Upanishad

Narada-pancaratra

Narada Purana, tr. by Ganesh Vasudeo Tagare, Banarsidass, Delhi, 1980

Narada Sutras, translated by Hari Prasad Shastri, Shanti Sadan, London, 1963

Narada-Bhakti-Sutra, A. C. Bhaktivedanta Swami, Bhaktivedanta Book Trust, Los Angeles, 1991

Padma Purana, tr. by S. Venkitasubramonia Iyer, Banarsidass, Delhi, 1988

Ramayana of Valmiki, tr. by Makhan Lal Sen, Oriental Publishing Co., Calcutta

Hymns of the Rig-veda, tr. by Griffith, Motilal Banarsidass, Delhi, 1973

Rig-veda Brahmanas: The Aitareya and Kausitaki Brahmanas of the Rigveda, translated by Arthur Keith, Motilal Banarsidass, Delhi, 1971

Samnyasa Upanisads, translated by Prof. A. A. Ramanathan, Adyar Library, Madras, India, 1978; contains Avadhutopanisad, Arunyupanisad, Katharudropanisad, Kundikopanisad, Jabalopanisad, Turiyatitopanisad, Narada-parivrajakopanisad, Nirvanopanisad, Parabrahmopanisad, Paramahamsa-parivrajakopanisad, Paramahamsopanisad, Brahmopanisad, Bhiksukopanisad, Maitreyopanisad, Yajnavalkyopanisad, Satyayaniyopanisad, and Samnyasopanisad.

Shiva Purana, edited by Professor J. L. Shastri, Banarsidass, Delhi, 1970

Sixty Upanisads of the Vedas, by Paul Deussen, translated from German by V. M.

Bedekar and G. B. Palsule, Motilal Banarsidass, Delhi, 1980;
contains Upanisads of the Rigveda: Aitareya and Kausitaki. Upanisads of the
Samaveda: Chandogya and Kena. Upanisads of the Black Yajurveda:
Taittiriya, Mahanarayan, Kathaka, Svetasvatara, and Maitrayana. Upanisads
of the White Yajurveda: Brihadaranyaka and Isa. Upanisads of the
Atharvaveda: Mundaka, Prasna, Mandukya, Garbha, Pranagnihotra, Pinda,
Atma, Sarva, Garuda; (Yoga Upanisads): Brahmavidya, Ksurika, Culik,
Nadabindu, Brahma-bindu, Amrtabindu, Dhyanabindu, Tejobindu,
Yoga-sikha, Yogatattva, Hamsa; (Samnyasa Upanisads): Brahma, Samnyasa,
Aruneya, Kantha-sruti, Paramahamsa, Jabala, Asrama; (Shiva Upanisads):
Atharvasira, Atharva-sikha, Nilarudra, Kalagnirudra, Kaivalya; (Vishnu
Upanisads): Maha, Narayana, Atmabodha, Nrisimhapurvatapaniya,
Nrisimhottara-tapaniya, Ramapurvatapaniya, Ramottaratapaniya.
(Supplemental Upanisads): Purusasuktam, Tadeva, Shiva-samkalpa, Baskala,
Chagaleya, Paingala, Mrtyu-langala, Arseya, Pranava, and Saunaka
Upanisad.

Skanda Purana

Sri Brihat Bhagavatamritam, by Sri Srila Sanatana Gosvami, Sree Gaudiya
Math, Madras, India, 1987

Sri Isopanisad, translated by A. C. Bhaktivedanta Swami, Bhaktivedanta Book
Trust, New York/Los Angeles, 1969

Srimad-Bhagavatam, translated by A. C. Bhaktivedanta Swami, Bhaktivedanta
Book trust, New York/Los Angeles, 1972

Srimad-Bhagavatam, translated by N. Raghunathan, Vighneswar Publishing
House, Madras, 1976

Srimad-Bhagavatam MahaPurana, translated by C. L. Goswami, M. A., Sastri,
Motilal Jalan at Gita Press, Gorkhapur, India, 1982

Svetasvatara Upanishad

Taittiriya Upanishad

Tantra of the Great Liberation (Mahanirvana Tantra), translated by Woodroffe,
Dover Publications, New York, 1972.

The Chaldean Account of Genesis, by Mr. George Smith.

The Pentateuch and Book of Joshua Critically Examined, by the Right Rev., John
William Colenso, Bishop of Natal, London. Longmans, Green & Co., 1863

Twelve Essential Upanishads, Tridandi Sri Bhakti Prajnan Yati, Sree Gaudiya
Math, Madras, 1982. Includes the *Isha, Kena, Katha, Prashna, Mundaka,
Mandukya, Taittiriya, Aitareya, Chandogya, Brihadaranyaka, Svetasvatara,*
and *Gopalatapani Upanishad* of the Pippalada section of the *Atharva-veda.*

The Upanishads, translated by Swami Prabhavananda and Frederick Manchester,
New American Library, New York, 1957; contains Katha, Isha, Kena, Prasna,

Mundaka, Mandukya, Taittiriya, Aitareya, Chandogya, Brihadaranyaka, Kaivalya, and Svetasvatara Upanishads.

The Upanisads, translated by F. Max Muller, Dover Publications; contains Chandogya, Kena, Aitareya, Kausitaki, Vajasaneyi (Isa), Katha, Mundaka, Taittiriya, Brihadaranyaka, Svetasvatara, Prasna, and Maitrayani Upanisads.

Varaha Purana, tr. by S.Venkitasubramonia Iyer, Banarsidass, Delhi, 1985

Vayu Purana, translated by G. V. Tagare, Banarsidass, Delhi, India, 1987

Veda of the Black Yajus School: Taitiriya Sanhita, translated by Arthur Keith, Motilal Banarsidass, Delhi, 1914

Vishnu Purana, translated by H. H. Wilson, Nag Publishers, Delhi

Vedanta-Sutras of Badarayana with Commentary of Baladeva Vidyabhusana, translated by Rai Bahadur Srisa Chandra Vasu, Munshiram Manoharlal, New Delhi, 1979

White Yajurveda, translated by Griffith, The Chowkhamba Sanskrit Series Office, Varanasi, 1976

Yajurveda, translated by Devi Chand, Munshiram Manoharlal, Delhi, 1980

Other references that were helpful are listed as follows:

A History of India, Hermann Kulke and Dietmar Rothermund, Dorset Press, New York, 1986

Elements of Hindu Iconography, by T. A. Gopinatha Rao, Motilal Banarsidass, Delhi, 1985

Harper's Dictionary of Hinduism, by Margaret and James Stutley, Harper & Row, San Francisco, 1917

Puranic Encyclopaedia, Vettam Mani, Motilal Banarsidass, Delhi, 1964

ABBREVIATIONS

Bhagavad-gita is abbreviated in this book as *Bg.*

Caitanya-caritamrita is *Cc.*

Manu-samhita is *Manu.*

Srimad-Bhagavatam or *Bhagavat Purana* is *Bhag.*

Vishnu Purana is *VP.*

Glossary

A

Acarya or *Acharya*--the spiritual master who sets the proper standard by his own example.

Acintya-bhedabheda-tattva--simultaneously one and different. The doctrine Lord Sri Caitanya taught referring to the Absolute as being both personal and impersonal.

Advaita--nondual, meaning that the Absolute is one with the infinitesimal souls with no individuality between them. The philosophy of Sankaracharya.

Agni--fire, or Agni the demigod of fire.

Agnihotra--the Vedic sacrifice in which offerings were made to the fire, such as ghee, milk, sesame seeds, grains, etc. The demigod Agni would deliver the offerings to the demigods that were referred to in the ritual.

Ahankara--false ego, identification with matter.

Ahimsa--nonviolence.

Akarma--actions which cause no *karmic* reactions.

Akasha--the ether, or etheric plane; a subtle material element in which sound travels.

Ananda--spiritual bliss.

Ananta--unlimited.

Ananta-Sesha--the Lord's incarnation as the thousand-headed serpent whose coiled body serves as the bed of Vishnu. He also sustains the planets of the universe on His heads. He is also known as the "Endless or Infinite One." The many coils of His body symbolize endless time. From His mouth comes the fire of universal annihilation and from between His eyebrows comes Lord Rudra who does his dance of dissolution which creates the clouds which create the universal flood.

Apara-prakrti--the material energy of the Lord.

Apsaras--the dancing girls of heaven.

Aranyaka--sacred writings that are supposed to frame the essence of the *Upanishads*.

Arati--the ceremony of worship when incense and ghee lamps are offered to the Deities.

Arca-vigraha--the worshipable Deity form of the Lord made of stone, wood, etc.

Atharva Veda--one of the four *Vedas*, the original revealed scriptures spoken by the Lord Himself.

Aryan--a noble person, one who is on the path of spiritual advancement.

Asana--postures for meditation, or exercises for developing the body into a fit

274

instrument for spiritual advancement.

Asat--that which is temporary.

Ashrama--one of the four orders of spiritual life, such as *brahmacari* (celibate student), *grihastha* (married householder), *vanaprastha* (retired stage), and *sannyasa* (renunciate); or the abode of a spiritual teacher or *sadhu*.

Astanga-yoga--the eightfold path of mystic yoga.

Asura--one who is ungodly or a demon.

Atma--the self or soul. Sometimes means the body, mind, and senses.

Atman--usually referred to as the Supreme Self.

Avatara--an incarnation of the Lord who descends from the spiritual world.

Avidya--ignorance or nescience.

Aum--*om* or *pranava*

Ayodhya--the town of Lord Rama in East India.

Ayurveda--the original wholistic form of medicine as described in the Vedic literature.

B

Babaji--wandering mendicant holy man.

Badrinatha--one of the holy places of pilgrimage in the Himalayas, and home of the Deity Sri Badrinatha along with many sages and hermits.

Balarama or Baladeva--the first plenary expansion of Lord Krishna, and His brother who appeared as the son of Rohini.

Bhagavad-gita--the Song of God, the conversation between Lord Krishna and His devotee Arjuna, which was one of the chapters in the *Mahabharata*.

Betel--a mildly intoxicating nut.

Bhagavan--one who possesses all opulences, God.

Bhajan--song of worship.

Bhajan kutir--a small dwelling used for one's worship and meditation.

Bhakta--a devotee of the Lord who is engaged in *bhakti-yoga*.

Bhakti--love and devotion for God.

Bhakti-yoga--the path of offering pure devotional service to the Supreme.

Bhang--pronounced bong, a sweet mixed with hashish.

Bhava--preliminary stage of love of God.

Bidi--an Indian cigarette.

Brahma--the demigod of creation who was born from Lord Vishnu, the first created living being and the engineer of the secondary stage of creation of the universe when all the living entities were manifested.

Brahmacari--a celebate student who is trained by the spiritual master. One of the four divisions or ashramas of spiritual life.

Brahmajyoti--the great white light or effulgence which emanates from the body of the Lord.

Brahmaloka--the highest planet or plane of existence in the universe; the planet where Lord Brahma lives.

Brahman--the spiritual energy; the all-pervading impersonal aspect of the Lord;
or the Supreme Lord Himself.

Brahmana or brahmin--one of the four orders of society; the intellectual class of
men who have been trained in the knowledge of the *Vedas* and initiated
by a spiritual master.

Brahmana--the supplemental books of the four primary *Vedas*. They usually
contained instructions for performing Vedic *agnihotras*, chanting the
mantras, the purpose of the rituals, etc. The *Aitareya* and *Kaushitaki
Brahmanas* belong to the *Rig-veda*, the *Satapatha Brahmana* belongs to
the *White Yajur-veda*, and the *Taittiriya Brahmana* belongs to the *Black
Yajur-veda*. The *Praudha* and *Shadvinsa Brahmanas* are two of the eight
Brahmanas belonging to the *Atharva-veda*.

Brahmastra--a nuclear weapon that is produced and controlled by *mantra*.

Brahminical--to be clean and upstanding, both outwardly and inwardly, like a
brahmana should be.

Brijbasi--a resident of Vraja, Vrindavan.

Buddha--Lord Buddha or a learned man.

C

Caitanya-caritamrta--the scripture by Krishnadasa Kaviraja which explains the
teachings and pastimes of Lord Caitanya Mahaprabhu.

Canakya Pandit--the prime minister of King Candragupta whose aphorisms are
noted for their logic and which is still famous throughout India.

Caranamrita--the water that has been used to bathe the Deity and is offered in
small spoonfuls to visitors in in the temple.

Chaitanya Mahaprabhu--the most recent incarnation of the Lord who appeared
in the 15th century in Bengal and who originally started the *sankirtana*
movement, based on congregational chanting of the holy names.

Chakra--a wheel, disk, or psychic energy center situated along the spinal column
in the subtle body of the physical shell.

Causal Ocean or Karana Ocean--is the corner of the spiritual sky where Maha-
Vishnu lies down to create the material manifestation.

Cit--eternal knowledge.

Chhandas--sacred hymns of the *Atharva-veda*.

D

Darshan--the devotional act of seeing and being seen by the Deity in the temple.

Deity--the *arca-vigraha*, or worshipful form of the Supreme in the temple, or
deity as the worshipful image of the demigod. A capital D is used in
refering to Krishna or one of His expansions, while a small d is used

when refering to a demigod or lesser personality.

Devas--demigods or heavenly beings from higher levels of material existence, or a godly person.

Devaloka--the higher planets or planes of existence of the devas.

Devaki--the devotee who acted as Lord Krishna's mother.

Dham--a holy place.

Dharma--the essential, spiritual nature or duty of the living being.

Dharmashala--a shelter or guesthouse for pilgrims at temples or holy towns.

Diksha--spiritual initiation.

Dualism--as related in this book refers to the Supreme as both an impersonal force as well as a person.

Durga--the form of Parvati, Shiva's wife, as a warrior goddess known by many names according to her deeds, such as Simhavahini when riding her lion, Mahishasuramardini for killing the demon Mahishasura, Jagaddhatri as the mother of the universe, Kali when she killed the demon Raktavija, Tara when killing Shumba, etc.

Dvapara-yuga--the third age which lasts 864,000 years.

Dvaraka--the island kingdom of Lord Krishna that was off the coast of Gujarat 5,000 years ago.

Dwaita--dualism, the principle that the Absolute Truth consists of the infinite Supreme Being and the infinitesimal individual souls.

E

Ekadasi--a fast day on the eleventh day of the waxing and waning moon.

G

Gandharvas--the celestial angel-like beings who have beautiful forms and voices, and are expert in dance and music, capable of becoming invisible and can help souls on the earthly plane.

Ganesh--a son of Shiva, said to destroy obstacles (as Vinayaka) and offer good luck to those who petition him.

Ganga--another name for the Ganges River.

Ganga Devi--the personified form of the Ganges River.

Ganges--the sacred and spiritual river which, according to the *Vedas*, runs throughout the universe, a portion of which is seen in India. The reason the river is considered holy is that it is said to be a drop of the Karana Ocean that leaked in when Lord Vishnu, in His incarnation as Vamanadeva, kicked a small hole in the universal shell with His toe. Thus, the water is spiritual as well as being purified by the touch of Lord Vishnu.

Gangapuja--the arati ceremony for worshiping the Ganges.

Gangotri--the source of the Ganges River in the Himalayas.

Garbhodakashayi Vishnu--the expansion of Lord Vishnu who enters into each
    universe.

Gaudiya--a part of India sometimes called Aryavarta or land of the Aryans,
    located south of the Himalayas and north of the Vindhya Hills.

Gaudiya *sampradaya*--the school of Vaishnavism founded by Sri Caitanya.

Gayatri--the spiritual vibration or *mantra* from which the other *Vedas* were
    expanded and which is chanted by those who are initiated as *brahmanas*
    and given the spiritual understanding of Vedic philosophy.

Ghat--a bathing place along a river or lake with steps leading down to the water.

Godasa--one who serves the senses.

Goloka Vrindavana--the name of Lord Krishna's spiritual planet.

Gompa--Buddhist monastery.

Gopuram--the tall ornate towers that mark the gates to the temples, often found
    in south India.

Gosvami--one who is master of the senses.

Govinda--a name of Krishna which means one who gives pleasure to the cows
    and senses.

Grihastha--the householder order of life. One of the four *ashramas* in spiritual
    life.

Gunas--the modes of material nature of which there is *sattva* (goodness), *rajas*
    (passion), and *tamas* (ignorance).

Guru--a spiritual master.

H

Hare--the Lord's pleasure potency, Radharani, who is approached for
    accessibility to the Lord.

Hare Krishna *mantra*--Hare Krishna, Hare Krishna, Krishna Krishna, Hare
    Hare/Hare Rama, Hare Rama, Rama Rama, Hare Hare.

Hari--a name of Krishna as the one who takes away one's obstacles on the
    spiritual path.

Haribol--a word that means to chant the name of the Lord, Hari.

Hari-kirtana--the chanting of the names of Lord Krishna.

Harinam--refers to the name of the Lord, Hari.

Har Ki Pauri--the holy bathing ghats in Hardwar where the Ganges leaves the
    mountains and enters the plains. It is at this spot where the Kumbha
    Mela is held every twelve years.

Hatha-yoga--a part of the yoga system which stresses various sitting postures and
    exercises.

Hiranyagarbha--another name of Brahma who was born of Vishnu in the
    primordial waters within the egg of the universe.

Holi--the festival that marks the end of winter, and is celebrated by throwing of colored dyes on all participants. The night before *holi*, bonfires are sometimes set to celebrate the destruction of Holika, the demoness who was the sister of the demon Hiranyakasipu. She tried to help her brother kill his son, Prahlada. She was immune from being burned and held Prahlada in a fire, but the power of his devotion to Vishnu, in the form of Narasimhadeva, was so great that she was burned to death while Prahlada was unharmed.

Hrishikesa--a name for Krishna which means the master of the senses.

I

Ikshvaku--the son of Manu who was king of the earth in ancient times and to whom Manu spoke *Bhagavad-gita*.

Impersonalism--the view that God has no personality or form, but is only an impersonal force.

Impersonalist--those who believe God has no personality or form.

Incarnation--the taking on of a body or form.

Indra--the King of heaven and controller of rain, who by his great power conquers the forces of darkness.

ISKCON--International Society for Krishna Consciousness.

J

Jai or *Jaya*--a term meaning victory, all glories.

Japa--the chanting one performs, usually softly, for one's own meditation.

Japa-mala--the string of beads one uses for chanting.

Jiva--the individual soul or living being.

Jivanmukta--a liberated soul, though still in the material body and universe.

Jiva-shakti--the living force.

Jnana--knowledge which may be material or spiritual.

Jnana-kanda--the portion of the *Vedas* which stresses empirical speculation for understanding truth.

Jnana-yoga--the process of linking with the Supreme through empirical knowledge and mental speculation.

Jnani--one engaged in *jnana-yoga*, or the process of cultivating knowledge to understand the Absolute.

K

Kala--eternal time.

Kali--the demigoddess who is the fierce form of the wife of Lord Shiva. The word *kali* comes from *kala*, the Sanskrit word for time: the power that dissolves or destroys everything.

Kali-yuga--the fourth and present age, the age of quarrel and confusion, which lasts 432,000 years and began 5,000 years ago.

Kalki--the incarnation of the Supreme who annihilates all of the miscreants and establishes the next age of Satya-yuga.

Kalpa--a day in the life of Lord Brahma which lasts a thousand cycles of the four *yugas*.

Kama--lust or inordinate desire.

Kama sutra--a treatise on sex enjoyment.

Kapila--an incarnation of Lord Krishna who propagated the Sankhya philosophy.

Karanodakashayi Vishnu (Maha-Vishnu)--the expansion of Lord Krishna who created all the material universes.

Karma--material actions performed in regard to developing one's position or for future results which produce *karmic* reactions. It is also the reactions one endures from such fruitive activities.

Karma-kanda--the portion of the *Vedas* which primarily deals with recommended fruitive activities for various results.

Karma-yoga--the system of yoga for dovetailing one's activities for spiritual advancement.

Karmi--the fruitive worker, one who accumulates more *karma*.

Kirtana--chanting or singing the glories of the Lord.

Krishna--the name of the original Supreme Personality of Godhead which means the most attractive and greatest pleasure. He is the source of all other incarnations, such as Vishnu, Rama, Narasimha, Narayana, Buddha, Parashurama, Vamanadeva, Kalki at the end of Kali-yuga, etc.

Krishnaloka--the spiritual planet where Lord Krishna resides.

Kshatriya--the second class of *varna* of society, or occupation of administrative or protective service, such as warrior or military personel.

Ksirodakashayi Vishnu--the Supersoul expansion of the Lord who enters into each atom and the heart of each individual.

Kumbha Mela--the holy festival in which millions of pilgrims and sages gather to bathe in the holy and purifying rivers for liberation at particular auspicious times that are calculated astrologically. The Kumbha Mela festivals take place every three years alternating between Allahabad, Nasik, Ujjain, and Hardwar.

Kuruksetra--the place of battle 5,000 years ago between the Pandavas and the Kauravas ninety miles north of New Delhi, where Krishna spoke the *Bhagavad-gita*.

Kurus--the family of Dhritarashtra who were the enemies of the Pandavas.

L

Lakshmi--the goddess of fortune and wife of Lord Vishnu.

Lila--pastimes.

Lilavataras--the many incarnations of God who appear to display various spiritual pastimes to attract the conditioned souls in the material world.

Linga--the phallic symbol of Lord Shiva.

M

Mahabhagavata--a great devotee of the Lord.

Mahabharata--the great epic of the Pandavas, which includes the *Bhagavadgita*, by Vyasadeva.

Maha-mantra--the best *mantra* for self-realization in this age, called the Hare Krishna *mantra*: Hare Krishna, Hare Krishna, Krishna Krishna, Hare Hare/Hare Rama, Hare Rama, Rama Rama, Hare Hare.

Mahatma--a great soul or devotee.

Mahat-tattva--the total material energy.

Maha-Vishnu or Karanodakasayi Vishnu--the Vishnu expansion of Lord Krishna from whom all the material universes emanate.

Mandir--a temple.

Mantra--a sound vibration which prepares the mind for spiritual realization and delivers the mind from material inclinations. In some cases a *mantra* is chanted for specific material benefits.

Manu--a demigod son of Brahma who is the forefather and lawgiver of the human race. A succession of 14 Manus exist during each day of Brahma.

Martya-loka--the earth planet, the place of death.

Maya--illusion, or anything that appears to not be connected with the eternal Absolute Truth.

Mayavadi--the impersonalist or voidist who believes that the Supreme has no form.

Mitra--the deity controlling the sun, and who gives life to earth.

Mleccha--a derogatory name for a low-born, uncivilized person, a meat eater, or those outside of Vedic society.

Moksha--liberation from material existence.

Murti--a Deity of the Lord or spiritual master that is worshiped.

Murugan--means the divine child, the Tamil name for Subramaniya, one of the sons of Shiva and Parvati, especially worshiped in South India.

N

Narada Muni--the universal sage and devotee of the Lord who travels throughout the universe in his eternal body. He is the spiritual master of Vyasadeva and many other devotees.

Narasimha--the incarnation of the Lord who appears as half-man, half-lion to display His anger toward the demons and provide protection to His devotees.

Narayana--the four-handed form of the Supreme Lord.

Nirguna--without material qualities.

Nirvana--the state of no material miseries, usually the goal of the Buddhists or voidists.

O

Om or *Omkara--pranava*, the transcendental *om mantra*, generally referring to the attributeless or impersonal aspects of the Absolute.

P

Pan--a concoction of ground betel nut and spices that acts as a mild stimulant or intoxicant. It is very popular and often leaves the teeth stained red.

Pandal--a large tent where religious gatherings are held.

Paramahamsa--the highest level of self-realized devotees of the Lord.

Paramatma--the Supersoul, or localized expansion of the Lord.

Parampara--the system of disciplic succession through which transcendental knowledge descends.

Parvati--Lord Shiva's spouse, daughter of Parvata. Parvata is the personification of the Himalayas. She is also called Gauri for her golden complexion, Candi, Bhairavi (as the wife of Bhairava, Shiva), Durga, Ambika, and Shakti.

Patanjali--the authority on the *astanga-yoga* system.

Pradhana--the total material energy in its unmanifest state.

Prajapati--deity presiding over procreation.

Prakriti--matter in its primordial state, the material nature.

Prana--the life air or cosmic energy.

Pranayama--control of the breathing process as in *astanga* or *raja-yoga*.

Pranava--same as *omkara*.

Prasada--food or other articles that have been offered to the Deity in the temple and then distributed amongst people as the blessings or mercy of the Deity.

Prema--matured love for Krishna.

Puja--the worship offered to the Deity.

Pujari--the priest who performs worship, *puja*, to the Deity.

Purusha or *Purusham*--the supreme enjoyer.

R

Raja-yoga--the eightfold yoga system.

Rajo-guna--the material mode of passion.

Ramachandra--an incarnation of Krishna as He appeared as the greatest of kings.

Ramayana--the great epic of the incarnation of Lord Ramachandra.

Rasa--an enjoyable taste or feeling, a relationship with God.

Rig Veda--one of the four *Vedas*, original scriptures spoken by the lord.

Rishi--saintly person who knows the Vedic knowledge.

S

Sacrifice--in this book it in no way pertains to human sacrifice, as many people tend to think when this word is used. But it means to engage in an austerity of some kind for a higher, spiritual purpose.

Sama Veda--one of the four original *samhitas*, consisting of Vedic hymns that were set to music.

Shabda-brahma--the original spiritual vibration or energy of which the *Vedas* are composed.

Sac-cid-ananda-vigraha--the transcendental form of the Lord or of the living entity which is eternal, full of knowledge and bliss.

Sadhana--a specific practice or discipline for attaining God realization.

Sadhu--Indian holy man or devotee.

Saguna Brahman--the aspect of the Absolute with form and qualities.

Samadhi--trance, the perfection of being absorbed in the Absolute.

Samsara--rounds of life; cycles of birth and death; reincarnation.

Sanatana-dharma--the eternal nature of the living being, to love and render service to the supreme lovable object, the Lord.

Sangam--the confluence of two or more rivers.

Sankarshana--one of the four original expansions of Lord Krishna in the spiritual world, and another name of Balarama who is also Krishna's brother.

Sankhya--analytical understanding of material nature, the body, and the soul.

Sankirtana-yajna--the prescribed sacrifice for this age: congregational chanting of the holy names of God.

Sannyasa--the renounced order of life, the highest of the four *ashramas* on the spiritual path.

Sarasvati--the goddess of knowledge and intelligence.

Sattva-guna--the material mode of goodness.

Satya-yuga--the first of the four ages which lasts 1,728,000 years.

Shaivites--worshipers of Lord Shiva.

Shakti--energy, potency or power, the active principle in creation. Also the active power or wife of a deity, such as Shiva/Shakti.

Shastra--the authentic revealed scripture.

Shiva--the benevolent one, the demigod who is in charge of the material mode
of ignorance and the destruction of the universe. Part of the triad of
Brahma, Vishnu, and Shiva who continually create, maintain, and
destroy the universe. He is known as Rudra when displaying his
destructive aspect.

Sikha--a tuft of hair on the back of the head signifying that one is a Vaishnava.

Smaranam--remembering the Lord.

Smriti--the traditional Vedic knowledge "that is remembered" from what was
directly heard by or revealed to the *rishis*.

Sravanam--hearing about the Lord.

Srimad-Bhagavatam--the most ripened fruit of the tree of Vedic knowledge
compiled by Vyasadeva.

Sruti--scriptures that were received directly from God and transmitted orally by
brahmanas or *rishis* down through succeeding generations. Traditionally,
it is considered the four primary *Vedas*.

Sudra--the working class of society, the fourth of the *varnas*.

Svami--one who can control his mind and senses.

T

Tamo-guna--the material mode of ignorance.

Tapasya--voluntary austerity for spiritual advancement.

Tilok--the clay markings that signify a person's body as a temple, and the sect
or school of thought of the person.

Tirtha--a holy place of pilgrimage.

Tirthankaras--the person who is the spiritual guide or teacher in Jainism.

Treta-yuga--the second of the four ages which lasts 1,296,000 years.

Tulasi--the small tree that grows where worship to Krishna is found. It is called
the embodiment of devotion, and the incarnation of Vrinda-devi.

U

Upanishads--the portions of the *Vedas* which primarily explain philosophically
the Absolute Truth. It is knowledge of Brahman which releases one
from the world and allows one to attain self-realization when received
from a qualified teacher. Except for the *Isa Upanishad*, which is the
40th chapter of the *Vajasaneyi Samhita* of the *Sukla* (*White*) *Yajur-veda*,
the *Upanishads* are connected to the four primary *Vedas*, generally
found in the *Brahmanas*.

V

Vaikunthas--the planets located in the spiritual sky.

Vaishnava--a worshiper of the Supreme Lord Vishnu or Krishna and His
 expansions or incarnations.

Vaishnava-*aparadha*--an offense against a Vaisnava or devotee, which can negate
 all of one's spiritual progress.

Vaisya--the third class of society engaged in business or farming.

Vanaprastha--the third of the four *ashramas* of spiritual life in which one retires
 from family life in preparation for the renounced order.

Varna--sometimes referred to as caste, a division of society, such as *brahmana*
 (a priestly intellectual), a *kshatriya* (ruler or manager), *vaisya* (a
 merchant, banker, or farmer), and *sudra* (common laborer).

Varnashrama--the system of four divisions of society, *varnas*, and four orders of
 spiritual life, *ashramas*. *Varnas* are the natural divisions of society,
 namely the *shudras* or laborer class, the *vaisyas* or farmers and
 merchants, the *kshatriyas* or warriors, military, and leaders, and the
 brahmanas or intellectual and priestly class. This is not the modern day
 caste system that is determined by family birth, which was inflicted on
 the people by the British to help cause dissension among the people and
 make it easier for the British to maintain control over them. But this is
 the natural tendencies, proclivities, and abilities that each individual has.
 When each individual is engaged in his natural tendencies and
 contributes to society that way, everyone is happy and appreciated. The
 ashramas are simply the divisions of life, consisting of *brahmacari* or
 celebate student life, the *grihasthas* of married life, the *vanaprasthas* or
 retired life, and the *sannyasis* or life of renunciation when one prepares
 for death by becoming as spiritually focused as possible.

Vedanta-sutras--the philosophical conclusion of the four *Vedas*.

Vedas--generally means the four primary *samhitas;* the *Rig, Yajur, Sama,* and
 Atharva.

Vidya--knowledge.

Vikarma--sinful activities performed without scriptural authority and which
 produce sinful reactions.

Virajanadi or Viraja River--the space that separates the material creation from
 the spiritual sky.

Vishnu--the expansion of Lord Krishna who enters into the material energy to
 create and maintain the cosmic world.

Vishnu Purana--one of the eighteen major *Puranas*, Vedic historical scriptures.

Vrindavana--the place where Lord Krishna displayed His village pastimes 5,000
 years ago, and is considered to be part of the spiritual abode..

Vyasadeva--the incarnation of God who appeared as the greatest philosopher who
 compiled all the *Vedas* into written form.

Y

Yadu dynasty--the dynasty in which Lord Krishna appeared.

Yajna--a ritual or austerity that is done as a sacrifice for spiritual merit, or ritual worship of a demigod for good *karmic* reactions.

Yajur Veda--one of the four *Vedas*, original revealed scriptures spoken by the Lord Himself.

Yamaraja--the demigod and lord of death who directs the living entities to various punishments according to their activities.

Yantra--a machine, instrument, or mystical diagram used in ritual worship.

Yoga--linking up with the Absolute.

Yoga-*siddhi*--mystic perfection.

Yogi--a transcendentalist striving for union with the Supreme.

Yuga-avataras--the incarnations of God who appear in each of the four *yugas* to explain the authorized system of self-realization in that age.

Index

ABOUT THE AUTHOR

Stephen Knapp grew up in a Christian family, during which time he seriously studied the Bible to understand its teachings. In his late teenage years, however, he sought answers to questions not easily explained in Christian theology. So he began to search through other religions and philosophies from around the world and started to find the answers for which he was looking. He also studied a variety of occult sciences, ancient mythology, mysticism, yoga, and the spiritual teachings of the East. After his first reading of the *Bhagavad-gita*, he felt he had found the last piece of the puzzle he had been putting together through all of his research. Therefore, he continued to study all of the major Vedic texts of India to gain a better understanding of the science of Vedanta.

It is known amongst all Eastern mystics that anyone, regardless of qualifications, academic or otherwise, who does not engage in the spiritual practices described in the Vedic texts cannot actually enter into understanding the depths of the Vedic spiritual science, nor acquire the realizations that should accompany it. So, rather than pursuing his research in an academic atmosphere at a university, Stephen directly engaged in the spiritual disciplines that have been recommended for hundreds of years. He continued his study of Vedic knowledge and spiritual practice under the guidance of a spiritual master. Through this process, and with the sanction of His Divine Grace A. C. Bhaktivedanta Swami Prabhupada, he became initiated into the genuine and authorized spiritual line of the Brahma-Madhava-Gaudiya *sampradaya*, which is a disciplic succession that descends back through Sri Caitanya Mahaprabhu and Sri Vyasadeva, the compiler of Vedic literature, and further back to Sri Krishna. Besides being *brahminically* initiated, Stephen has also been to India several times and traveled extensively throughout the country, visiting most of the major holy places and gaining a wide variety of spiritual experiences that only such places can give.

Stephen has been writing *The Eastern Answers to the Mysteries of Life* series, which includes *The Secret Teachings of the Vedas*, *The Universal Path to Enlightenment*, *The Vedic Prophecies: A New Look into the Future*, and now concludes with this volume, *How the Universe was Created and Our Purpose In It*. He has also written such books as *Toward World Peace: Seeing the Unity Between Us All*, and *Facing Death: Welcoming the Afterlife*, as well as *Proof of Vedic Culture's Global Existence*. He has also written a novel, *Destined for Infinity*, for those who prefer lighter reading, or learning spiritual knowledge in the context of a spiritual adventure. Stephen has put the culmination of over twenty-five years of continuous research and travel experience into his books in an effort to share it with those who are also looking for higher levels of spiritual understanding.

If you have enjoyed this book, or if you are serious about finding higher levels of real spiritual Truth, you will also want to get:

The Secret Teachings of the Vedas

This book presents the essence of the ancient Eastern philosophy and summarizes some of the most elevated and important of all spiritual knowledge. This enlightening information is explained in a clear and concise way and is essential for all who want to increase their spiritual understanding, regardless of what their religious background may be. If you are looking for a book to give you an in-depth introduction to the Vedic spiritual knowledge, and to get you started in real spiritual understanding, this is the book!

The topics include: What is your real spiritual identity; the Vedic explanation of the soul; scientific evidence that consciousness is separate from but interacts with the body; the real unity between us all; how to attain the highest happiness and freedom from the cause of suffering; the law of karma and reincarnation; the karma of a nation; where you are really going in life; the real process of progressive evolution; life after death--heaven, hell, or beyond; a description of the spiritual realm; the nature of the Absolute Truth--personal God or impersonal force; recognizing the existence of the Supreme; the reason why we exist at all; and much more. This book provides the answers to questions not found in other religions or philosophies, and condenses information from a wide variety of sources that would take a person years to assemble. It also contains many quotations from the Vedic texts to let the texts speak for themselves, and to show the knowledge the Vedas have held for thousands of years. It also explains the history and origins of the Vedic literature. This book has been called one of the best reviews of Eastern philosophy available.

There is also a special section on traveling to the major historical holy sites of South India with over 75 photographs of art work, sculptures, deities, architecture, and some of the most amazing temples you will see anywhere. This section elaborates on the many ancient legends connected with these important places and what it is like to travel and see them today.

To get your copy, order it from your local bookstore (ISBN:0-9617410-1-5), or simply send $14.95, plus $2.50 for postage and handling ($7.50 for overseas orders) to:

The World Relief Network, P. O. Box 15082, Detroit, Michigan, 48215-0082, U. S. A.

Much rare information is also found in Volume Two of this series:

The Universal Path to Enlightenment

Although all religions and spiritual processes are meant to lead you toward enlightenment, they are not all the same in regard to the methods they teach, nor in the level of philosophical understanding they offer. So an intelligent person will make comparisons between them to understand the aims and distinctions of each religion, and which may give the most complete philosophy. This book presents a most interesting and revealing survey of the major spiritual paths of the world and describes their origins, histories, philosophical basis, and goals. This book will help you decide which path may give you the highest levels of spiritual understanding, and to see the similarities between all religions.

You Will Discover

--the essential similarities of all religions that all people of any culture can practice, which would bring about a united world religion, or "THE UNIVERSAL PATH TO ENLIGHTENMENT."

--how Christianity and Judaism were greatly influenced by the early "pagan" religions and adopted many of their legends, holidays, and rituals that are still practiced today.

--about evidence that shows Jesus may have traveled to the East and learned its spiritual knowledge, and then made bhakti-yoga the essence of his teachings.

--who were the real Vedic Aryans, the founders of the earliest of religions and organized cultures, and how widespread and influential their civilization was to other cultures, such as Egyptian, Greek, Oriental, etc., and how their Vedic teachings are still found in Christianity and other traditions today, which makes them the source of the world's spiritual heritage.

--the philosophical basis and origin of Christianity, Judaism, Islam, Hinduism, Buddhism, Zoroastrianism, Jainism, Sikhism, and many others.

--about the different yoga systems, such as raja-yoga, hatha-yoga, bhakti-yoga, mantra-yoga, etc., what their goals are, and how practical they are in this age.

--about the different mystic powers and experiences that can be attained through yoga.

--what the qualifications are of a genuine spiritual teacher.

--the bliss and results of attaining spiritual enlightenment or experiencing the Absolute.

--and, most importantly, what is the real purpose of a spiritual path that you should strive for, and how to practice the path that is especially recommended as the easiest and most effective for the people of this age to attain real spiritual enlightenment.

--and much more information not easily found elsewhere.

There is also a special section on seeing spiritual India. You will tour the famous temples and holy places of Eastern India, from Madras in the South to New Delhi in the North. You will learn about some of the most important and sacred temples and towns in the world where several of the major religions originated. Almost 100 photographs are included of a variety of temples, holy sites, art, sculptures, and people engaged in all aspects of life in India and Nepal. A great adventure and reference for those who want to travel in this area.

To get your copy, see your local book store to order it (ISBN 0-9617410-2-3), or simply send $14.95, plus $2.50 for postage and handling ($7.50 for overseas orders) to: The World Relief Network, P. O. Box 15082, Detroit, Michigan, 48215-0082, U. S. A.

The Vedic Prophecies:
A New Look into the Future

The Vedic prophecies take you to the end of time! This is the first book ever to present the unique predictions found in the ancient Vedic texts of India. These prophecies are like no others and will provide you with a very different view of the future and how things fit together in the plan for the universe. These prophecies will surprise you.

Now you can discover the amazing secrets that are hidden in the oldest spiritual writings on the planet. Find out what they say about the distant future, and what the seers of long ago saw in their visions of the destiny of the world.

This book will reveal predictions of deteriorating social changes and how to avoid them; future droughts and famines; low-class rulers and evil governments; whether there will be another appearance (second coming) of God; and predictions of a new spiritual awareness and how it will spread around the world. You will also learn the answers to such questions as:

- Does the future get worse or better?
- Will there be future world wars or global disasters?
- What lies beyond the predictions of Nostradamus, the Mayan prophecies, or the Biblical apocalypse?
- Are we in the end times? How to recognize them if we are.
- Does the world come to an end? If so, when and how?

Now you can find out what the future holds. The Vedic Prophecies carry an important message and warning for all humanity, which needs to be understood now!

There is also a special section on seeing spiritual India. This takes you through the famous temples and holy places of Western India, from Jaipur in Central India all the way to Bangalore in the South. Now you can tour them through their histories, legends, and miraculous stories, along with over 65 photographs of temples, holy sites, art, sculptures, sages and people of India. A wonderful addition!

To get your copy, order it from your bookstore (ISBN:0-9617410-4-X) or simply send $14.95 plus $2.50 for postage and handling ($3.50 for Canada, or $7.50 for overseas orders) to: The World Relief Network, P.O.Box 15082, Detroit, Michigan, 48215-0082, U.S.A.

Toward World Peace:
Seeing the Unity Between Us All

This book points out the essential reasons why peace in the world and cooperation amongst people, communities, and nations have been so difficult to establish. It also advises the only way real peace and harmony amongst humanity can be achieved.

In order for peace and unity to exist we must first realize what barriers and divisions keep us apart. Only then can we break through those barriers to see the unity that naturally exists between us all. Then, rather than focusing on our differences, it is easier to recognize our similarities and common goals. With a common goal established, all of humanity can work together to help each other reach that destiny.

This book is short and to the point. It is a thought provoking book and will provide inspiration for anyone. It is especially useful for those working in politics, religion, interfaith, race relations, the media, the United Nations, teaching, or who have a position of leadership in any capacity. It is also for those of us who simply want to spread the insights needed for bringing greater levels of peace, acceptance, unity, and equality between friends, neighbors, and communities. Such insights include:

- The factors that keep us apart.
- Breaking down cultural distinctions.
- Breaking down the religious differences.
- Seeing through bodily distinctions.
- We are all working to attain the same things.
- Our real identity: The basis for common ground.
- Seeing the Divinity within each of us.
- What we can do now to bring unity between everyone we meet.

This book carries an important message and plan of action that we must incorporate into our lives and plans for the future if we intend to ever bring peace and unity between us.

To get your copy, order it from your bookstore (ISBN:0-9617410-5-8), or send $5.95 plus $2.00 for postage and handling ($3.00 for Canada, $5.00 for overseas orders) to: The World Relief Network, P.O.Box 15082, Detroit, Michigan, 48215-0082, U.S.A.

Facing Death
Welcoming the Afterlife

Many people are afraid of death, or do not know how to prepare for it nor what to expect. So this book is provided to relieve anyone of the fear that often accompanies the thought of death, and to supply a means to more clearly understand the purpose of it and how we can use it to our advantage. It will also help the survivors of the departed souls to better understand what has happened and how to cope with it. Furthermore, it shows that death is not a tragedy, but a natural course of events meant to help us reach our destiny.

This book is short and easy to read, with soothing and comforting wisdom, along with stories of people who have been with departing souls and what they have experienced. It is written especially for those who have given death little thought beforehand, but now would like to have some preparedness for what may need to be done regarding the many levels of what might take place during this transition.

To assist you in preparing for your own death, or that of a loved one, you will find guidelines for making one's final days as peaceful and as smooth as possible, both physically and spiritually. Preparing for death, no matter what stage of life you are in, can transform your whole outlook in a positive way, if understood properly. This will make things clearer in regard to what matters most in this life, especially when you know the remainder of your life may be short. It is like looking into the Truth of yourself, and taking a pilgrimage to the edge of the spiritual dimension. Some of the topics in the book include:

- The fear of death and learning to let go.
- The opportunity of death: The portal into the next life.
- This earth and this body are no one's real home, so death is natural.
- Being practical and dealing with the final responsibilities.
- Forgiving yourself and others before you go.
- Being the assistant of one leaving this life.
- Connecting with the person inside the disease.
- Surviving the death of a loved one.
- Stories of being with dying, and an amazing near-death-experience.
- Connecting to the spiritual side of death.
- What happens while leaving the body.
- What difference the consciousness makes during death, and how to attain the best level of awareness to carry you through it.

So no matter whether you are afraid of death or concerned about surviving the death of a loved one, or are worried about those that you will leave behind if you depart, or what death will be like and how to prepare for it, this book will help you.

Order your copy today! Send $6.95 plus $2.00 for shipping and handling to: The World Relief Network, P. O. Box 15082, Detroit, Michigan 48215-0082, or available through your local bookstore. ISBN: 0-9617410-7-4, trim size 5 ½" x 8 ½", 110 pages.

Proof of Vedic Culture's Global Existence

This book provides evidence which makes it clear that the ancient Vedic culture was once a global society. Even today we can see its influence in any part of the world. Thus, it becomes obvious that before the world became full of distinct and separate cultures, religions and countries, it was once united in a common brotherhood of Vedic culture, with common standards, principles, and representations of God.

No matter what we may consider our present religion, society, or country, we are all descendants of this ancient global civilization. Thus, the Vedic culture is the parent of all humanity and the original ancestor of all religions. In this way, we all share a common heritage.

This book is offered as an attempt to allow humanity to see more clearly its universal roots. This book provides a look into:

* How Vedic knowledge was given to humanity by the Supreme Being.
* The history and traditional source of the *Vedas* and Vedic Aryan society.
* Who were the original Vedic Aryans. How Vedic society was a global influence and what shattered this world-wide society. How Sanskrit faded from being a global language, and how the Vedic culture slowly diminished.
* The many scientific discoveries over the past several centuries that are only rediscoveries of what the Vedic culture already knew.
* How the origins of world literature are found in India and Sanskrit.
* The links between the Vedic and other ancient cultures, such as the Sumerians, Persians, Egyptians, Romans, Greeks, and others.
* Links between the Vedic tradition and Judaism, Christianity, Islam, and Buddhism.
* How many of the western holy sites, churches, and mosques were once the sites of Vedic holy places and sacred shrines.
* The Vedic influence presently found in such countries as Britain, France, Russia, Greece, Israel, Arabia, China, Japan, and in areas of Scandinavia, the Middle East, Africa, the South Pacific, and the Americas.
* Uncovering the truth of India's history: Powerful evidence that shows how many mosques and Muslim buildings were once opulent Vedic temples, including the Taj Mahal, Delhi's Jama Masjid, Kutab Minar, as well as buildings in many other cities, such as Agra, Ahmedabad, Bijapur, and Allahabad.
* How there is presently a need to plan for the survival of Vedic culture.

This book is sure to provide some amazing facts and evidence about the truth of world history and the ancient, global Vedic Culture. This book has enough startling information and historical evidence to cause a major shift in the way we view religious history and the basis of world traditions.

Order your copy today!! Send $14.95, plus $2.50 for shipping and handling, ($3.50 in Canada, $7.50 overseas surface mail) to: The World Relief Network, P.O.Box 15082, Detroit, MI 48215-0082, U.S.A. The book is 6" x 9" trim size, over 325 pages, ISBN: 0-9617410-6-6, LC # 98-061106.